Scales
for viola

by Simon Fischer

Scales and scale studies for the viola

Leipzig · London · New York

Peters Edition Limited
2–6 Baches Street
London
N1 6DN

First published 2017

© 2017 by Peters Edition Limited London

ISMN 979-0-57700-794-6

A catalogue record for this book is available from the British Library

The right of Simon Fischer to be identified as the author of this work has been asserted by him in accordance with the Copyright, Designs and Patents Act, 1988.

All rights reserved. No part of this publication may be reproduced, stored in a retrieval system or transmitted in any form or by any means, electronic, mechanical, photocopying, recording or otherwise, without the prior written permission of the publisher.

Cover image: Still Life with Violin and Guitar, 1913 (oil on canvas), Gris, Juan (1887–1927) / Museo Nacional Centro de Arte Reina Sofía, Madrid, Spain / The Bridgeman Art Library

Contents

Introduction v

How to use *Scales* vii

Part 1
Scales and arpeggios in low positions without shifting
Notes, page 2

1	How to tune each note of the scale	4
2	One-octave scales	6
3	One-octave arpeggio sequence	18
4	Chromatic scales	22
5	Warm-up exercise: fourth-finger extensions	25
6	Two-octave scales and arpeggios	26
7	Two-octave broken thirds and fourths	40

Part 2
Three-octave scales and arpeggios: preparatory practice
Notes, page 48

8	Three-octave scales: structuring intonation	52
9	Tone-semitone patterns	64
10	Scales: exercise for overlapping the first and fourth fingers	68
11	One-octave scales in all positions without shifting	70
12	The turning-point at the top of the scale	82
13	Three-octave scales: exercise for timing shifts	83
14	Harmonic minor scale: exercise for augmented 2nd, fourth to first finger	89
15	Warm-up exercise: smooth bowing	89
16	Exercise to develop 'fast fingers'	90
17	Warm-up exercise: moving fingers independently of the hand	90
18	Placing fingers in blocks	91
19	One-octave arpeggio sequence in all positions without shifting	96
20	Starting at the top	101
21	Three-octave arpeggios: exercise for timing shifts	102

	22 Three-octave diminished sevenths	106
	23 Three-octave dominant sevenths	109
	24 Arpeggios: shifting exercise	112
	25 Practice method: 'trilling' the shift	113
	26 Practice method: uniform intonation in arpeggios	113
	27 Arpeggios: placing fingers in blocks	114
	28 Chromatic scales: exercise for 321 or 123 fingering	118

Part 3

Three-octave scales, arpeggios and chromatic scales

Notes, page 120

29 Rhythm, accent, bowing and dynamic patterns	122
30 Speeding up with the metronome	124
31 Three-octave scales, arpeggios and chromatic scales	129

Part 4

Scales and arpeggios on one string

Notes, page 142

32 Single-finger scales and arpeggios	144
33 Two-finger scales	152
34 One-octave scales	156
35 One-octave arpeggios	168
36 Broken thirds on the A string	180
37 Arpeggios: strengthening the top octave	182
38 Two-octave scales and arpeggios	183

Part 5

Four-octave scales and arpeggios

Notes, page 194

39 Speeding up with the metronome	195
40 Four-octave scales and arpeggios	196

Introduction

Building the scale in stages

An important and original feature of this book is that scales are built up in stages, with notes added in a particular harmonic order. The word "scale" comes from the Latin word "scala", which means "ladder". But whereas when we climb a ladder we need only focus on one rung at a time, a scale should be built and structured so that each note is felt according to its position in the key, and its relationship with the rest of the scale.

The Catalan cellist Pablo Casals, widely regarded as one of the most influential musicians of the 20th century, taught scales in this way, as did the American violinist Dorothy DeLay, one of the foremost violin teachers at the end of the 20th century. She devised the same approach as Casals, without knowing that he had thought along the same lines. "All I was trying to do," she said, "was to find a way of getting my students to play their scales in tune!"

We are taught that the major scale is made up of the series tone–tone–semitone–tone–tone–tone–semitone. But this obscures the true symmetry of the scale, which is revealed if you think of it as two groups of four notes (tetrachords), each comprising tone–tone–semitone, which are joined by a tone. Minor scales are similarly made up of two tetrachords and can also be thought of as two equal halves, even though the pattern of tones and semitones are not the same in each half.

Casals and DeLay structured the scale as follows. Begin with the notes of the perfect intervals (the first and fourth notes in each half of the scale): I, IV; V, VIII (in A major: A, D; E, A), all the way up the scale and down again. Then add the leading note (G♯ in A major), feeling what Casals called its "gravitational attraction" upward to the tonic and the third (C♯), feeling it as a "leading note" to the fourth. Of course, the third is not a leading note like the seventh, but for the purposes of tuning the scale it can be treated as such.

Next, add the second and the sixth (in A major: B and F♯). These should be tuned according to how high you pitch the third and the seventh – which, to some degree, is a matter of taste. If you choose to play the thirds and sevenths higher, the seconds and sixths have to be higher too, otherwise you will have adjacent whole tones which are unequal.

The sequence taught by Casals and DeLay is musically satisfying in both major and minor keys, but in the major it is particularly effective because you can measure the third and the seventh in relation to the fourth and the octave. It is not quite so satisfactory for helping to measure the flattened thirds and flattened sevenths in the minor scale. So, in some sections I have added a further stage before stage 2: after playing I, IV; V, VIII, play I, III; V, VII, i.e. the first and third notes of each half. In other words, first play perfect fourths starting on the tonic and on the fifth; and then play major or minor thirds starting on the tonic and the fifth.

When I first began to add this new stage it was intended to be used only in minor scales. Soon it became obvious, because of the new light it casts on the third and seventh, that it is also very helpful in the major scale too.

Writing out the stages in each scale

The basic outline of the Carl Flesch Scale System first appeared in Volume 1 of Flesch's *Art of Violin Playing* (1924). It was written out only in C major in the belief that players would naturally apply the same patterns to the other keys as well. However, some years later

Flesch realised that because the system was shown only in C major, most of his students practised scales only in that key and rarely, if ever, in any other. So he wrote out the scale and arpeggio sequences in all the keys, added bowing and rhythm patterns, and *Das Skalensystem* came into existence.

Similarly, while I saw Dorothy DeLay teach how to tune the scales in individual lessons, in master classes and in her technique classes at the Aspen Music Festival, I only ever saw her demonstrate it in A major. Having shown how to do it, she expected students to apply the same logic to all the other keys. I do not know how many of her students did, but I have always suspected that few of mine do so without needing constant reminders.

For this reason, I have followed Carl Flesch's example and, until the final few sections of *Scales*, written out the stages of building the scale into each key. It seems an obvious, desirable and long overdue solution to have the scales written out in this form so that you can simply read them off the page.

Held-down finger lines

Another original feature of *Scales* is the indication of where and for how long to hold fingers down. Some of these fingers (e.g. the first finger) you would hold down in the normal course of playing to give stability to the hand; others are for the purposes of 'beneficial exaggeration' so that afterwards, playing naturally without holding them down, everything feels much easier and more secure than before. These can be adapted to suit the individual hand, with any which feel unnatural or awkward simply ignored. Equally, in some instances you may wish to add extra lines, or to hold fingers down for longer than marked. The habit of holding fingers down, with all the measuring between fingers that then takes place, is one of the foundations of a secure left hand.

Finger preparation

While we usually blame the bow when the tone of a note is not clean, many impure sounds are caused not by the bow but by the fingers not being ready on the string.

In natural, musical playing, the fingers prepare themselves and stop the string an instant before the bow moves. 'Just in time' is usually the right moment for the finger to be ready on the string. But in many sections of *Scales*, the important fingers to prepare are shown as stemless, diamond-headed notes: place these fingers extra early, again using beneficial exaggeration. Play slowly and prepare the fingers very deliberately: prepare then play. Afterwards, when you play normally, your fingers will again prepare themselves instinctively but with a new reliability.

Often, the prepared fingers should be exactly in tune without needing adjustment before sounding them. But just as often – especially when preparing fingers a semitone apart – if you were to play the prepared fingers without first adjusting them, they would probably not be exactly in tune.

To play semitones in tune, the fingers often need to be squeezed closer together than they are when placed side-by-side on the string. It all depends on the width of your fingertips and how high up the fingerboard you are. In those cases where it is impossible to prepare fingers in tune, still begin to get ready early, as marked by the diamond-headed notes, but the fingers will not find their true place on the string until the instant before the note is sounded.

What is a scale like when it is played well?

The three basic building blocks of music are pitch, sound and rhythm. When a scale or arpeggio is played at the highest standard it is entirely even in all three. The pitch is even – the same letter-names in the different octaves are in tune with each other, with a consistent logic behind the tuning of each note. The sound is even – undisturbed by changes of string, bow, position or finger. The rhythm is even – again undisturbed by changes of string, bow, position or finger.

Evenness does not mean that the scale is played purely mechanically. Each note has its own musical character due to its place in the scale (which becomes clear when you build the scale in stages). A well-played scale is not musically empty, but full of inner tensions. And in performance it is usually desirable to crescendo to the top of the scale or arpeggio, with a sense of arrival there, unless there are particular reasons to shape it differently.

After evenness of pitch, sound and rhythm, and playing musically, the last element to achieve is effortlessness. Until something feels easy, needing little physical or mental effort, there is more you can do to improve it. One simple approach is that whenever you are pleased with anything, see if you can get that same result but with half the effort. And then the same result with half the effort again.

How to use *Scales*

Which exercise to practise?
How long to practise it?
How often to practise it?

The basic aim is to be fluent in three-octave scales and arpeggios in every key, and then also in the few four-octave keys, playing them all with good intonation, sound and rhythm, and with a lack of effort. The question is how to get the scales to that level.

Instead of practising only the scale itself, raise your standard of pitch-sound-rhythm-ease by working on the elements of the scale (Parts 1 and 2 of this book). The one-octave scales at the beginning are intended not only for less advanced players, but also for those who can already play the four octaves at the end.

Decide which section (or pages within a section) to practise, and cover many keys or variations within one practice. Or choose a particular key and work on each section of the book in that key only.

Return frequently to the pure three- or four-octave scales themselves, either to practise them or just to see how they sound and feel compared with the last time you played them. But, to improve them at the fastest possible rate, do not spend the bulk of your time practising them; work instead on the practice methods. Foundation work like this is still time spent practising scales: it is simply written-out, excellent practice.

A simple principle of training is to learn to do more than you need, so that what you have to do feels relatively easy. To improve three-octave scales and arpeggios, regularly spend time on the one- and two-octave scales on one string (Part 4). It does not matter if at first they seem difficult, or if your current stage or repertoire does not use those areas of the fingerboard. The point is that after playing them, the three- and four-octave scales feel so much more straightforward and approachable.

Practising *Scales* on viola

In transcribing *Scales* from the violin to the viola, the obvious question was how much the book's range and detail should be reduced because of the viola's larger dimensions. In the end I decided that the most sensible approach would be to preserve everything from the violin book.

Since the dimensions of full-size violas vary dramatically compared to full-size violins, and since hands come in all sizes and shapes, none of the scales in this book could be described as necessarily being more difficult on the viola than on the violin.

Larger stretches on the viola are only a factor in the lower positions. If any of the held-down finger lines in the lower positions feel too difficult, simply omit them. By the middle positions the spacing is the same as when playing in first position on the violin. In the upper positions everything depends on the width of the instrument's shoulders. The player will naturally change some of the fingerings (for example, 1-2-3-4 at the top octave of arpeggios), if the shoulder of the instrument is too wide.

There is also the question of whether it is necessary to practise in the second octave on any string except the A. Surely very little viola repertoire requires skill at the very top of the lower strings? However, as is the case for the violin, it is good to practise in those higher regions because they make the normal areas of the fingerboard feel so much easier afterwards. If any sections feel too precarious to be practicable, simply omit them.

Part 1

Scales and arpeggios in low positions without shifting

Notes

part 1

1. How to tune each note of the scale *Page 4*

Tune each C, G, D and A exactly with the open strings.

Measure sharps relative to the natural note one semitone above, flats relative to the natural note one semitone below. Sharps may be higher, and flats lower, than their tuning on a keyboard, where B♭ and A♯ are the same.

Whether a sharp or flat is higher or lower than the tempered pitch of a keyboard, or is the same, depends on the key or the place of the note in the scale.

Think of B in relation to C; think of F in relation to E.

Measure F from the perfect fourth above open C, or perfect fifth below C on the G string.

2. One-octave scales *Page 6*

Place the prepared fingers, shown with diamond noteheads, decisively. Afterwards, when playing without thinking about preparation, the fingers will automatically perform the correct, light, just-in-time placement naturally.

3. One-octave arpeggio sequence *Page 18*

This is the arpeggio sequence used by Otakar Ševčík, later borrowed by Carl Flesch, and used in many standard scale books since:

1. Minor
2. Major
3. Relative minor, 1st inversion
4. Sub-dominant major, 2nd inversion
5. Sub-dominant minor, 2nd inversion
6. Diminished seventh
7. Dominant seventh

Held-down finger lines that end with 'etc' mean that the finger should continue to be held down throughout the following bars.

4. Chromatic scales *Page 22*

An important principle of tuning chromatic scales is the rule of semitones, which decides whether the two notes are played close (diatonic semitone, notated as a minor second), or played wide (chromatic semitone, notated as an augmented unison):

- If the letter names of the semitone are the same (e.g. C–C♯, E–E♭), the semitone is played wide
- If the letter names of the semitone are different (e.g. C–D♭, E–D♯), the semitone is played close

That leaves the question of how the chromatic scale should be spelt. The usual principle is to use sharps ascending and flats descending, but this varies in different scale books.

So while a chromatic scale in a piece has a clear musical context (although even then one might sometimes disagree with a composer and intentionally play a ♯ instead of a ♭), in a neutral chromatic scale the player can feel a certain degree of freedom of choice.

Keep the left hand still during chromatic scales played in first position. Whether the fingering is sliding or shifting, keep the thumb in one place. For example, in the sliding fingering do not begin on first finger C♯ in half position but keep the hand in first position and reach back with the first finger to find the C♯. Then, moving from E♭ to E with the second finger, do not keep the shape of the finger the same and shift the whole hand: keep the hand still and move only the finger.

In the shifting fingering, keep the hand in first position throughout, without being in half position for the first two notes, then in second position on the E♭, then first position again once the second finger E is played.

5. Warm-up exercise: fourth-finger extensions *Page 25*

In the next section, no. 6, the fingering starting on the third finger demands a fourth-finger extension at the top of the scale. Play this exercise a few times first to make it feel easy.

6. Two-octave scales and arpeggios *Page 26*

This section is an excellent exercise for uniform intonation. The point is to make all three fingerings (the same notes played starting on the first, second and third fingers) sound exactly the same, since the right tuning of a note is the same no matter which finger you play it with. When you repeat a group of notes but use a different fingering each time, notes that are not in tune stand out clearly.

The results are often surprising, since it is all too easy to get used to an out-of-tune note if it is always the same degree sharp or flat when played with a particular finger. It is only when you try a different fingering that you realise that the previous pitch which you had accepted as being in tune, actually needs to be adjusted.

Play the harmonic minor by flattening the minor thirds in the major scales.

7. Two-octave broken thirds and fourths *Page 40*

See no. 6: *Two-octave scales and arpeggios*

How to tune each note of the scale

- ⊙ exactly in tune with the open string of the same name
- ↑ tune high, or relative to natural above
- ↓ tune low, or relative to natural below
- P4 Perfect fourth
- P5 Perfect fifth
- ↕ midway (in pitch) between the notes either side
- ↔ tune midway like a keyboard

One-octave scales

C major

melodic minor

harmonic minor

Part 1: Scales and arpeggios in low positions without shifting   See notes, page 2

One-octave scales

Part 1: Scales and arpeggios in low positions without shifting   See notes, page 2

One-octave scales

E♭ major

melodic minor

harmonic minor

Part 1: Scales and arpeggios in low positions without shifting See notes, page 2

One-octave scales

E major

melodic minor

harmonic minor

Part 1: Scales and arpeggios in low positions without shifting   See notes, page 2

One-octave scales

F major

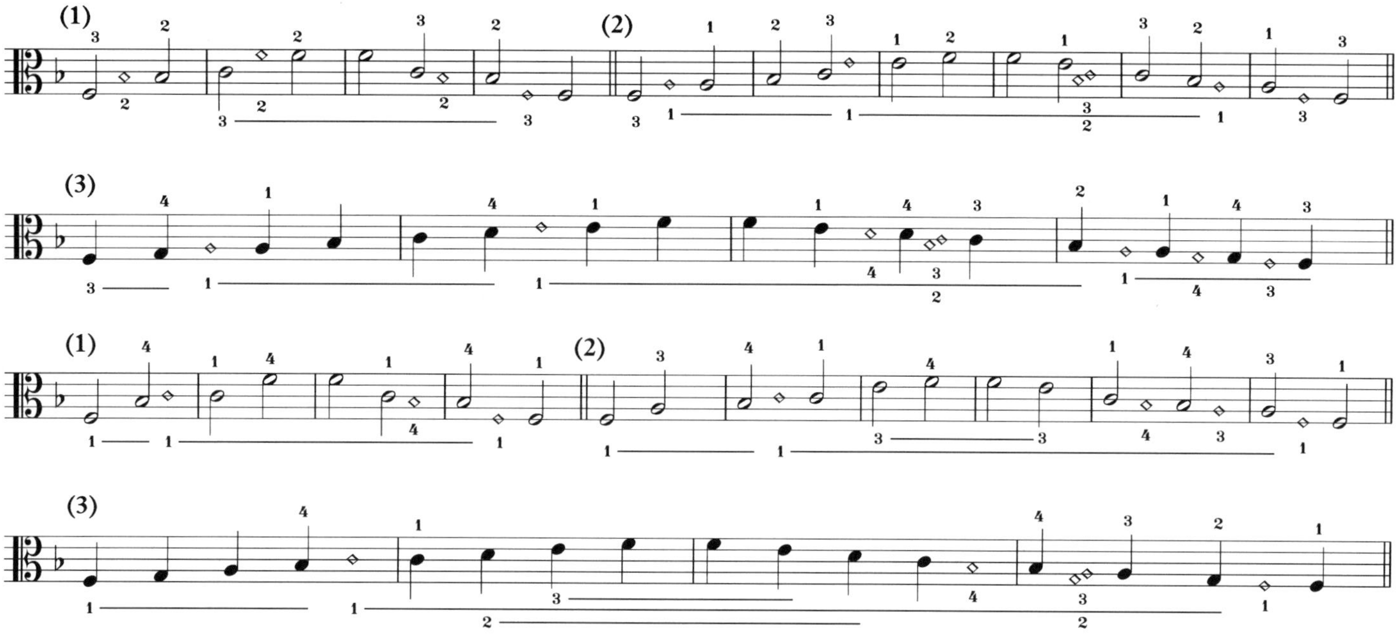

melodic minor

harmonic minor

Part 1: Scales and arpeggios in low positions without shifting   See notes, page 2

One-octave scales

14 Part 1: Scales and arpeggios in low positions without shifting   See notes, page 2

One-octave scales

A major

melodic minor

harmonic minor

Part 1: Scales and arpeggios in low positions without shifting   See notes, page 2

One-octave scales

B♭ major

melodic minor

harmonic minor

Part 1: Scales and arpeggios in low positions without shifting   See notes, page 2

One-octave scales

B

major

melodic minor

harmonic minor

Part 1: Scales and arpeggios in low positions without shifting   See notes, page 2

One-octave arpeggio sequence

One-octave arpeggio sequence

Part 1: Scales and arpeggios in low positions without shifting   See notes, page 2

One-octave arpeggio sequence

4 Chromatic scales

Slow fingering (sliding)

Base the hand position on the first finger D, and reach back with the first finger for the C♯   Reach back with the first finger for the D♭

Leave the fingers down on the string

Exercise for sliding

Hold down without playing. Balance the hand on the fourth finger and reach back.

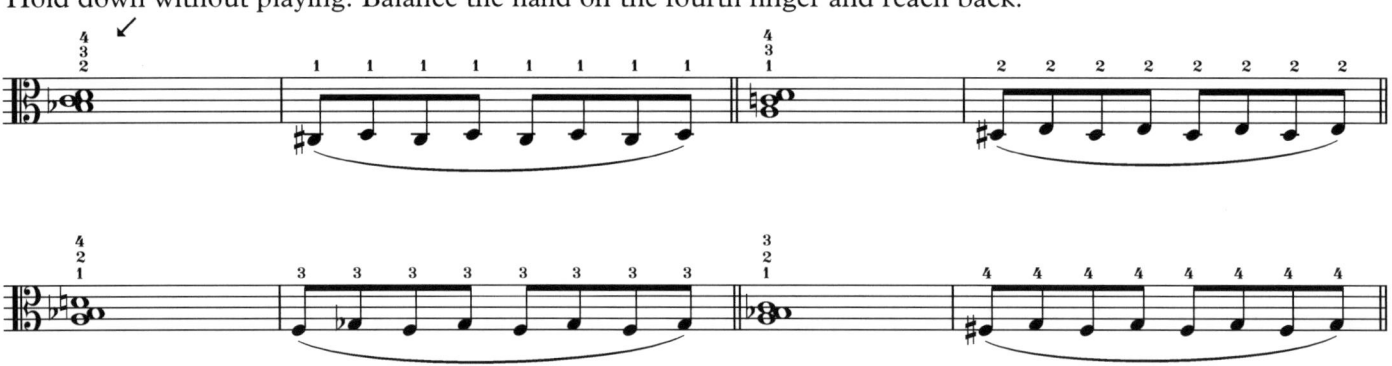

Play the same patterns on the other pairs of strings:

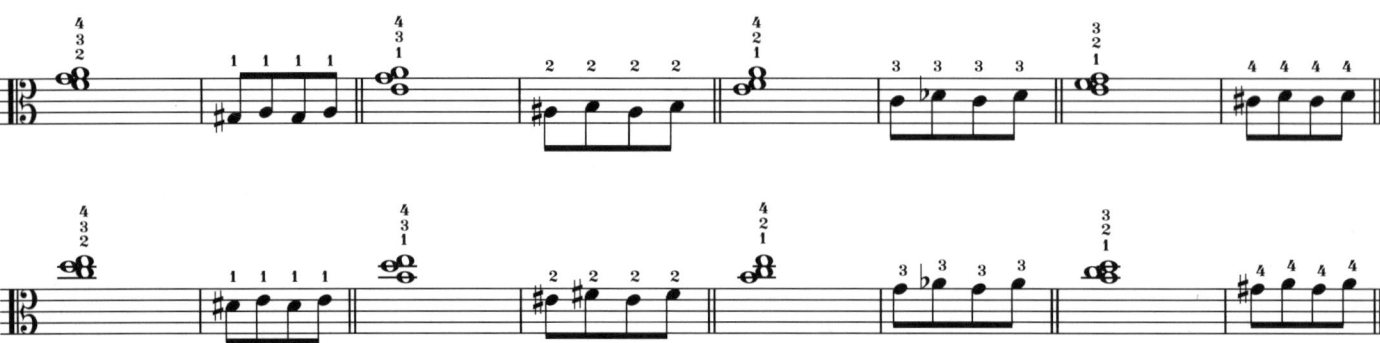

Co-ordination exercise for separate bows

Play the dotted notes as long as possible, the short notes as short as possible.
Aim for 128th notes rather than 32nd notes (demisemiquavers).

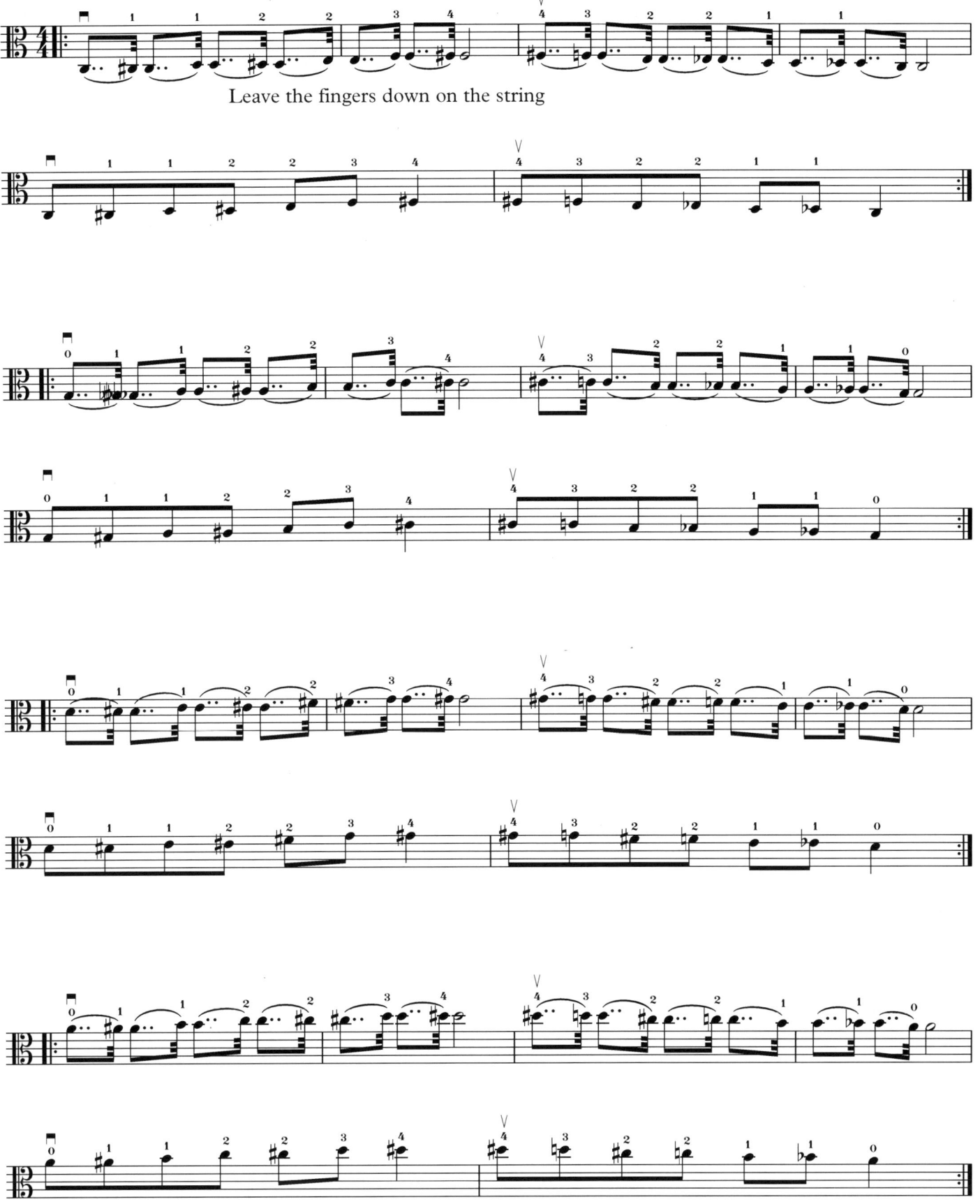

Leave the fingers down on the string

Chromatic scales

Fast fingering (shifting)

Keep the hand and thumb in one place; move only the fingers. Do not 'shift up' from the second to the first finger. Aim for 128th notes rather than 32nd notes (demisemiquavers). 'Ghost' the x-notes by lightening the finger as if to play a harmonic.

Co-ordination exercise for separate bows

Aim for 128th notes rather than 32nd notes (demisemiquavers).

Exercise for timing the shift: missing out the note before the shift

Use fast *spiccato* or *sautillé*. The exercise also works well with a fast, short stroke on the string.
Place each finger quickly so that it is ready for the bow.

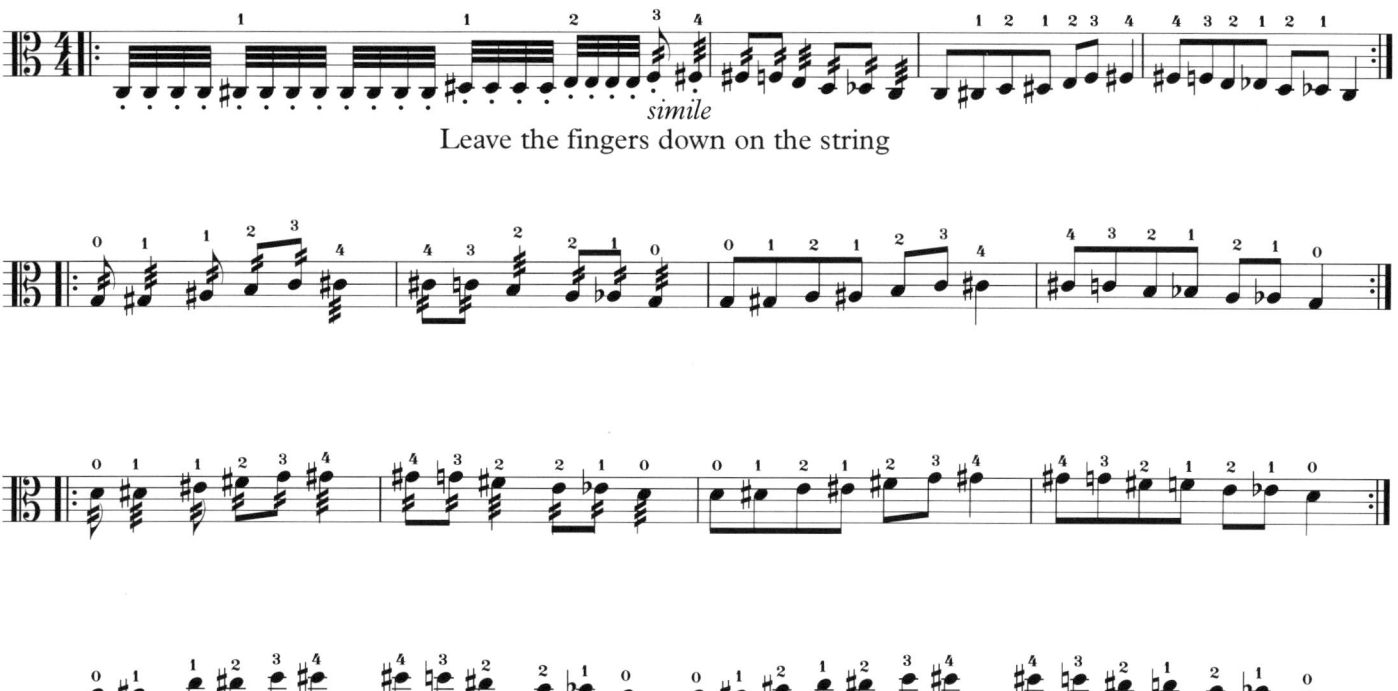

Leave the fingers down on the string

Repeat the sequence on the C, G and D strings.

6 Two-octave scales and arpeggios

F major

First finger

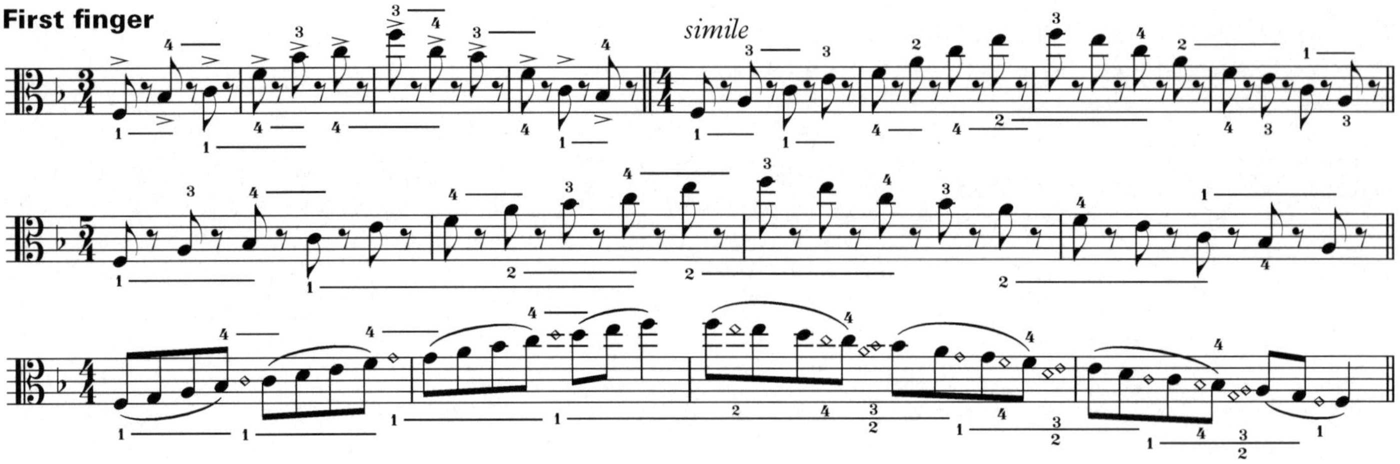

Second finger

Third finger

Arpeggio

26 Part 1: Scales and arpeggios in low positions without shifting See notes, page 2

Two-octave scales and arpeggios

 minor

First finger

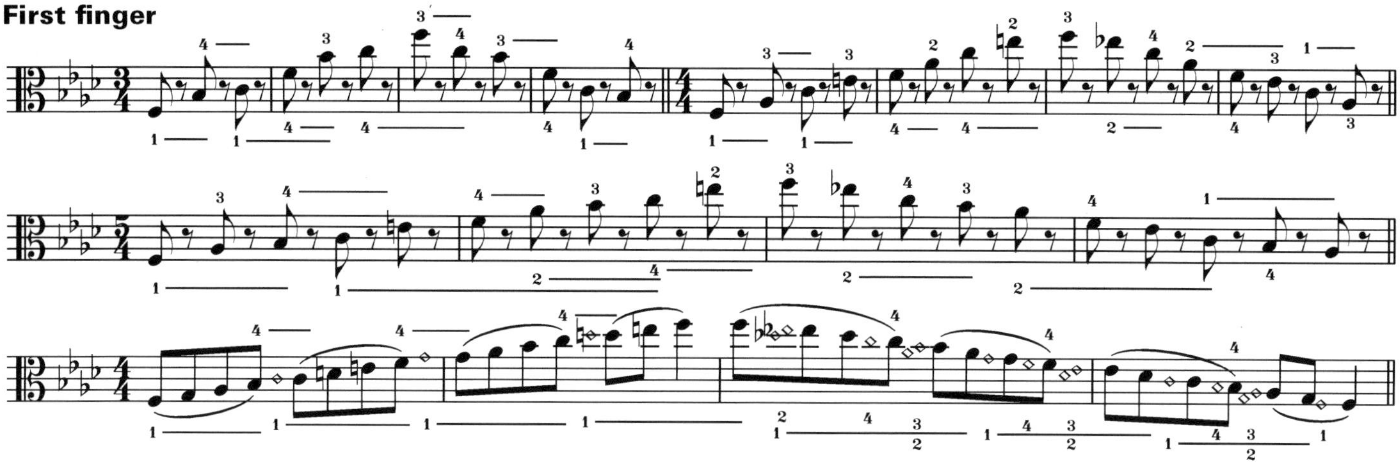

Second finger

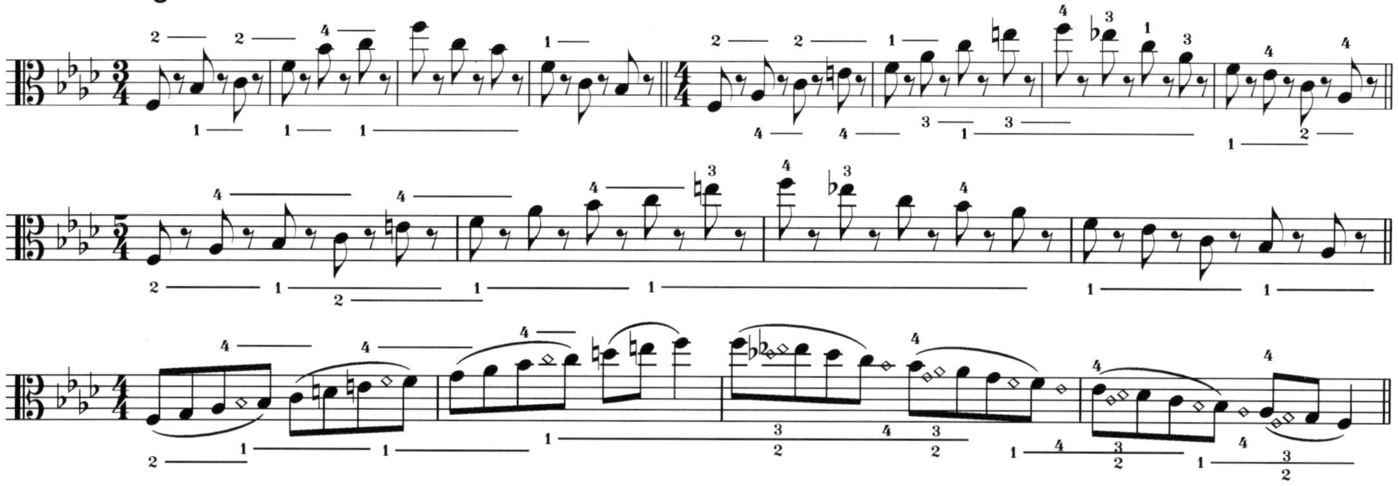

Third finger

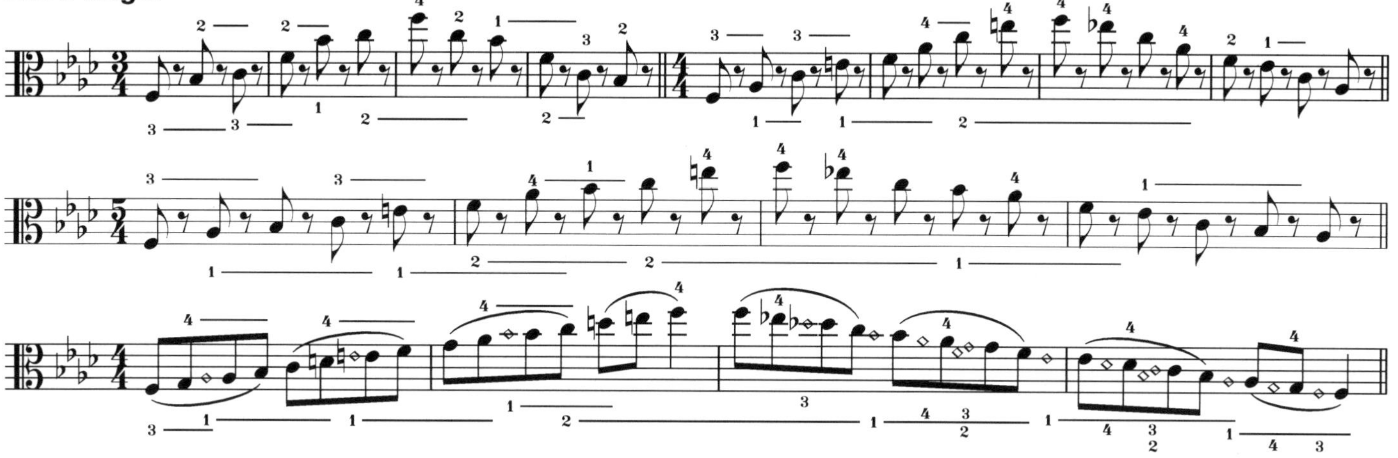

Arpeggio

Part 1: Scales and arpeggios in low positions without shifting See notes, page 2

G♭ major

First finger

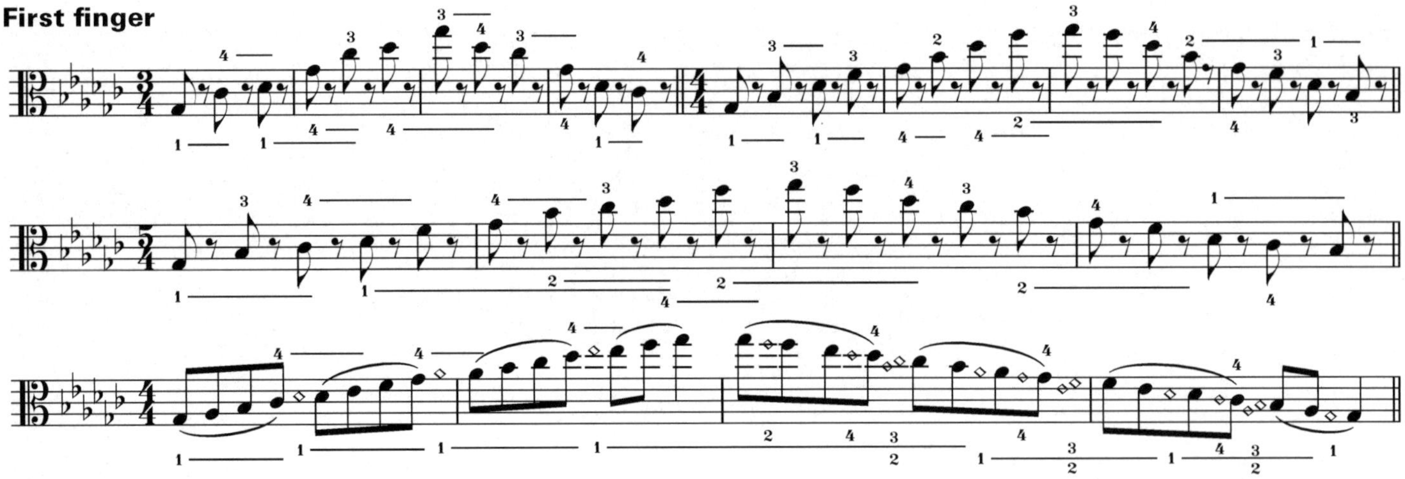

Second finger

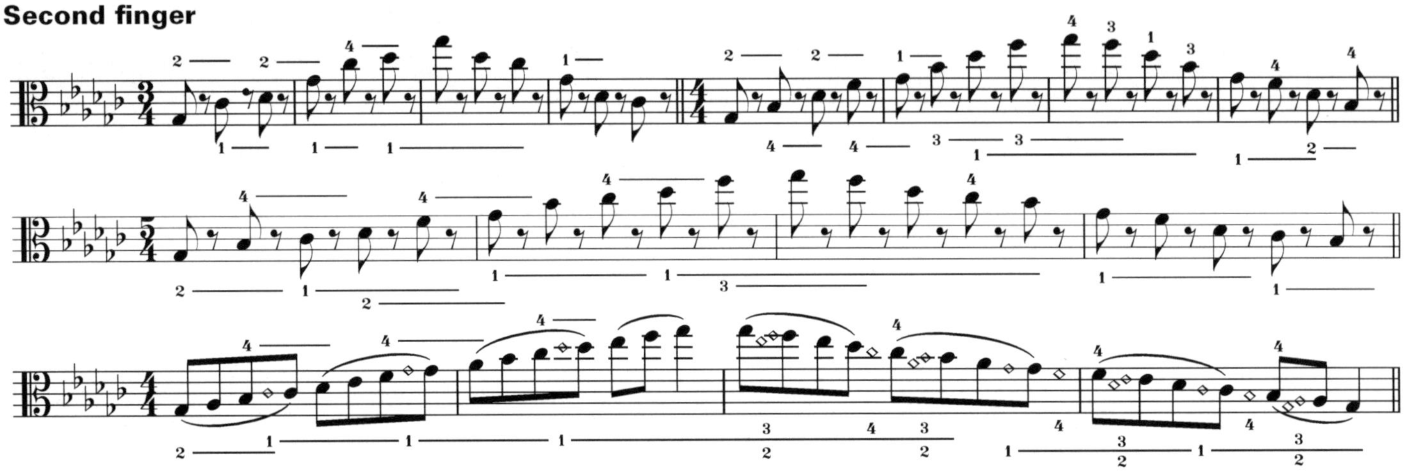

Third finger

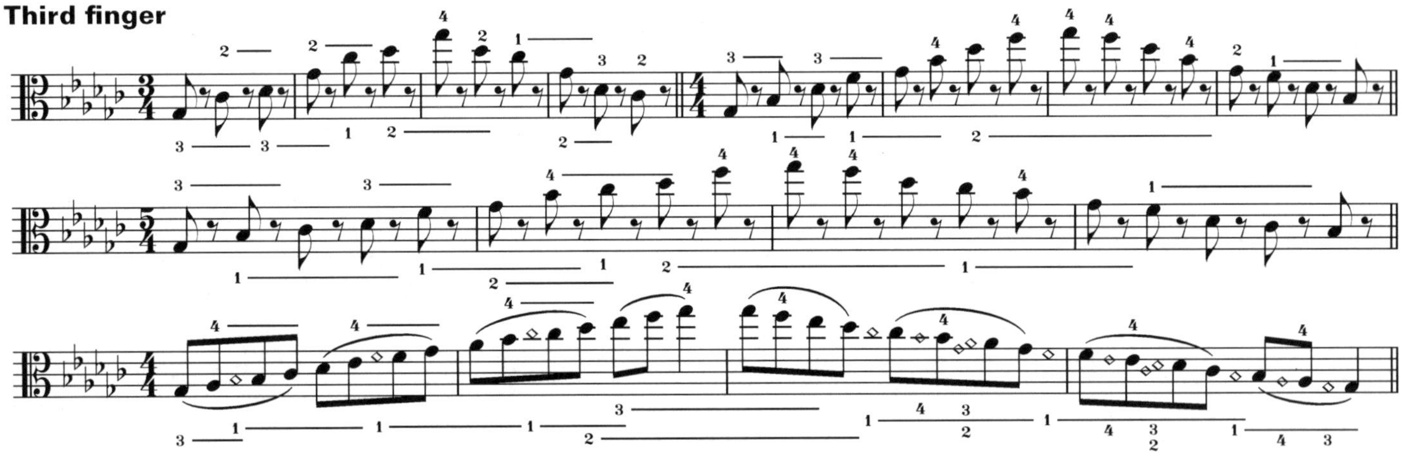

Arpeggio

Two-octave scales and arpeggios

F# minor

First finger

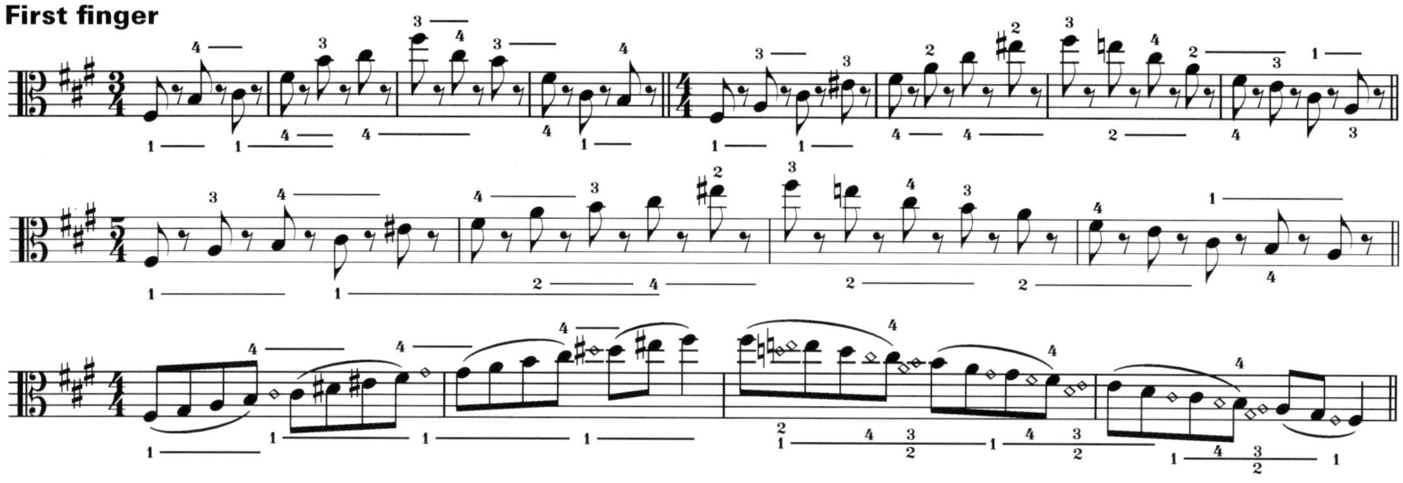

Second finger

Third finger

Arpeggio

Part 1: Scales and arpeggios in low positions without shifting   See notes, page 2

G minor

Two-octave scales and arpeggios

First finger

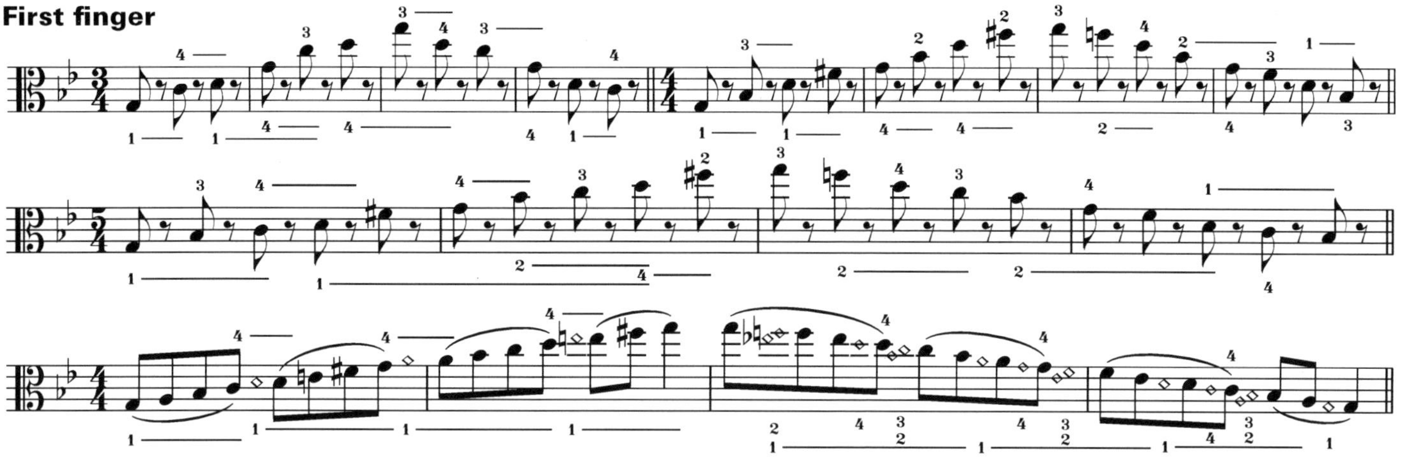

Second finger

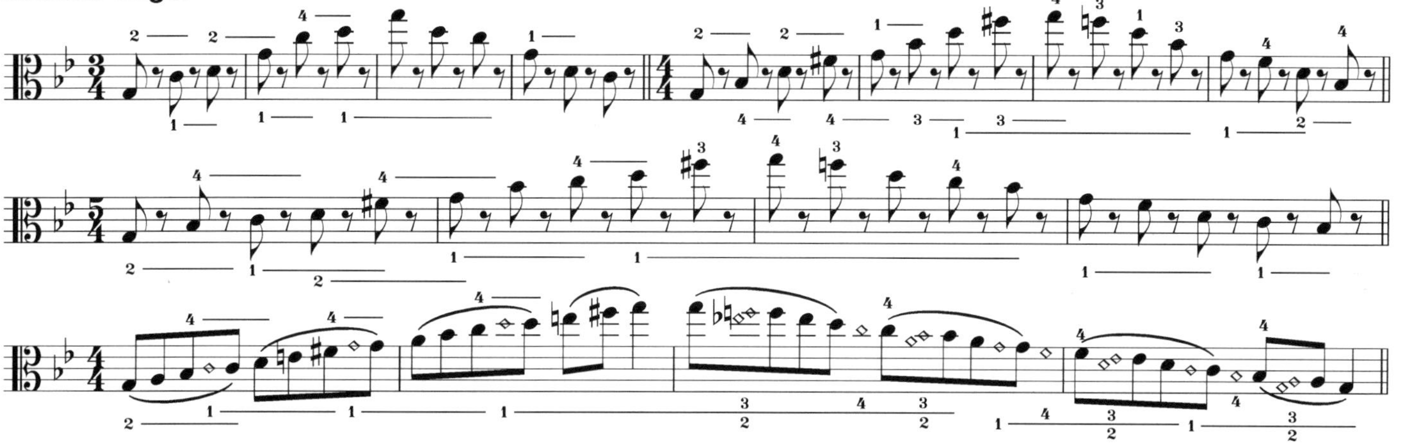

Third finger

Arpeggio

Part 1: Scales and arpeggios in low positions without shifting   See notes, page 2

Two-octave scales and arpeggios

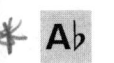 

First finger

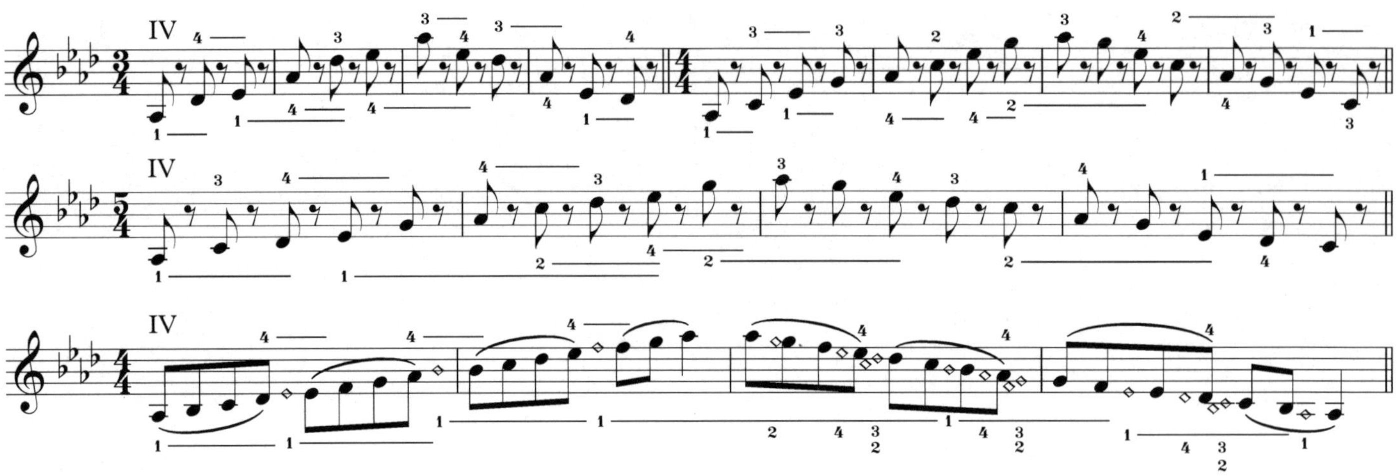

Second finger

Third finger

Arpeggio

A minor

Two-octave scales and arpeggios

First finger

Second finger

Third finger

Arpeggio

Part 1: Scales and arpeggios in low positions without shifting   See notes, page 2

Two-octave scales and arpeggios

B♭ major

First finger

Second finger

Third finger

Arpeggio

Part 1: Scales and arpeggios in low positions without shifting   See notes, page 2

B♭ minor

Two-octave scales and arpeggios

First finger

Second finger

Third finger

Arpeggio

B minor

7 Two-octave broken thirds and fourths

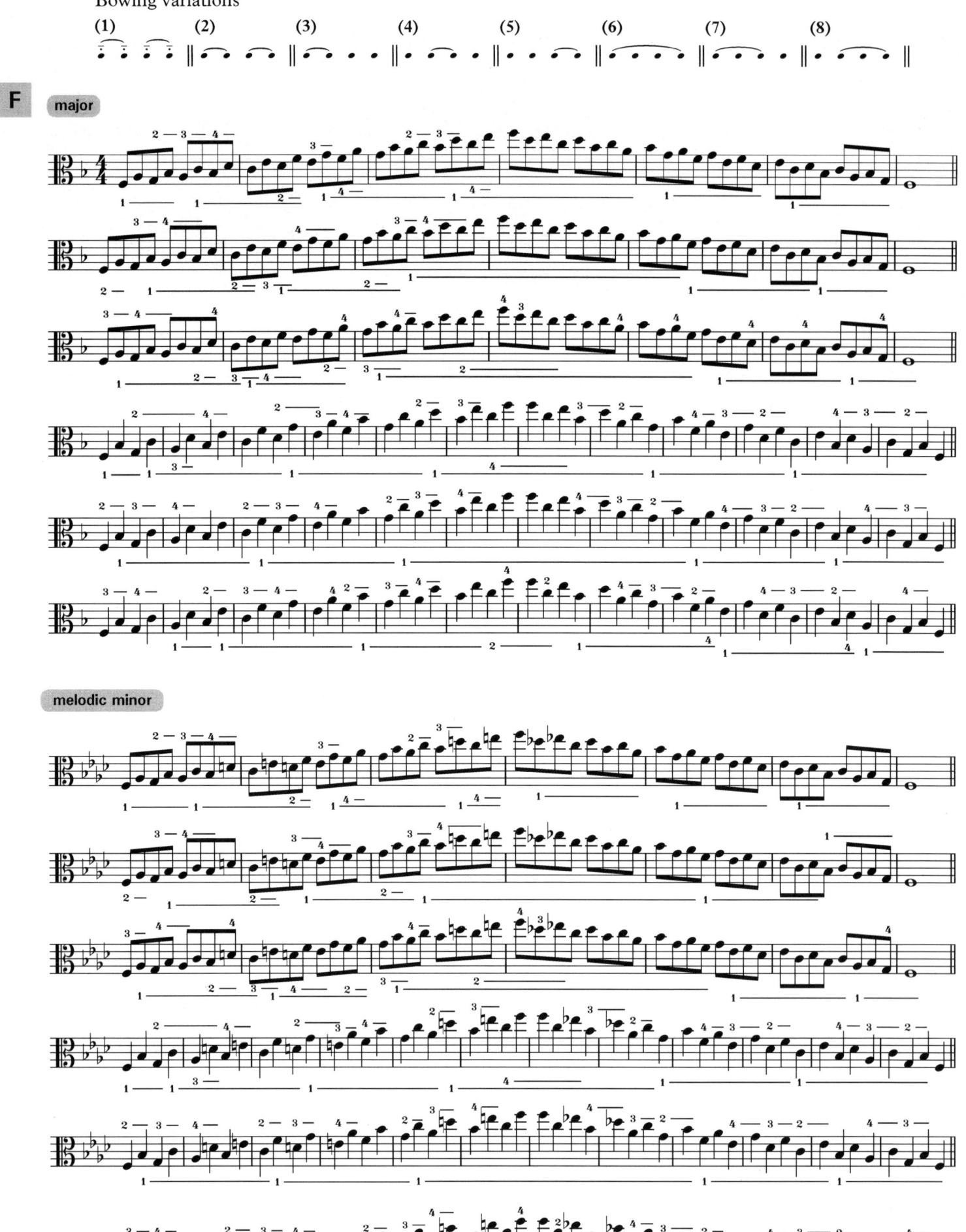

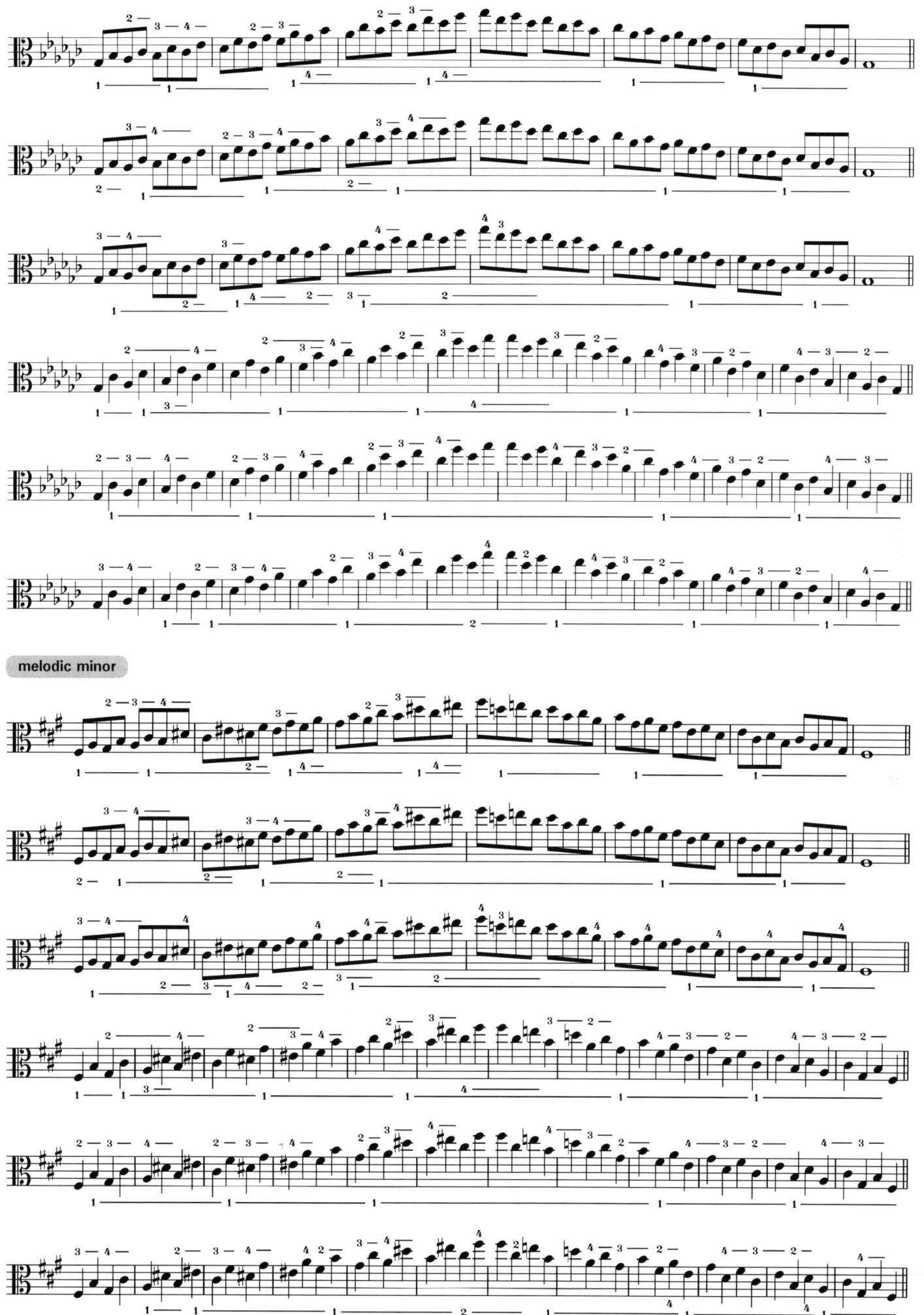

Two-octave broken thirds and fourths

G major

melodic minor

Two-octave broken thirds and fourths

A major

melodic minor

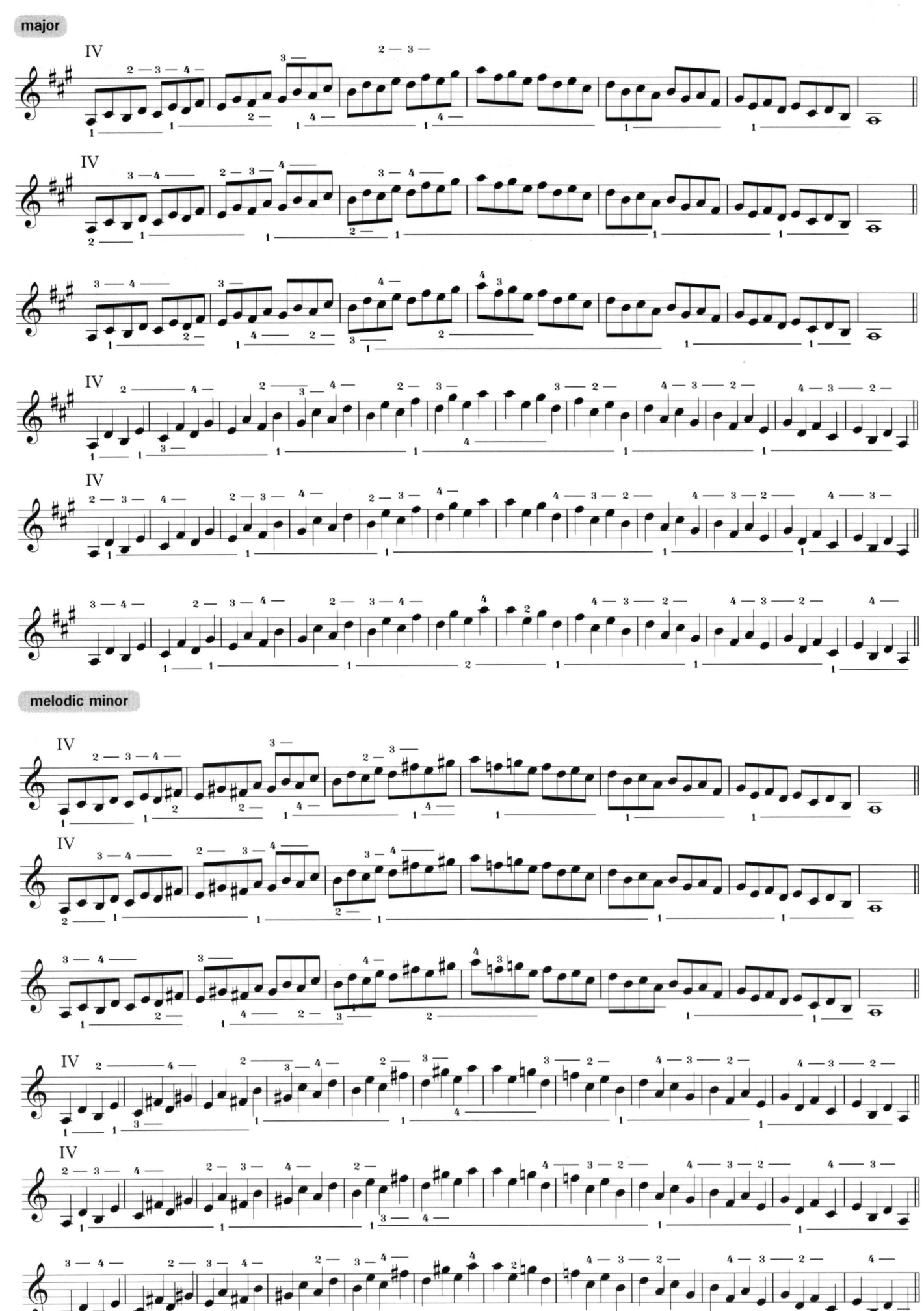

Part 1: Scales and arpeggios in low positions without shifting   See notes, page 2

Two-octave broken thirds and fourths

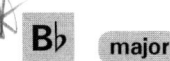**major**

melodic minor

Part 1: Scales and arpeggios in low positions without shifting See notes, page 2

Two-octave broken thirds and fourths

B major

melodic minor

Part 1: Scales and arpeggios in low positions without shifting   See notes, page 2

Part 2

Three-octave scales and arpeggios: preparatory practice

Notes

part 2

8 — Three-octave scales: structuring intonation — *Page 52*

The notes of the three building stages, before the complete scale, do not need to be played as a continuous sequence with regular rhythm. At first, to act as guides for placing the notes you play, finger the missed-out notes without sounding them.

9 — Tone-semitone patterns — *Page 64*

This simple exercise helps the hand learn the spacing of each tone-semitone pattern in each position. Once you have become fluent with the exercise there is a feeling of the entire hand being in tune, each finger knowing exactly where to go in each position, rather than a sense of having to aim each finger in tune one at a time.

10 — Scales: exercise for overlapping the first and fourth fingers — *Page 68*

This exercise trains five essential elements of smooth scale-playing:

1. Holding down the fourth finger momentarily, in ascending, when crossing to the first finger on the next string.
2. Holding down the first finger in descending when crossing to the fourth finger on the lower string.
3. Preparing the first finger on the new string in ascending.
4. Preparing the fourth finger in descending.
5. Smooth string crossings: moving early to the next string avoids a sudden movement which may cause an accent.

11 — One-octave scales in all positions without shifting — *Page 70*

This exercise is one of the best in the whole repertoire of intonation exercises. Include it in any practice of three or four octave scales, playing the exercise in the key of the scale. To play the harmonic minor, use the same patterns and fingerings as the major.

As in no. 6, page 26, make each fingering sound identical to each other. Omit nos. 4-6 if the positions are too high for you, and if you do not normally play at the top of the fingerboard (as you do in the music of Paganini, Wieniawski et al). But do play through the higher positions occasionally, however awkward they may feel, since one reason for doing them is so that the same patterns in lower positions feel much easier afterwards.

These scales are very useful for helping young players get used to playing in high positions early on, without needing to give them pieces that are too difficult.

12 The turning-point at the top of the scale — *Page 82*

Strengthen the top of the scale.

13 Three-octave scales: exercise for timing shifts — *Page 83*

To focus on the exact timing of the shift, this practice method misses out the note before the shift. The point is to arrive on the shifted-to note precisely in time, with absolute regularity and continuity. The resulting note pattern should be as rhythmically even as it would be if you played it without shifting.

This method of practice derives from the fact that the time for the shift must be taken from the note before the shift. The shift must not begin at the very moment that the finger is actually meant to be arriving on the new note.

Play a slurred arpeggio with a metronome click on each beat. The incorrect timing can be illustrated like this:

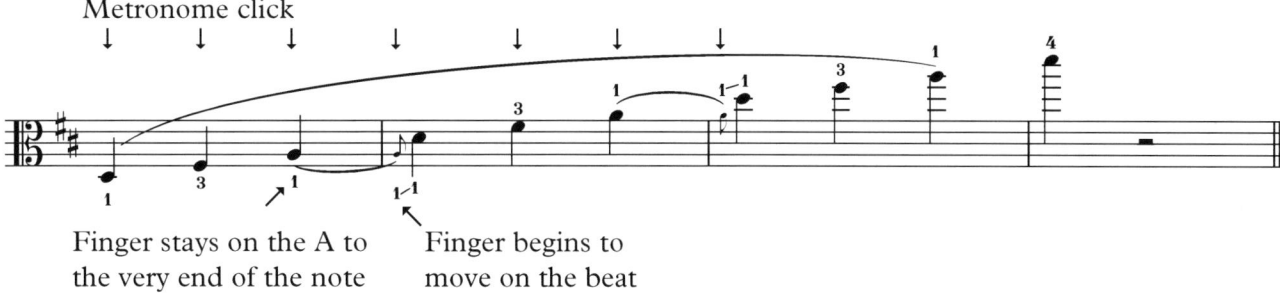

Finger stays on the A to the very end of the note   Finger begins to move on the beat

Instead, in order to arrive in time exactly on the beat you have to begin to shift during the previous note, not at the end of it:

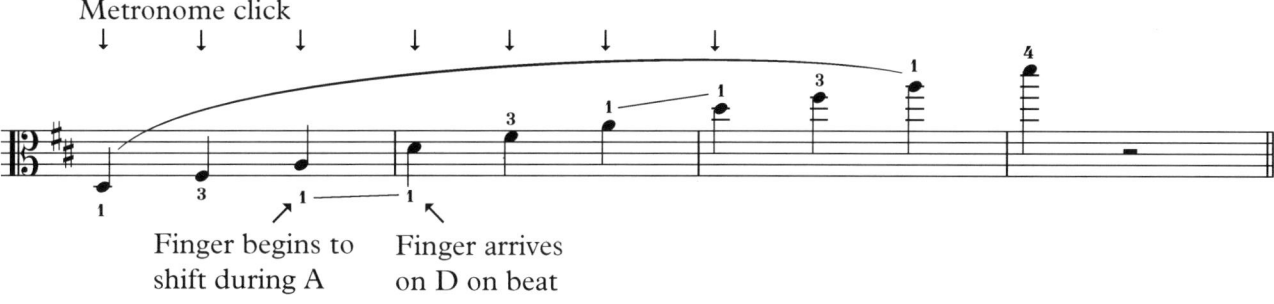

Finger begins to shift during A   Finger arrives on D on beat

Rather than thinking about shifting at all, focus on the rhythm of the actual notes. In a scale or arpeggio, or any group of notes that includes a shift, you need a rhythmic feeling of '*now, now, now, now*' as you sound each note; not '*now, now, shift…now, now*'. If you concentrate on the musical rhythm, the timing of the shift takes care of itself.

14 Harmonic minor scale: exercise for the augmented 2nd — *Page 89*

This sequence focuses on the unusual contraction of the hand caused by the augmented 2nd between the fourth and first fingers. The normal 'frame' of the hand is a perfect 4th but here it becomes a diminished 4th.

15 Warm-up exercise: smooth bowing — *Page 89*

The basic action of the fingers is vertical; the bow horizontal. The one must not affect the other. Playing *forte* should not make the left fingers over-press; the finger action should not disturb the bow. This exercise for independence instantly produces the perfect legato tone. Apply it constantly throughout all your work on scales and arpeggios – briefly bow on another string while continuing to finger the notes you are practising – and to phrases or passages in pieces.

16 Exercise to develop 'fast fingers' *Page 90*

Play repeated fast strokes on each note. The fingers must drop and lift very quickly to co-ordinate with the bow. The faster the stroke, the faster the finger action must be. The more strokes on each note, the longer the left finger must wait before moving. This forces you to wait, and then to move the finger very fast.

Sautillé is best, since the shorter the stroke the more precise the co-ordination must be; but you can get the same result with fast, short strokes along the string. Occasional practice like this, on any scale or arpeggio, quickly transforms the timing of the left fingers, making them quicker, easier and more efficient.

17 Warm-up exercise: moving fingers independently of the hand *Page 90*

The best action of the fingers is a movement from the base knuckle joint. In simple down-and-up movements on one string, the curved shape of the finger should remain basically the same, with no movement from the middle joint and without partly dropping the finger with a movement of the hand. A simple way to train this is simply to hold down three fingers on the strings and to silently tap down and up with the remaining finger. Use this as a constant warm-up exercise, and occasionally return to it during the course of practising a scale if you sense that your fingers could be moving more freely.

18 Placing fingers in blocks *Page 91*

While you can play each finger individually at slower speeds, at the fastest speeds you often have to drop or lift two or more fingers at the same time in a 'block'. Then instead of two, three or four notes requiring two, three or four mental commands and actions, you can play all of them with one command and one action. Make the fingers into a fan-like shape so that they touch or leave the string separately.

In all the descending lift-offs, make sure you place the fingers on the string first, in their correct tone–semitone pattern, before lifting them together with one action.

19 One-octave arpeggio sequence in all positions without shifting *Page 96*

Make each fingering sound identical to the others. See also no. 11, page 70.

20 Starting at the top *Page 101*

Starting at the top of the scale or arpeggio, while seeming to go against gravity, presents many new challenges that lead to greater security and control when playing the normal scale. Practise in all keys, using the patterns in Parts 3 and 5 as a guide.

21 Three-octave arpeggios: exercise for timing shifts *Page 102*

In the first two bars, the note before the shift is left out. Play exactly in time, shifting to the new note so that the arrival of the finger is perfectly co-ordinated with the bow. Do not wait with the bow for the finger. The bow must play on regardless, and the shifting finger must get there in time. The aim is for it to sound the same as if you were playing across the strings in one position without shifting.

Also practise this exercise without the repeated notes, either playing separate bows or long slurs (with ties when adjacent notes are the same).

22 Three-octave diminished sevenths — *Page 106*

In the first two bars the double-stops force the left fingers to prepare, and the bow to pivot early to the next string. Then find the same leading in the left hand as you cross to the next string, and the same smooth leading in the bow, when you play without the double-stops.

23 Three-octave dominant sevenths — *Page 109*

Be careful to tune the notes of the double-stops as if they were single-stops. For example, if in the first bar you play the C–E double-stops 'in tune' as an interval, the E would have to be played rather flat and would be too low when played on its own afterwards.

24 Arpeggios: shifting exercises — *Page 112*

Strengthen typical shifts used in arpeggios. Play the same patterns in many different areas of the fingerboard on each string.

25 Practice method: 'trilling' the shift — *Page 113*

'Trill' each shift: begin slowly and speed up. Keep the hand and fingers soft and repeat many times until it is as clean as possible. Remind yourself of how good the 'trill' could be by playing it with a proper, non-shifting fingering. Then make the shifting, 'trilling' fingering sound the same.

Do this exercise on troublesome shifts not only in scale or arpeggios but also in phrases or passages in pieces.

26 Practice method: uniform intonation in arpeggios — *Page 113*

'Uniform intonation' means that every tonic, third and fifth in an arpeggio is exactly in tune with every other. For example, there should not be a wider major third in one octave and a narrower major third in the next. Finger the diamond noteheads without sounding them. Play only the normal notes and tune them to each other exactly.

27 Arpeggios: placing fingers in blocks — *Page 114*

This practice-method is related to no. 18, but in this case do not drop the fingers in a fan-like shape. Place the x-notes at exactly the same time as the top (sounding) note, and keep them down on the string until they are played on the descent.

28 Chromatic scales: exercise for 321 or 123 fingering — *Page 118*

The two usual fingerings for playing the ascending chromatic scale on the A string are 12 and 123. Descending, the usual fingering is 321.

The 123 or 321 fingering may seem uncomfortable at first because after playing two semitones, the first and third fingers are a tone apart in spacing instead of the usual minor or major third. These exercises quickly help the fingers learn the unfamiliar contracted position, and afterwards the normal chromatic scale feels natural and easy.

Three-octave scales: structuring intonation

Three-octave scales: structuring intonation

D♭ major

C♯ melodic minor

harmonic minor

Part 2: Three-octave scales and arpeggios: preparatory practice See notes, page 48

Three-octave scales: structuring intonation

Three-octave scales: structuring intonation

E major

melodic minor

harmonic minor

Part 2: Three-octave scales and arpeggios: preparatory practice   See notes, page 48

Three-octave scales: structuring intonation

F

Three-octave scales: structuring intonation

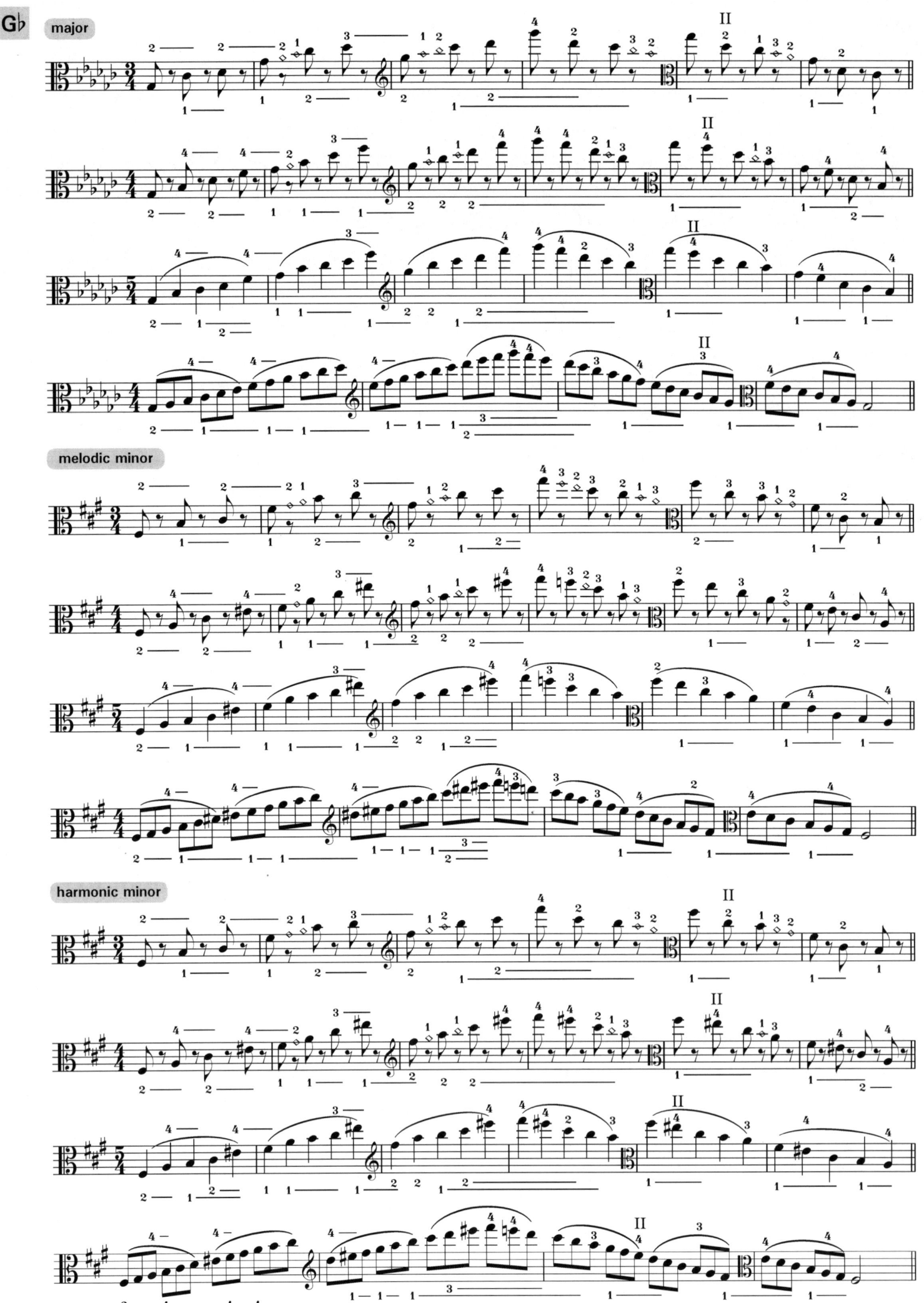

Three-octave scales: structuring intonation

Ab major

G# melodic minor

harmonic minor

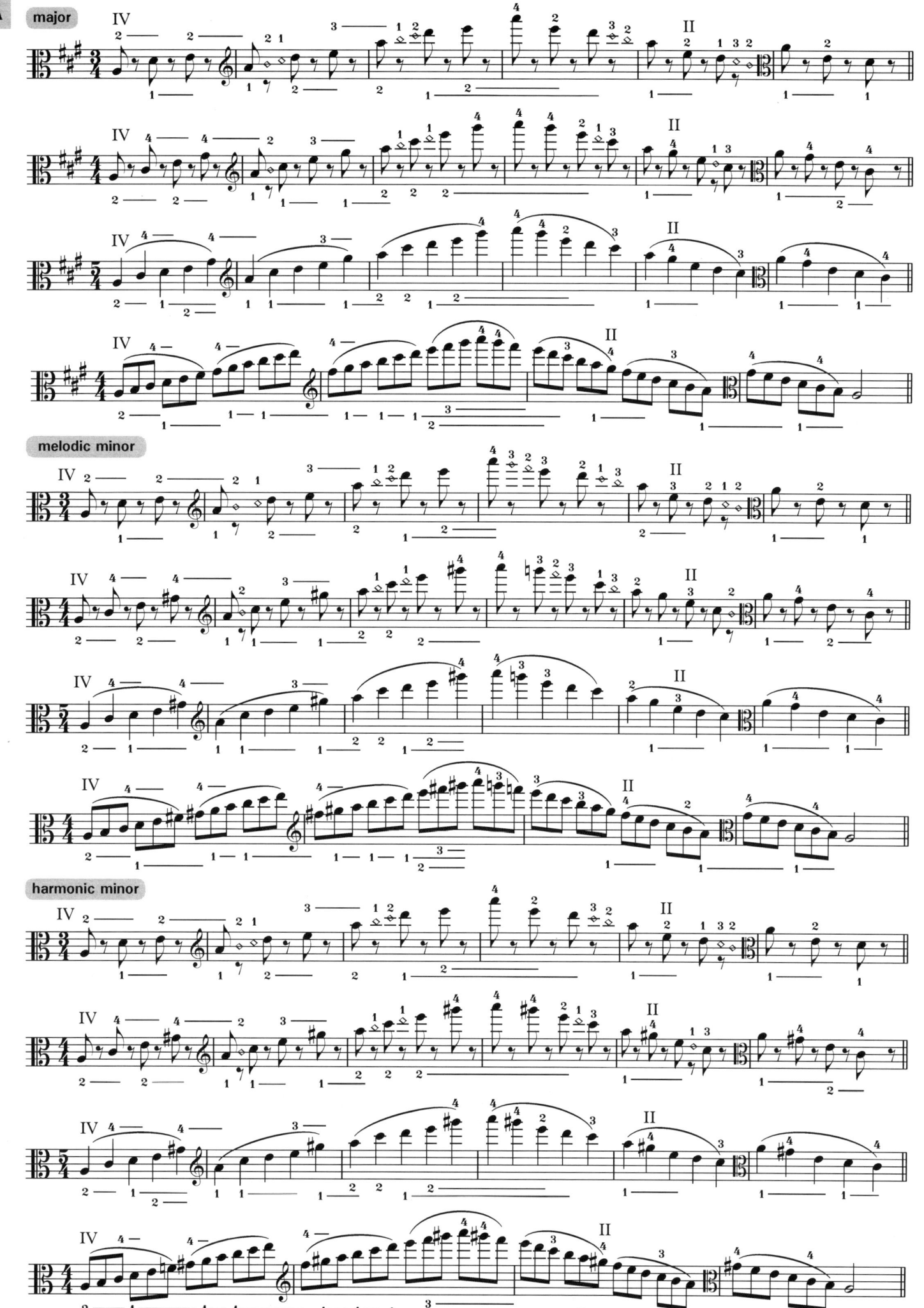

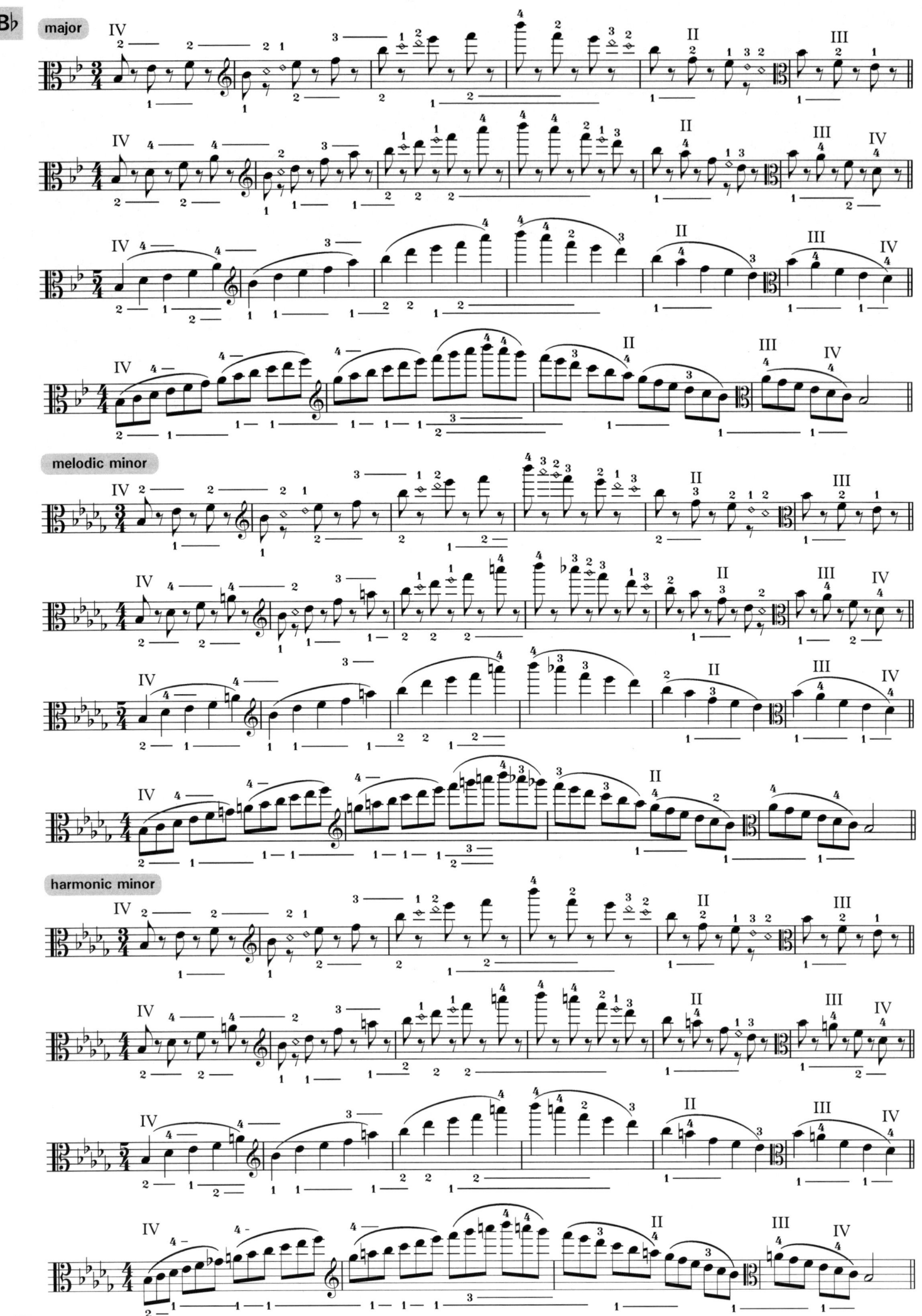

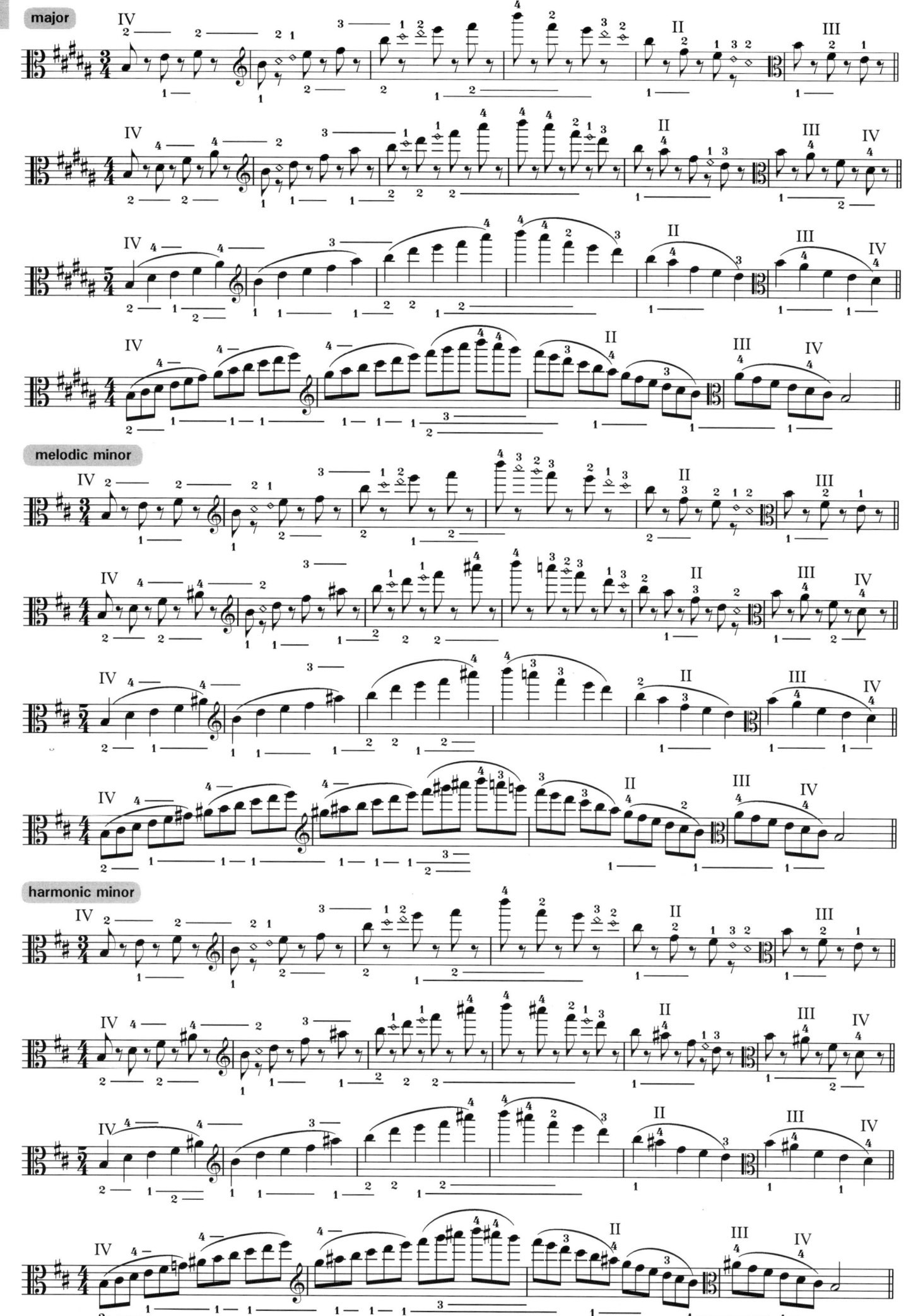

9 Tone-semitone patterns

- ○ exactly in tune with the open string of the same name
- ↑ tune high, or relative to natural above
- ↓ tune low, or relative to natural below
- P4 Perfect fourth above open string or first note of group
- ↕ midway (in pitch) between the notes either side
- ↔ tune midway like a keyboard

Variations

Semitone – tone – tone

simile

(Continue on C string as far up as possible)

Sul III

Sul II

(Continue on G string as far up as possible)

Sul I

(Continue on D string as far up as possible)

(Continue as far up as possible)

Part 2: Three-octave scales and arpeggios: preparatory practice   See notes, page 48

Tone-semitone patterns

Tone – semitone – tone

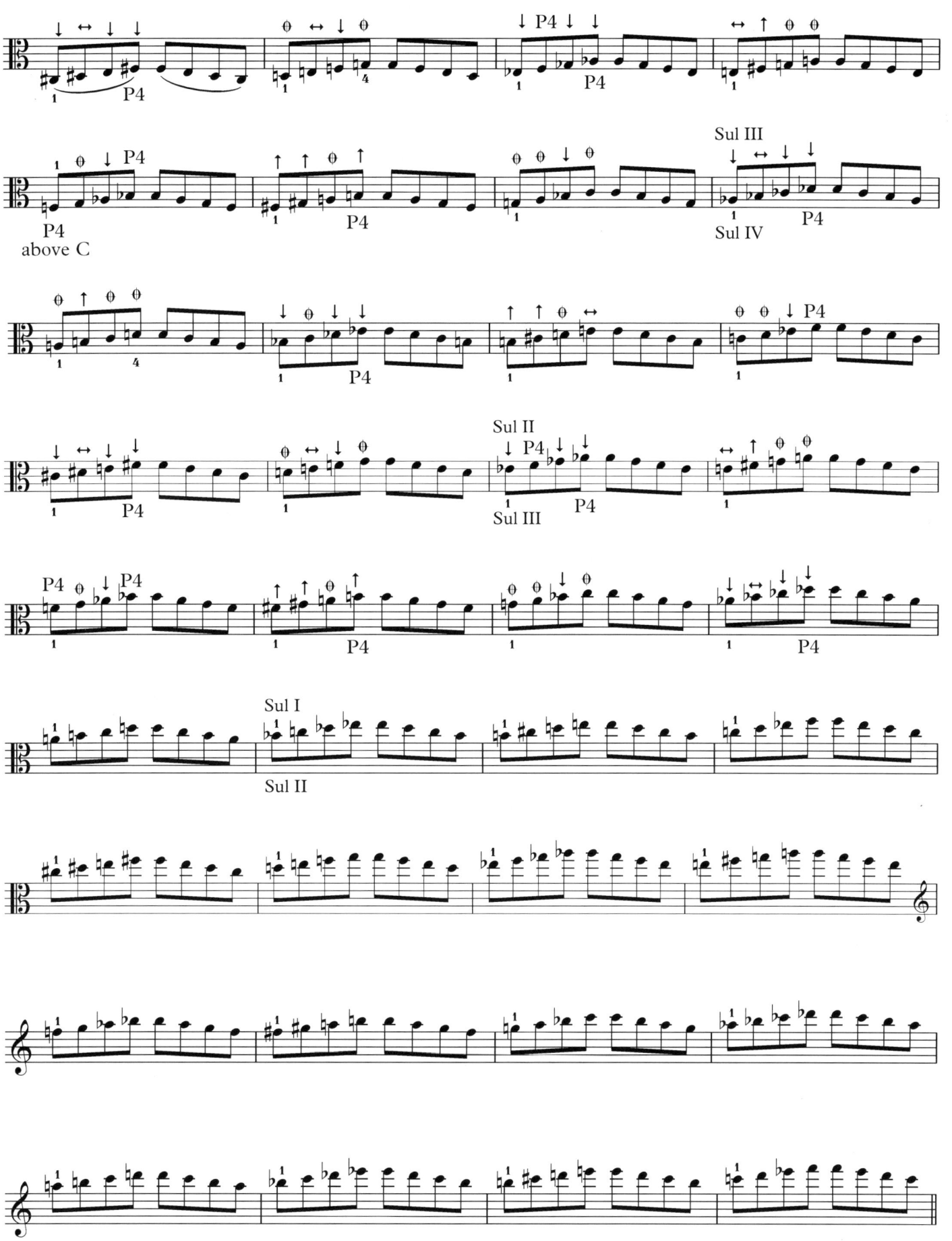

Tone-semitone patterns

- ⊕ exactly in tune with the open string of the same name
- ↑ tune high, or relative to natural above
- ↓ tune low, or relative to natural below
- P4 Perfect fourth above open string or first note of group
- ↕ midway (in pitch) between the notes either side
- ↔ tune midway like a keyboard

Tone – tone – semitone

Tone – tone – tone

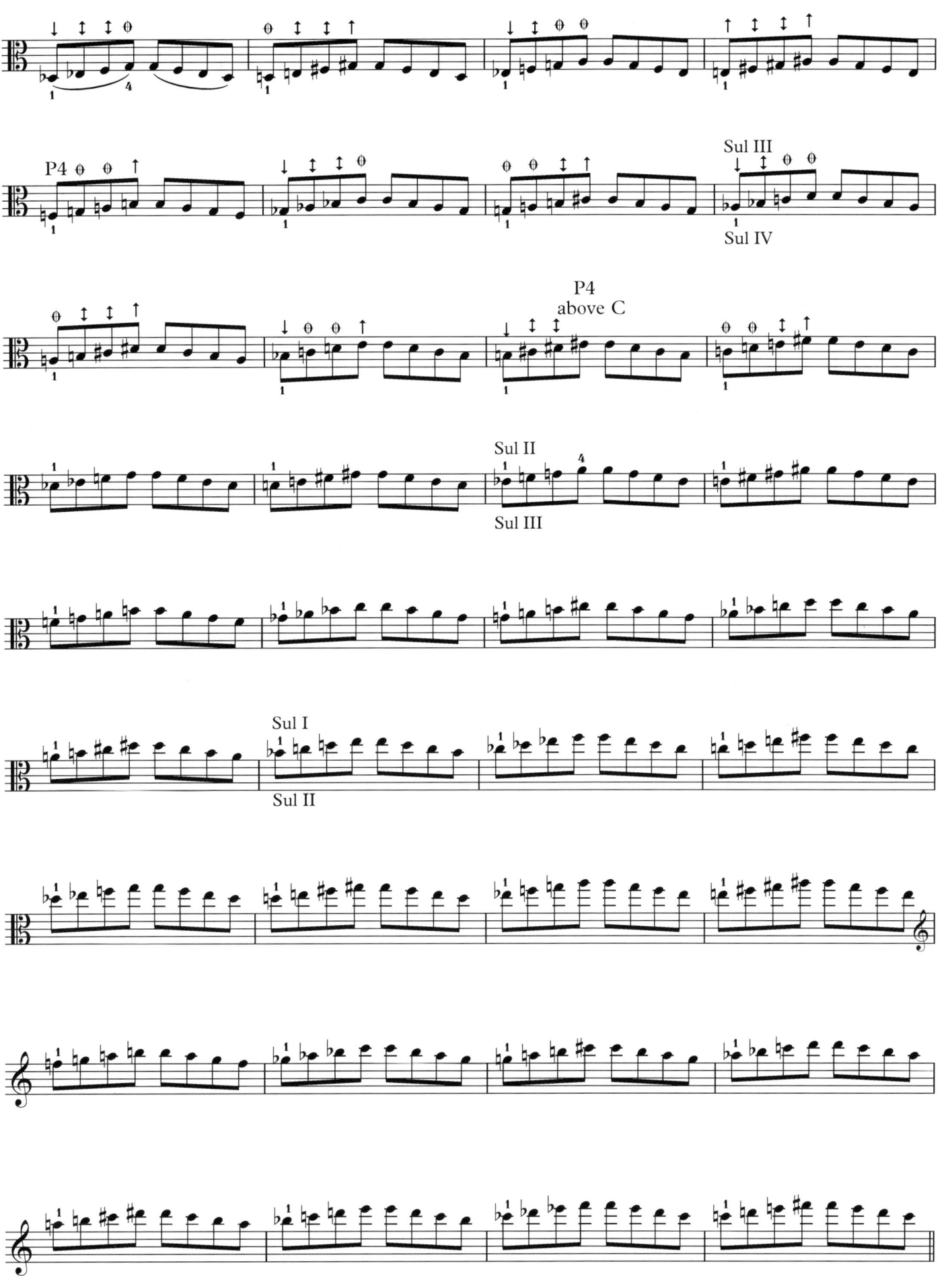

Scales: exercise for overlapping the first and fourth fingers

Keep the first finger on the string throughout, lifting only when it is needed on the next string.

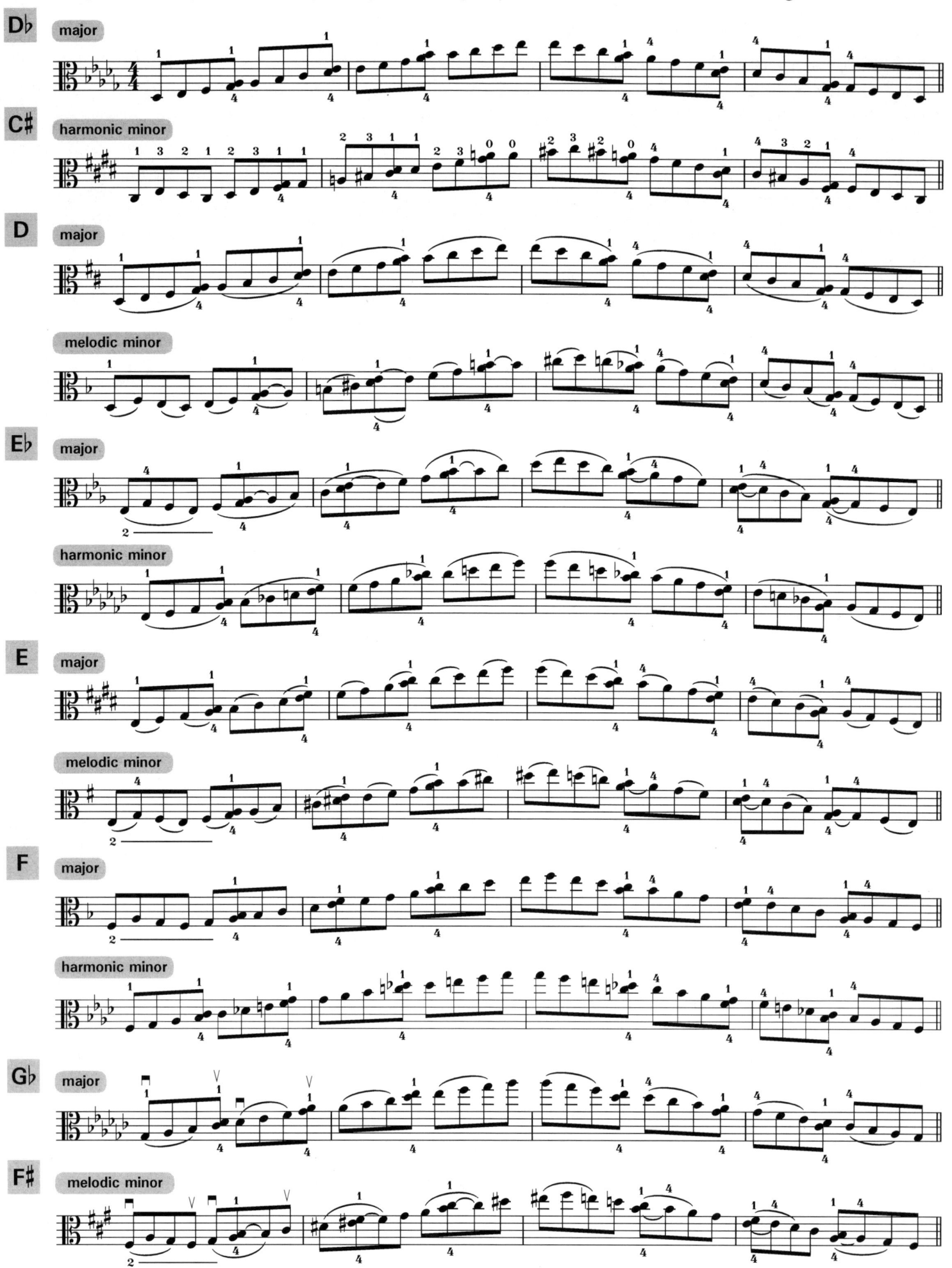

Part 2: Three-octave scales and arpeggios: preparatory practice   See notes, page 48

11. One-octave scales in all positions without shifting

Practice method: at each string crossing place the first and fourth fingers together as in no. 10, page 68.

C major

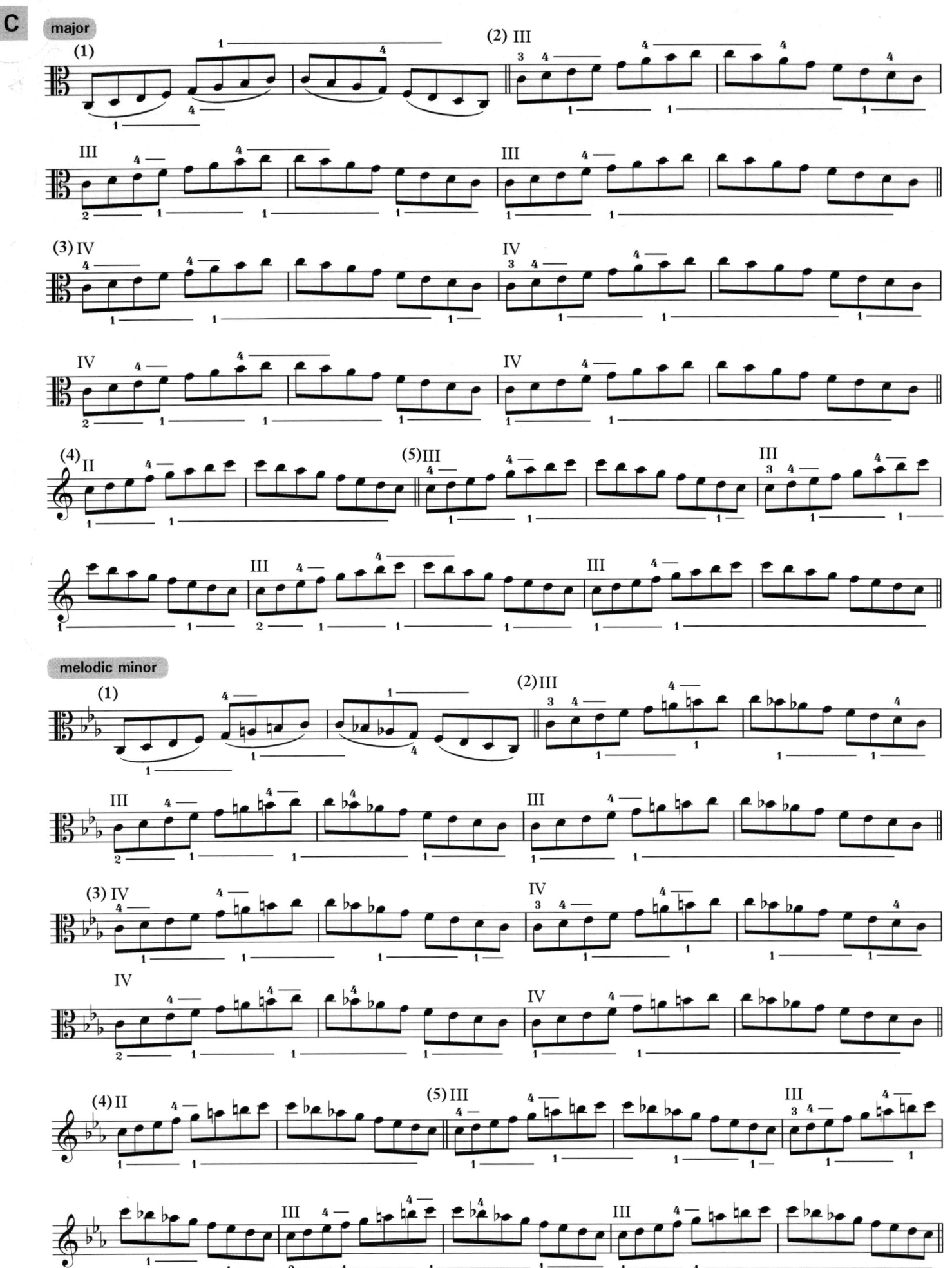

melodic minor

One-octave scales in all positions without shifting

Part 2: Three-octave scales and arpeggios: preparatory practice   See notes, page 48

One-octave scales in all positions without shifting

D major

melodic minor

Part 2: Three-octave scales and arpeggios: preparatory practice   See notes, page 48

One-octave scales in all positions without shifting

E♭ major

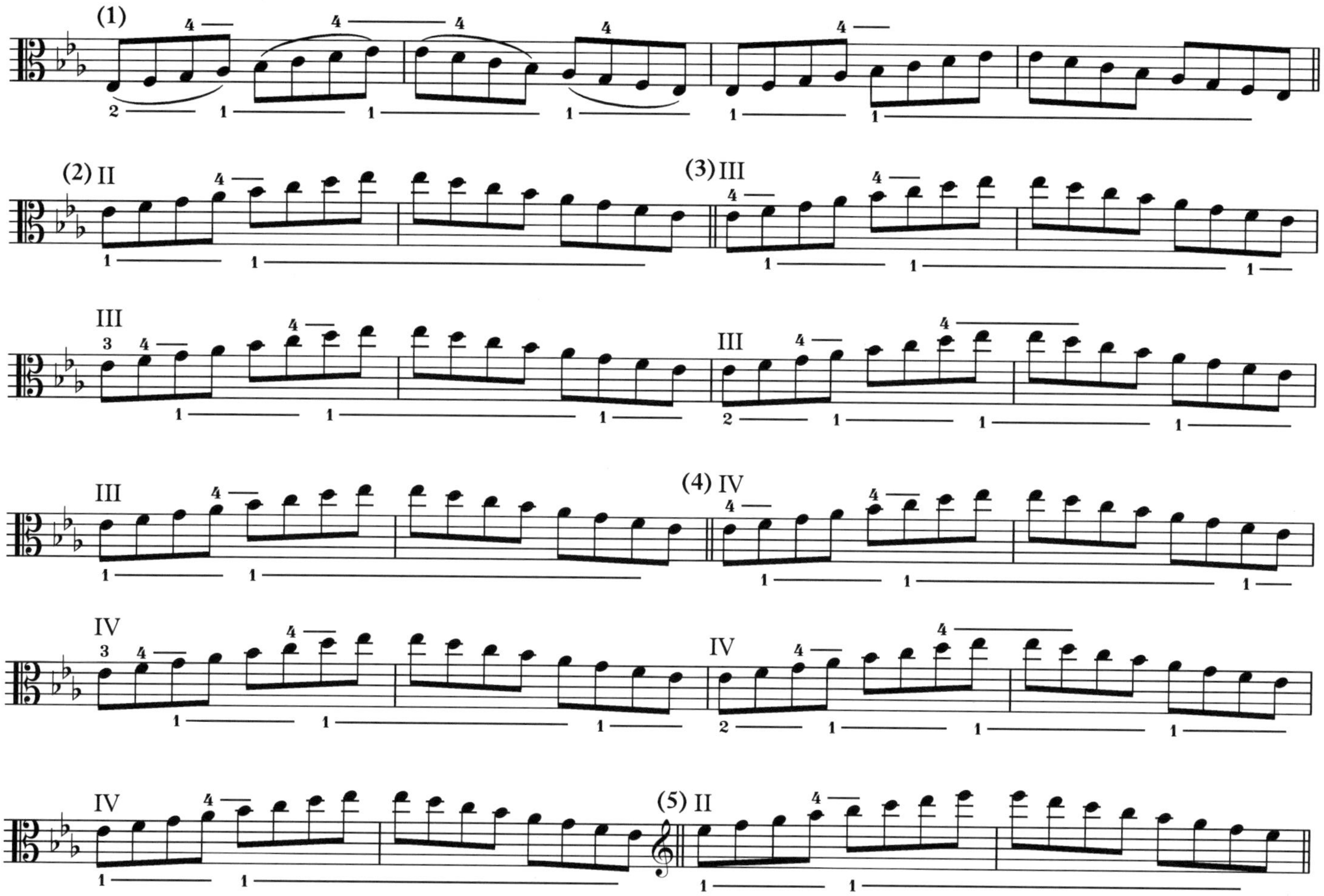

melodic minor

Part 2: Three-octave scales and arpeggios: preparatory practice See notes, page 48

One-octave scales in all positions without shifting

E major

melodic minor

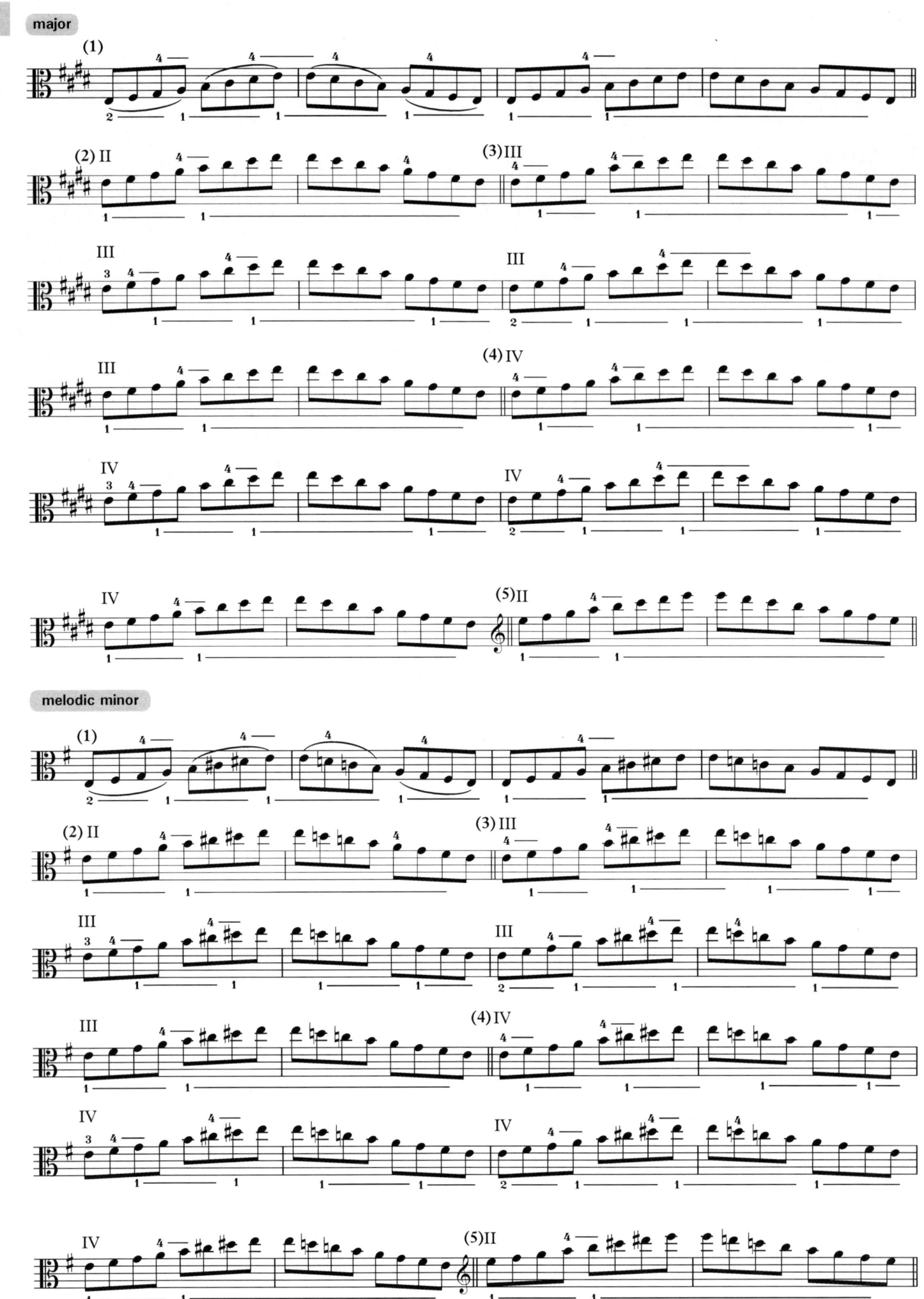

One-octave scales in all positions without shifting

F major

One-octave scales in all positions without shifting

G♭ major

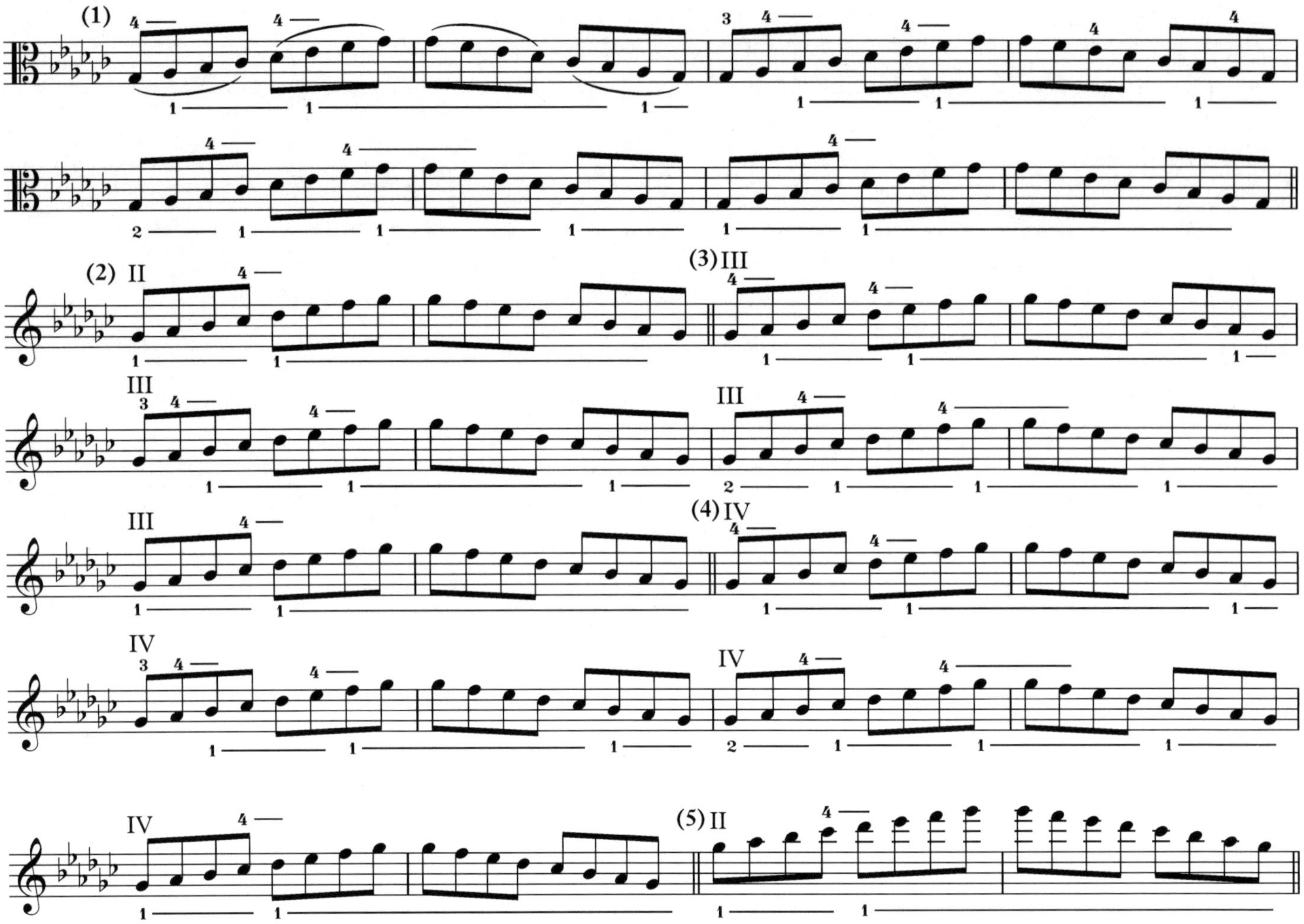

F♯ melodic minor

Part 2: Three-octave scales and arpeggios: preparatory practice   See notes, page 48

One-octave scales in all positions without shifting

A One-octave scales in all positions without shifting

major

melodic minor

One-octave scales in all positions without shifting

B♭ major

One-octave scales in all positions without shifting

B major

melodic minor

Part 2: Three-octave scales and arpeggios: preparatory practice   See notes, page 48

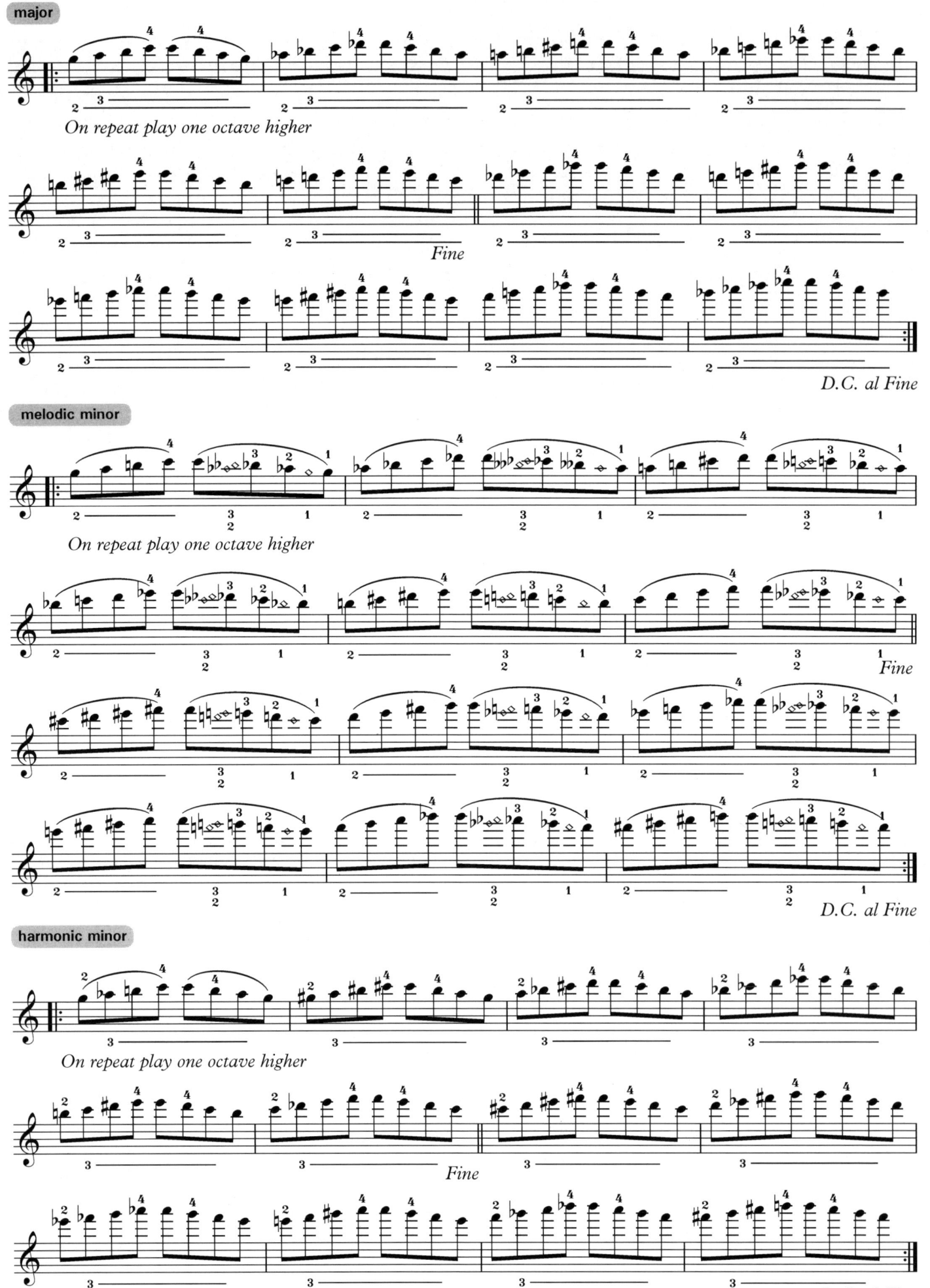

Three-octave scales: exercise for timing shifts

Part 2: Three-octave scales and arpeggios: preparatory practice   See notes, page 48

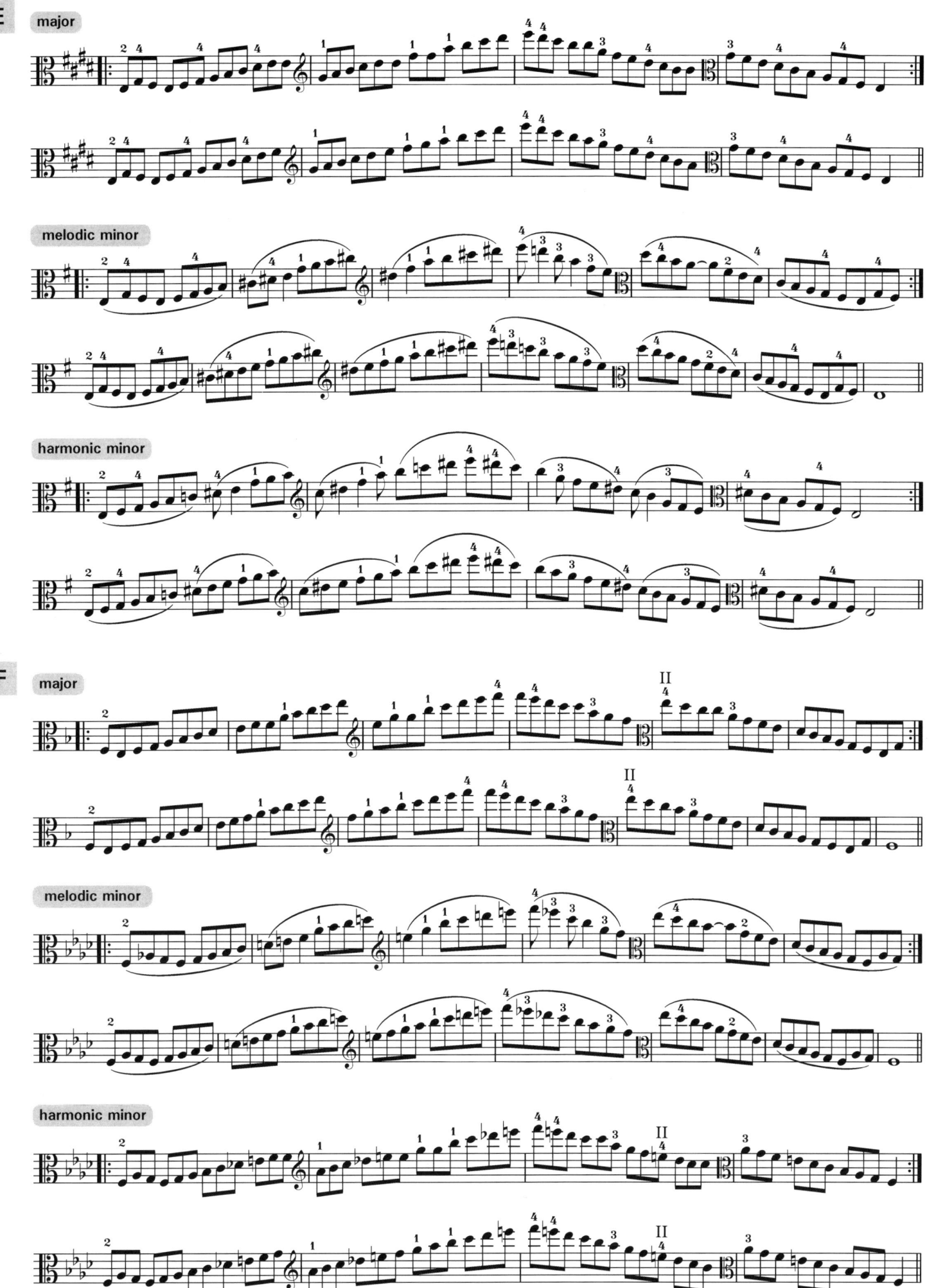

Three-octave scales: exercise for timing shifts

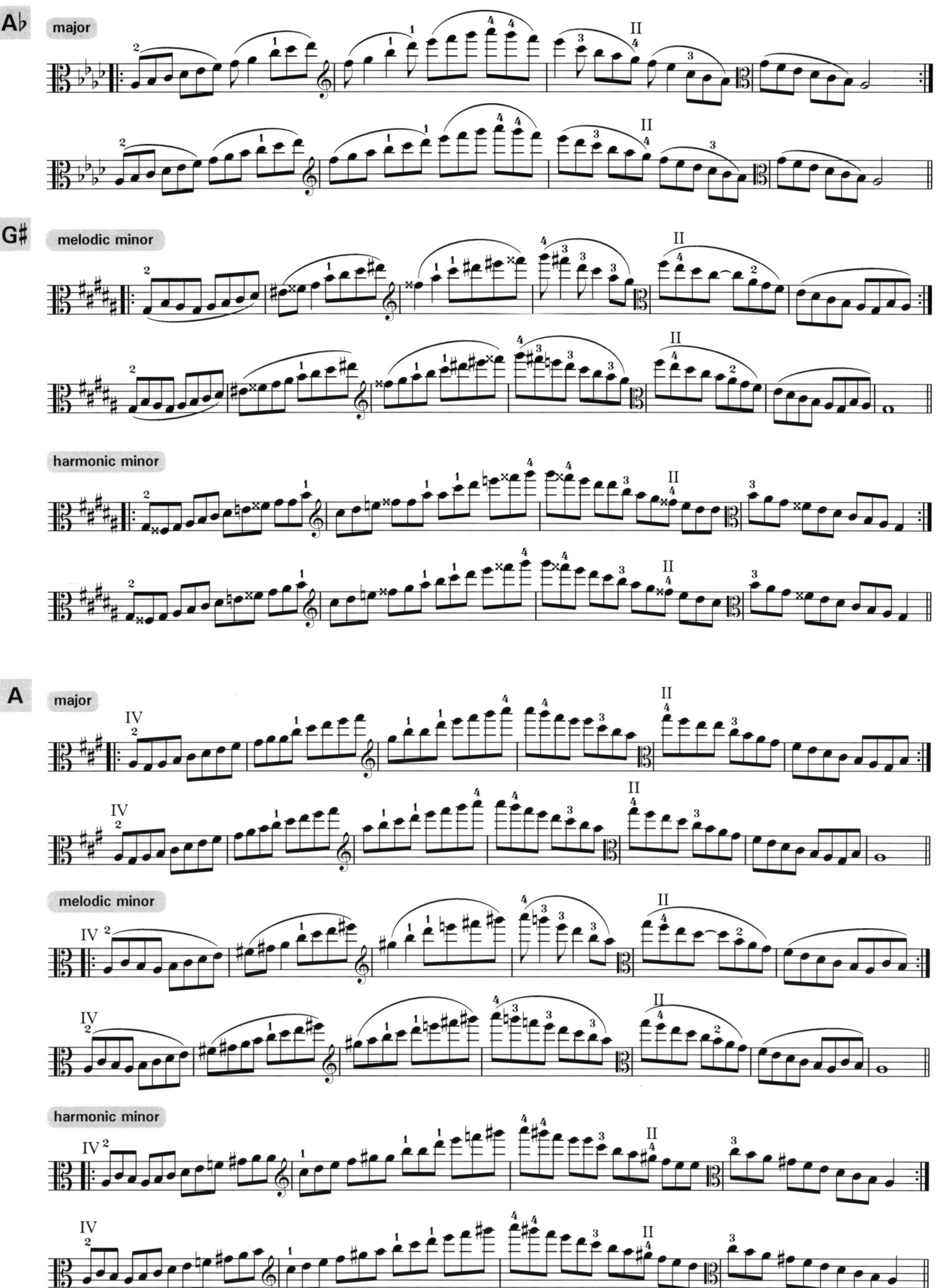

Three-octave scales: exercise for timing shifts

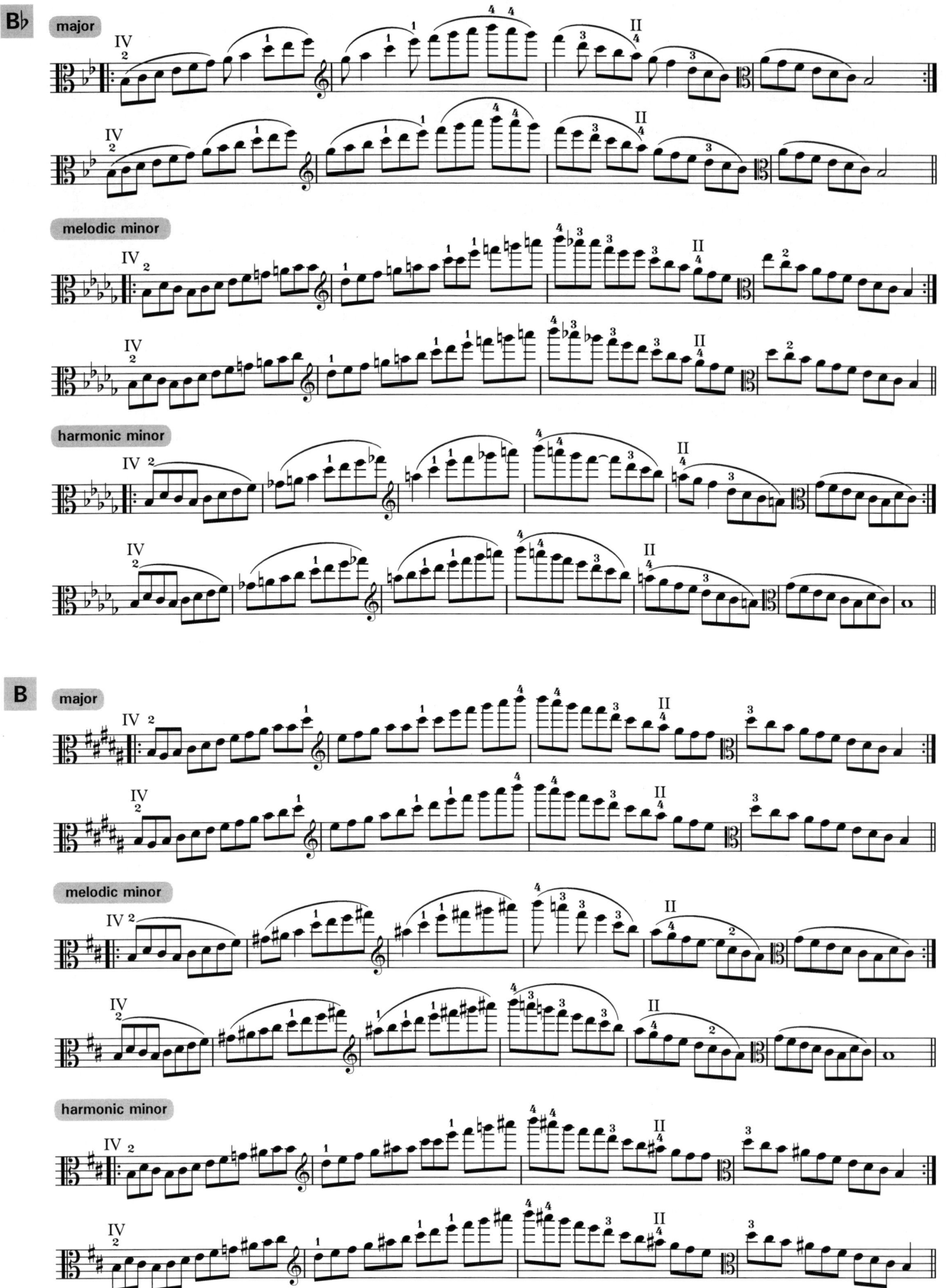

Harmonic minor scale: exercise for augmented 2nd, fourth to first finger

Warm-up exercise: smooth bowing

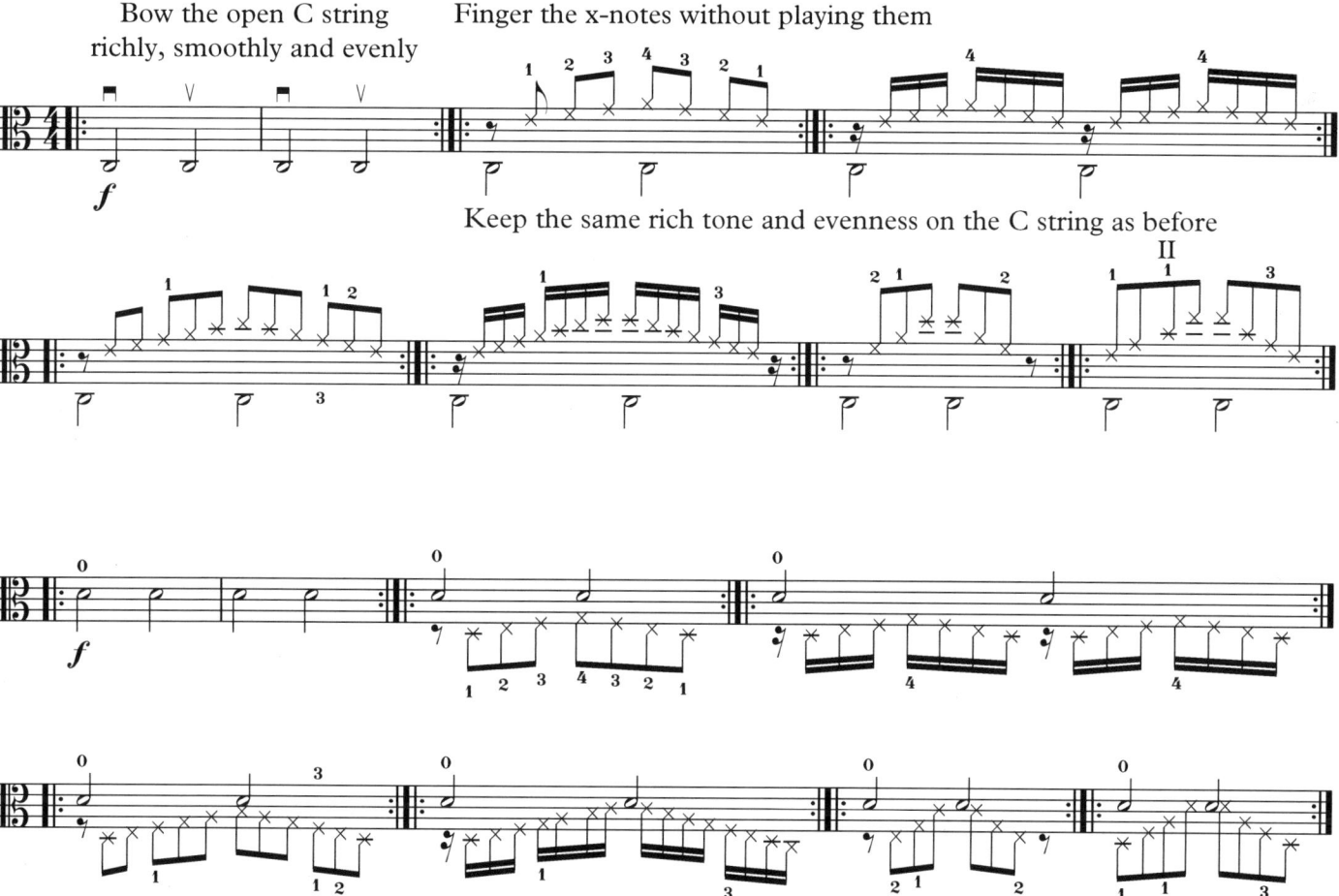

16 Exercise to develop 'fast fingers'

Also practise with fast triple and double strokes on each note:

17 Exercise for moving fingers independently of the hand

Hold down without playing

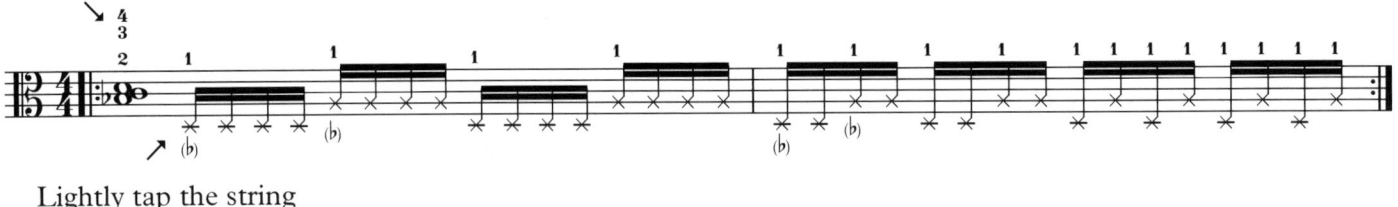

Lightly tap the string

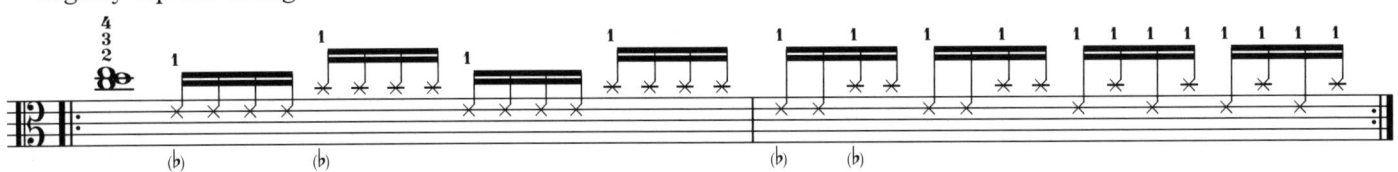

Repeat the sequence with the other fingers:

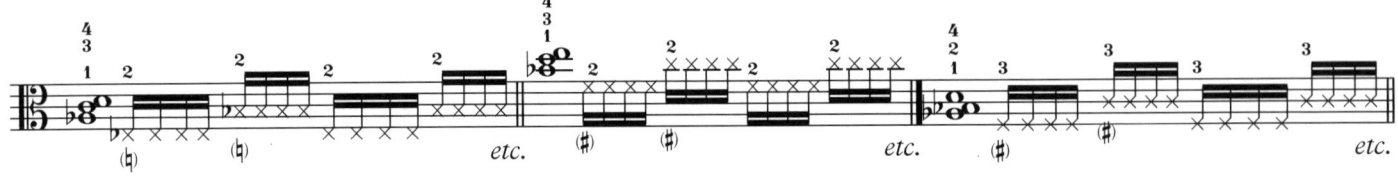

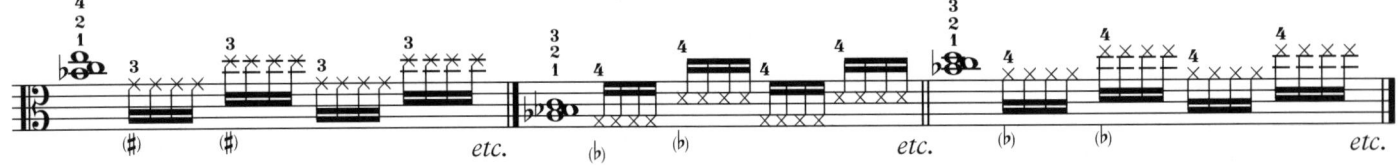

Placing fingers in blocks

92 Part 2: Three-octave scales and arpeggios: preparatory practice   See notes, page 48

Placing fingers in blocks

Part 2: Three-octave scales and arpeggios: preparatory practice   See notes, page 48

Placing fingers in blocks

G melodic minor

A♭ major

G# melodic minor

A major

melodic minor

Part 2: Three-octave scales and arpeggios: preparatory practice See notes, page 48

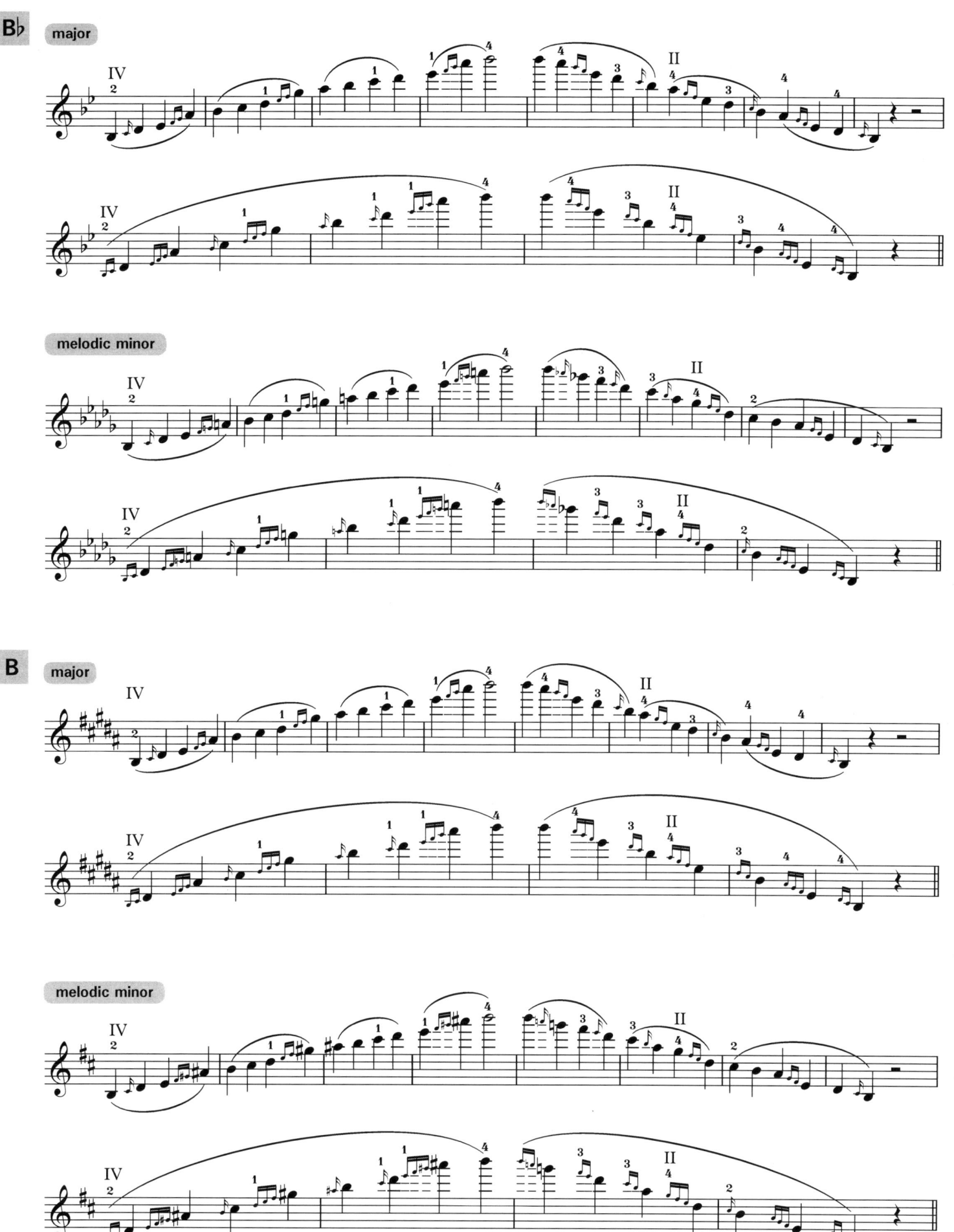

19 One-octave arpeggio sequence in all positions without shifting

Refer to the fingerings and the held-down finger lines on this page when starting on the same finger in other keys.

One-octave arpeggio sequence in all positions without shifting

E

F

One-octave arpeggio sequence in all positions without shifting

One-octave arpeggio sequence in all positions without shifting

A

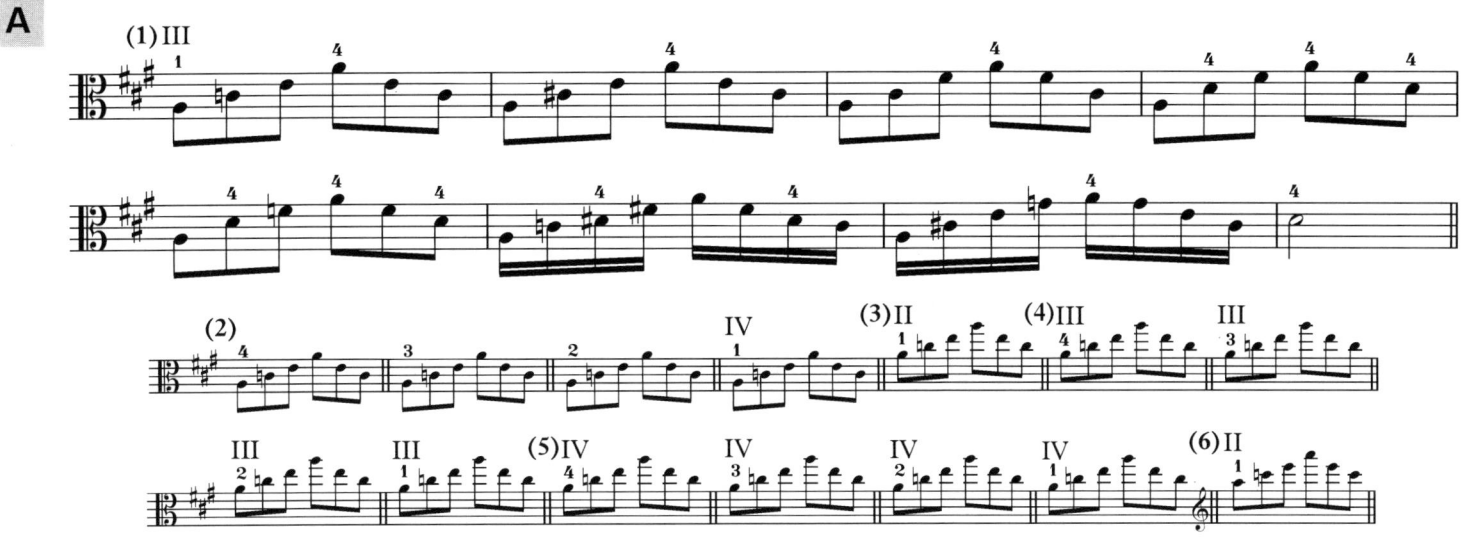

B♭

B

One-octave arpeggio sequence in all positions without shifting

Starting at the top

F major

melodic minor

harmonic minor

arpeggios

chromatic

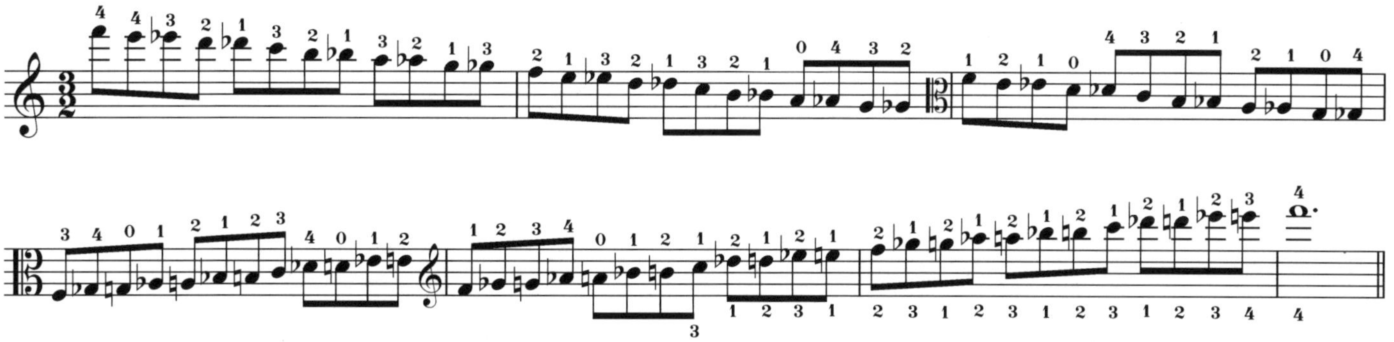

Part 2: Three-octave scales and arpeggios: preparatory practice   See notes, page 48

21 — Three-octave arpeggios: exercise for timing shifts

For the purposes of this exercise, leave the first finger down on the string for as long as possible.

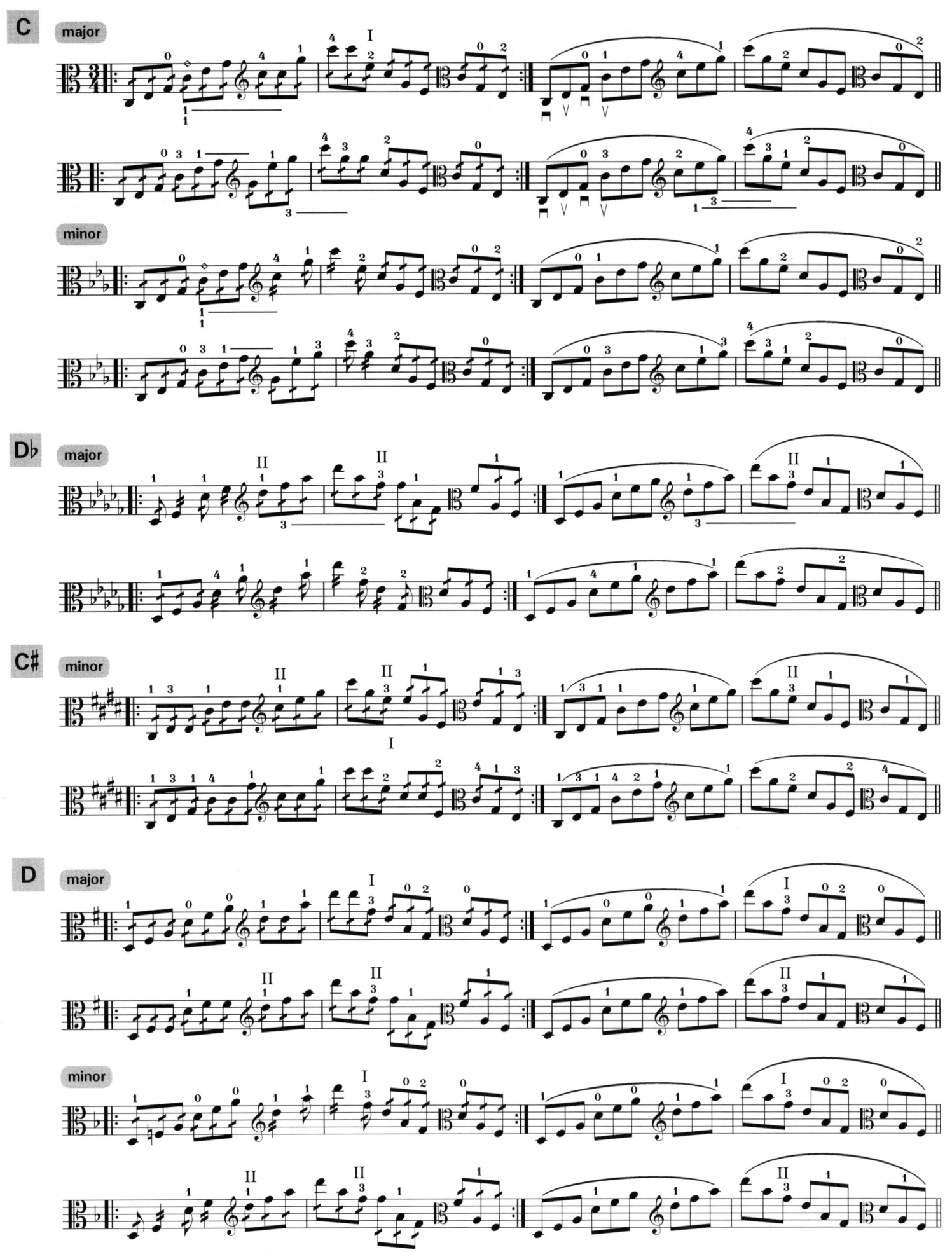

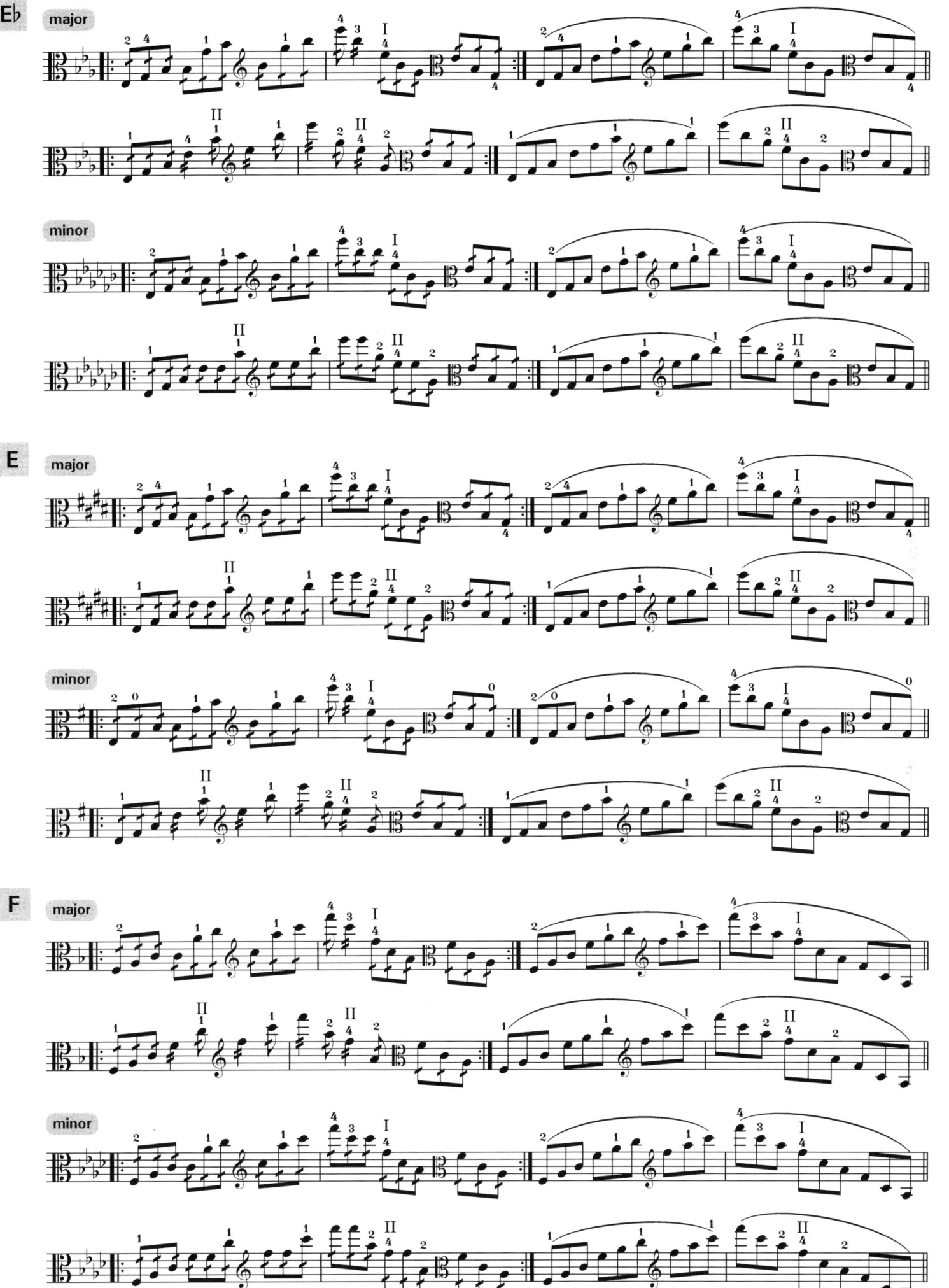

Three-octave arpeggios: exercise for timing shifts

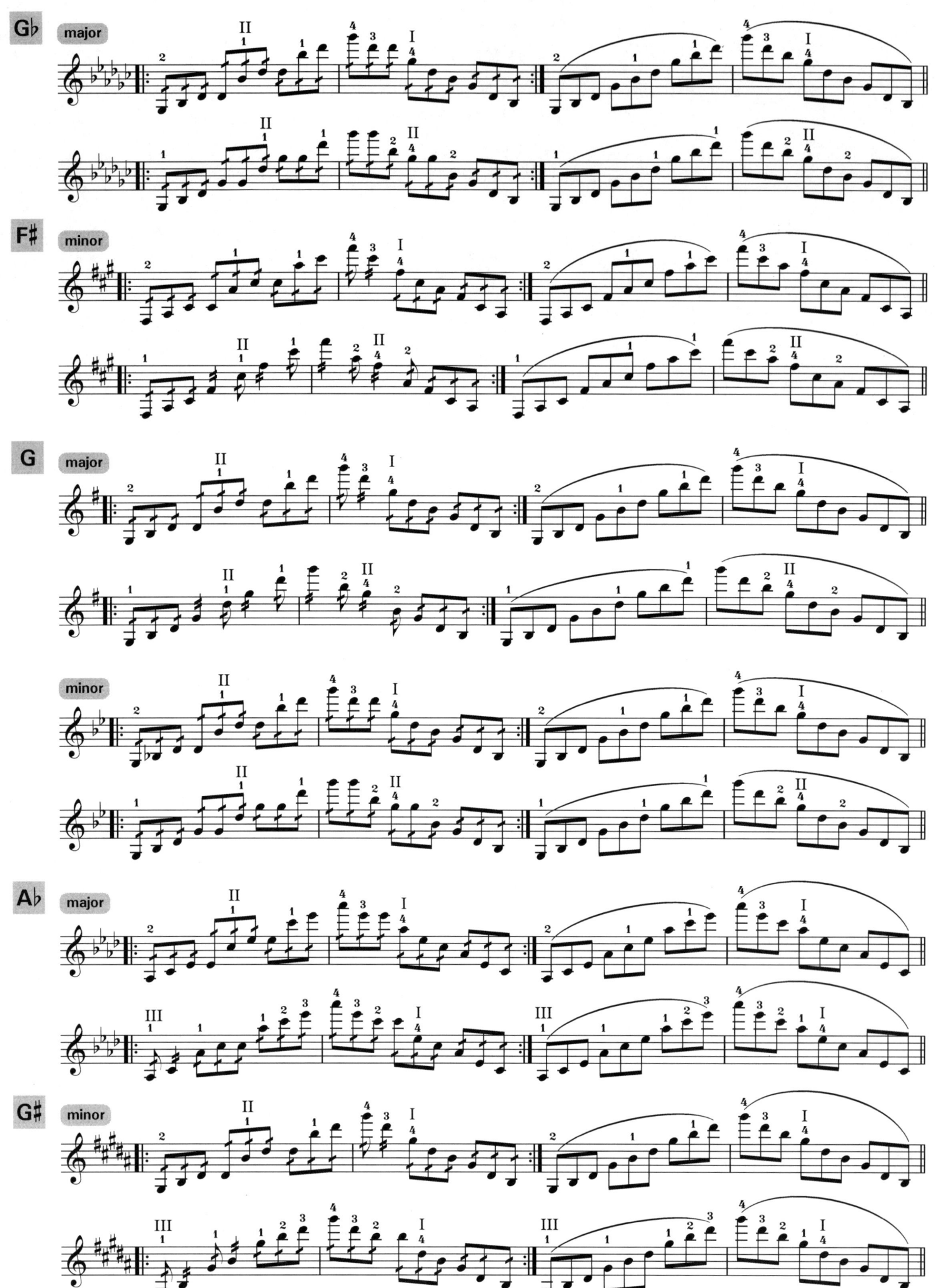

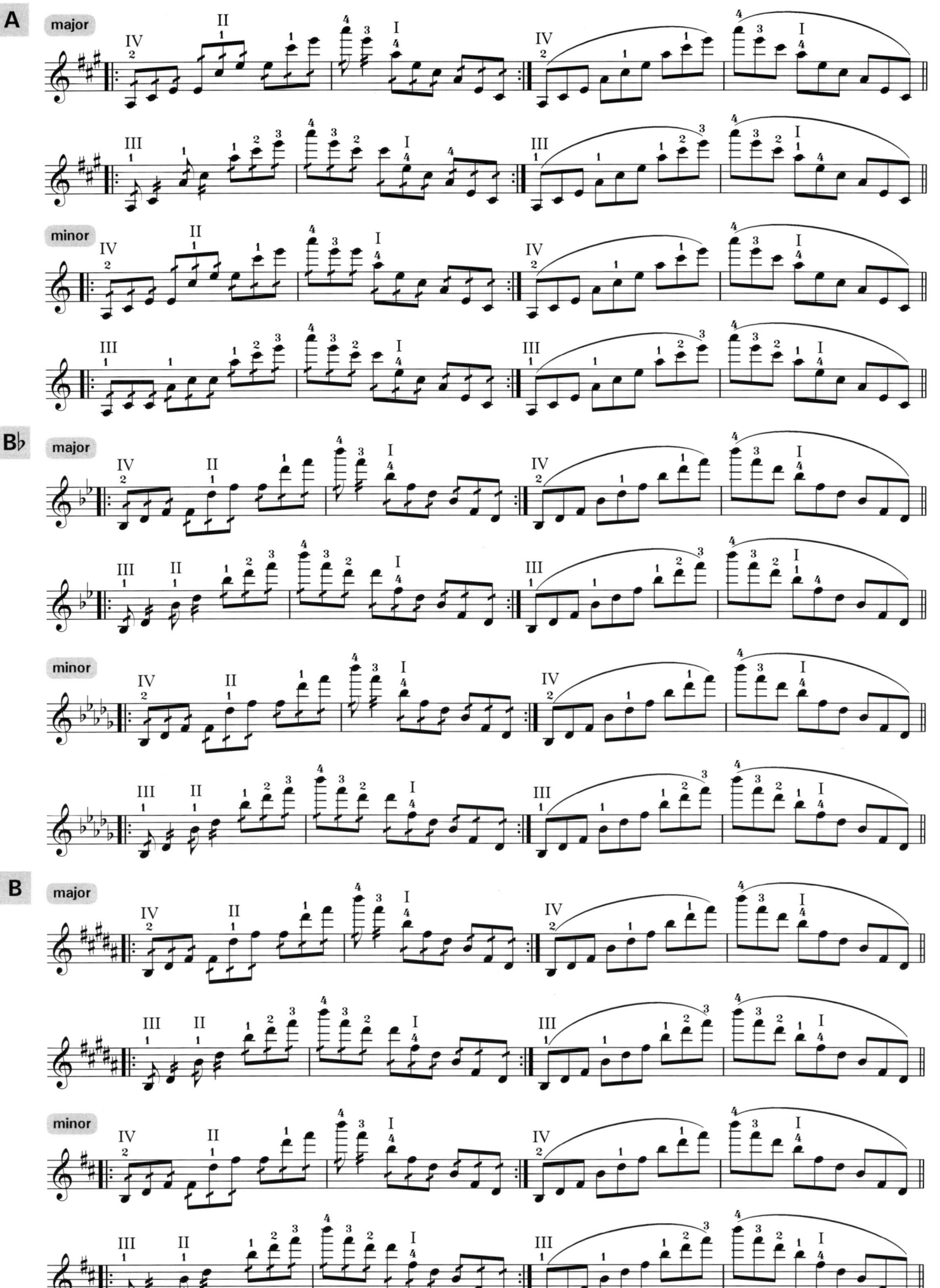

Three-octave diminished sevenths

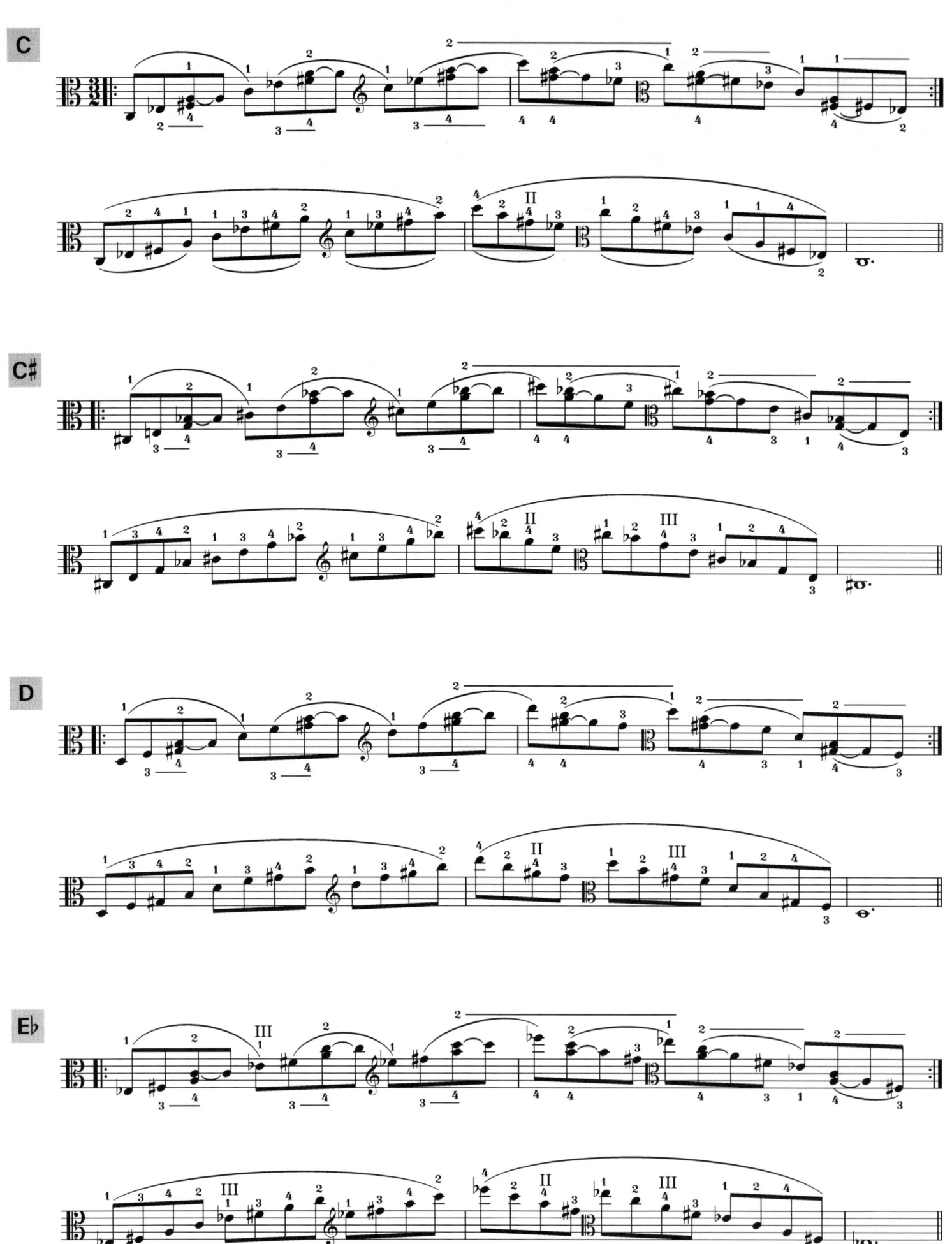

Three-octave diminished sevenths

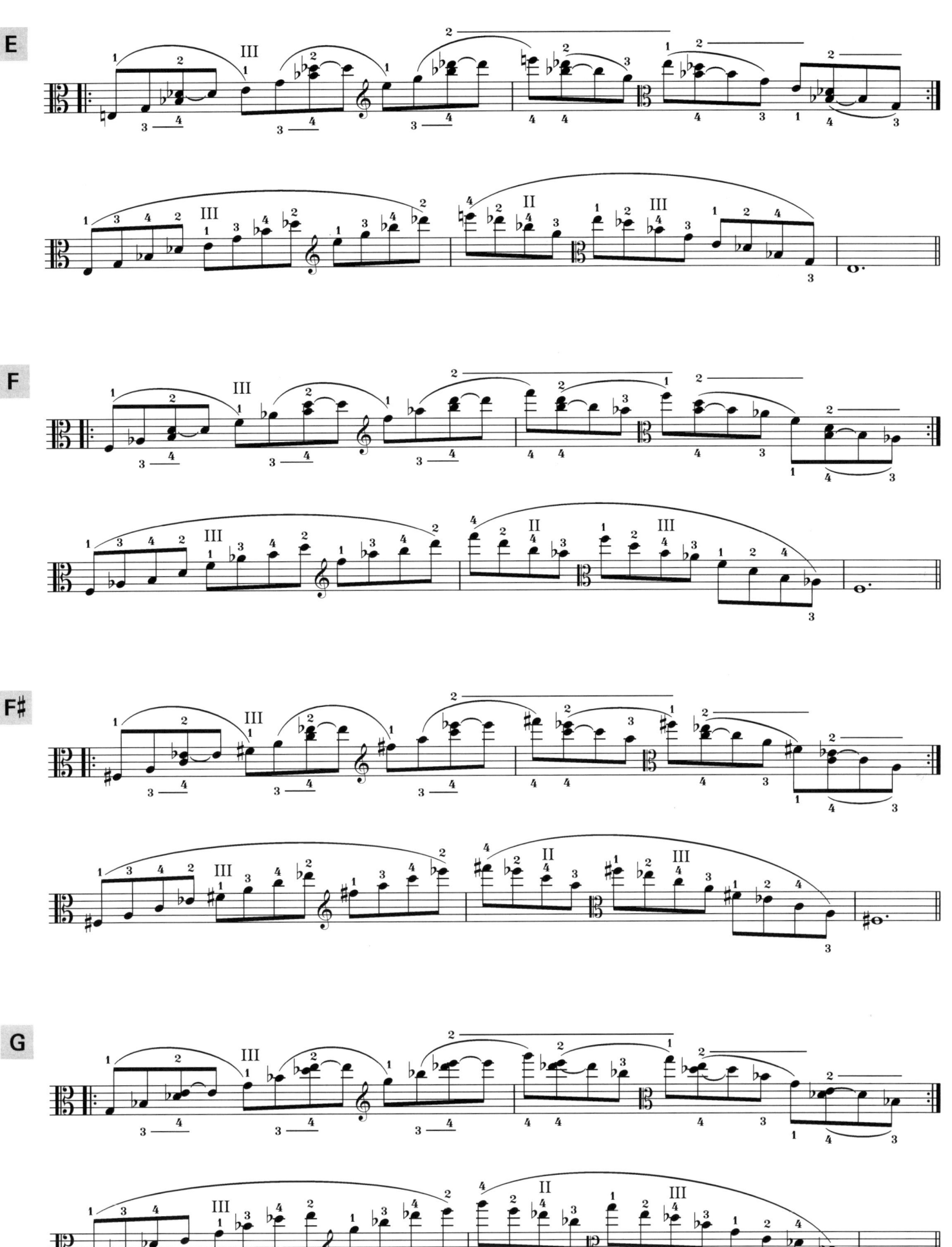

Part 2: Three-octave scales and arpeggios: preparatory practice   See notes, page 48

Three-octave diminished sevenths

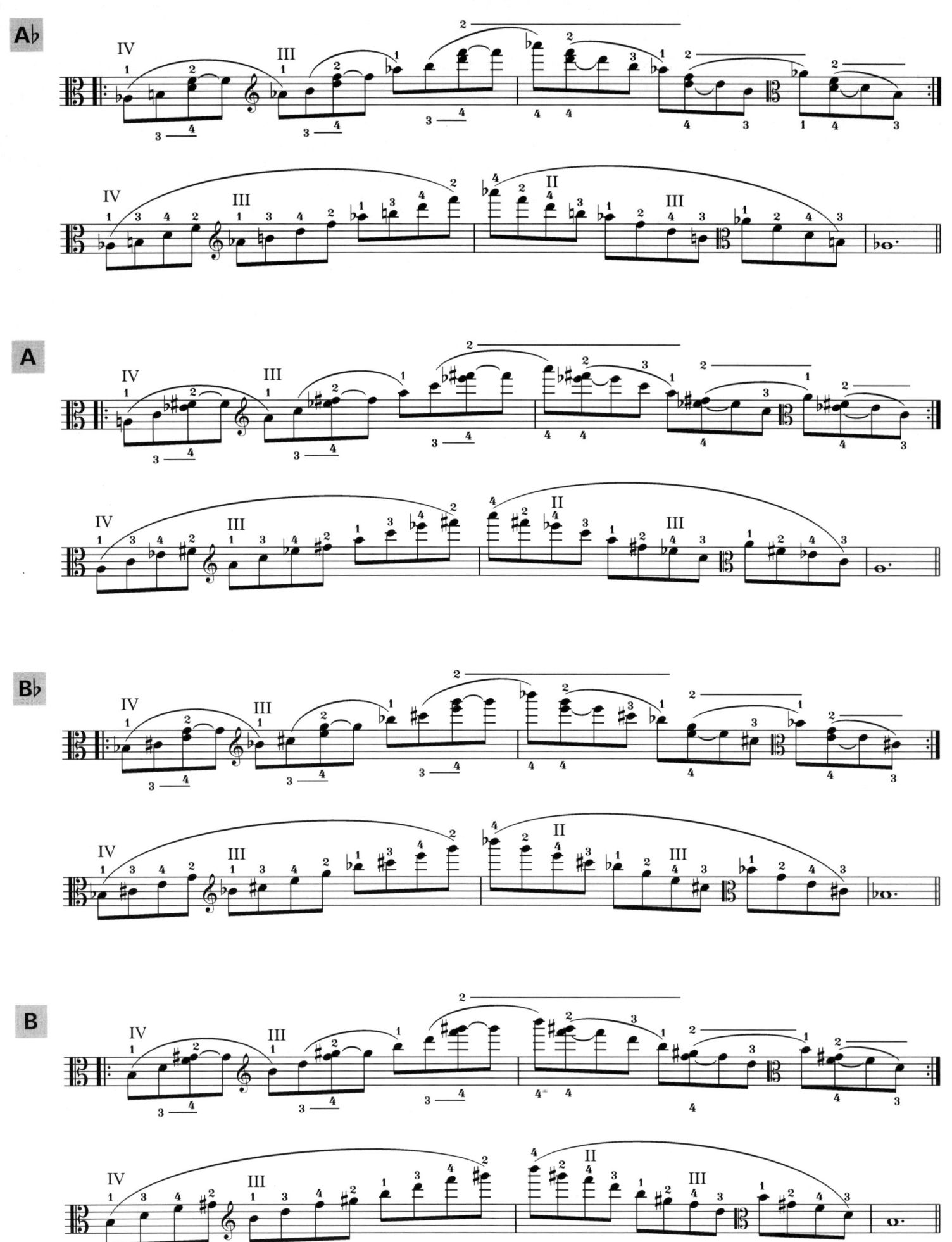

108 Part 2: Three-octave scales and arpeggios: preparatory practice   See notes, page 48

Three-octave dominant sevenths

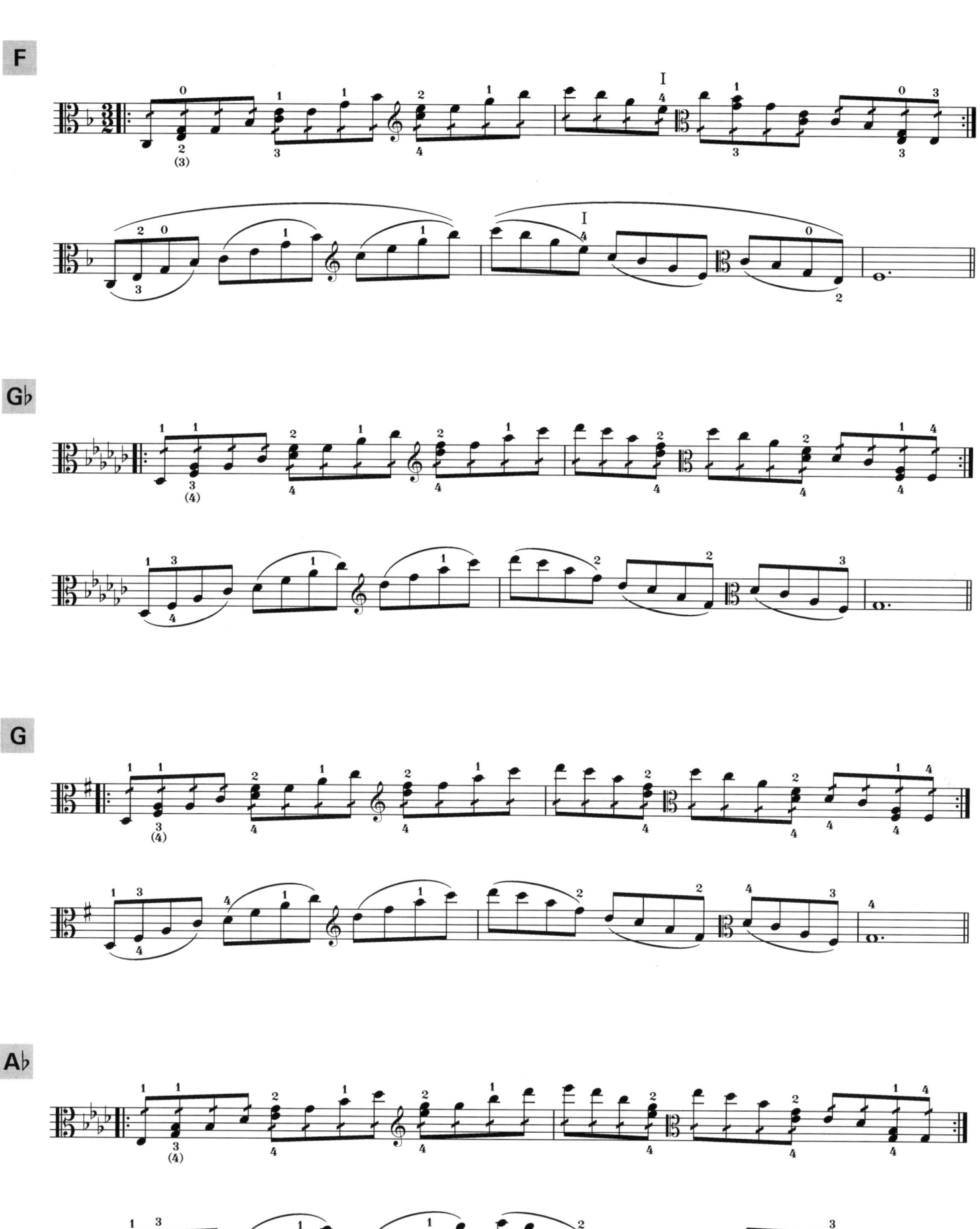

Three-octave dominant sevenths

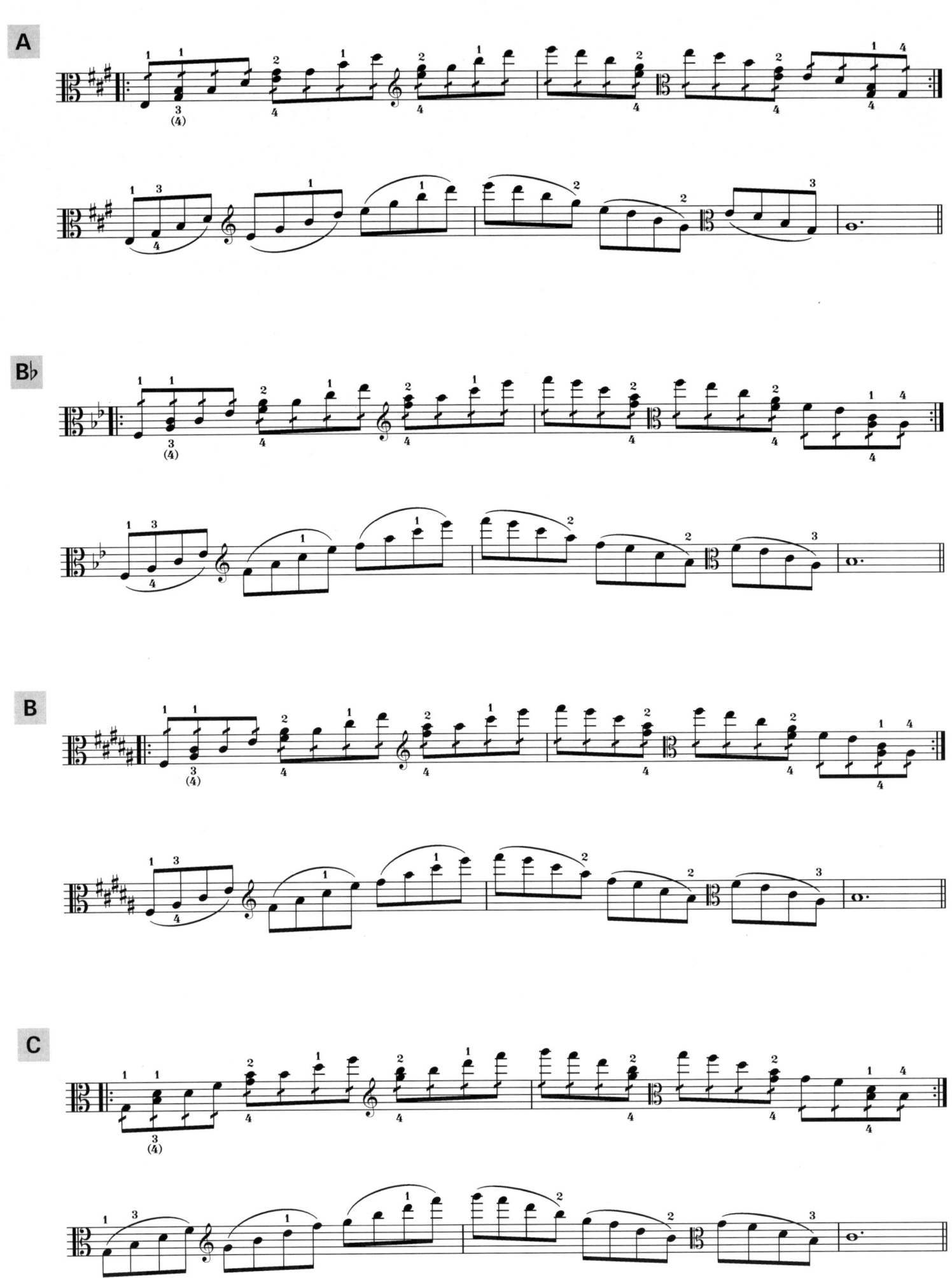

Part 2: Three-octave scales and arpeggios: preparatory practice See notes, page 48

Three-octave dominant sevenths

D♭
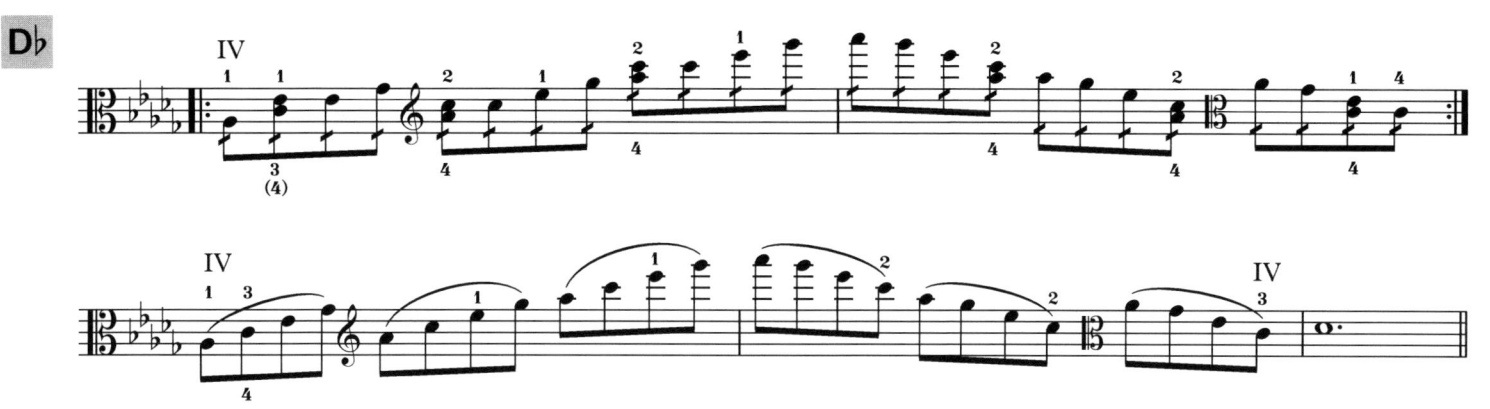

D
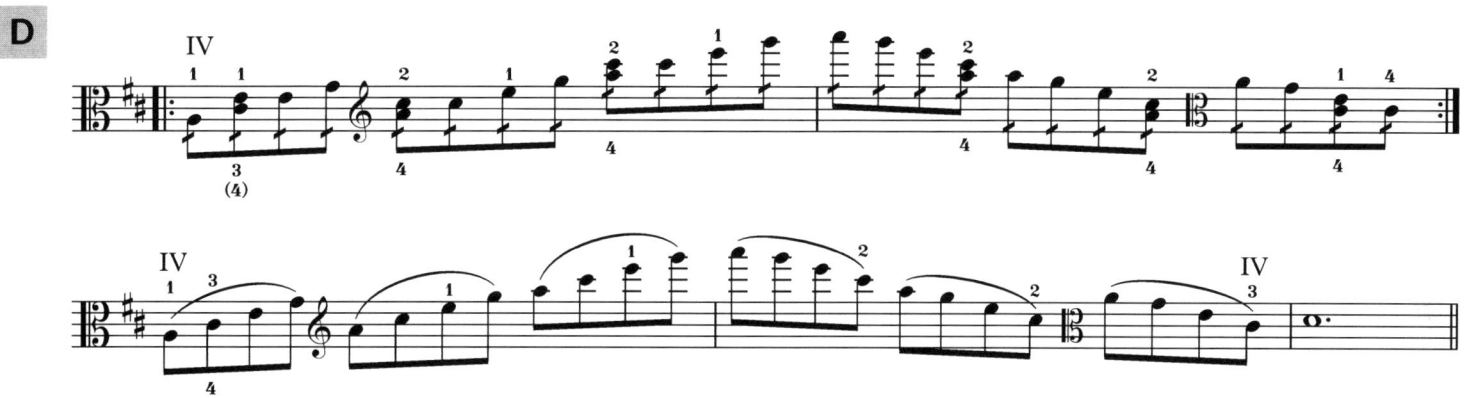

E♭
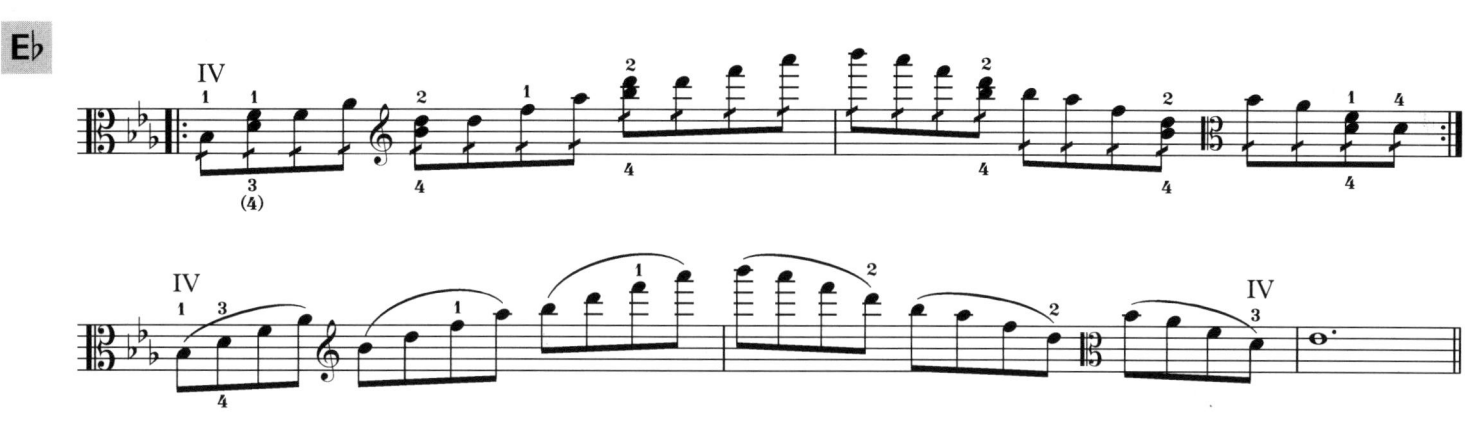

E
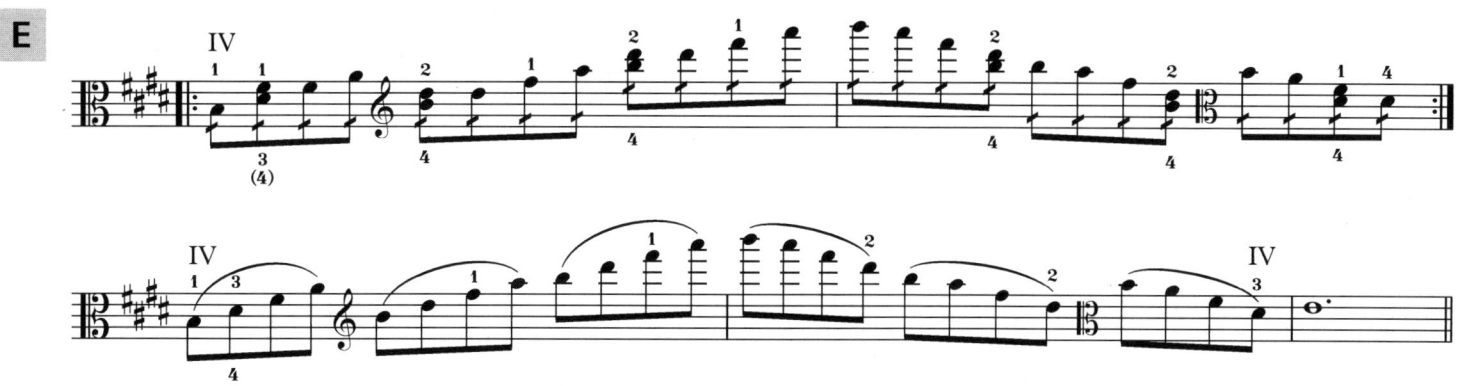

Arpeggios: shifting exercise

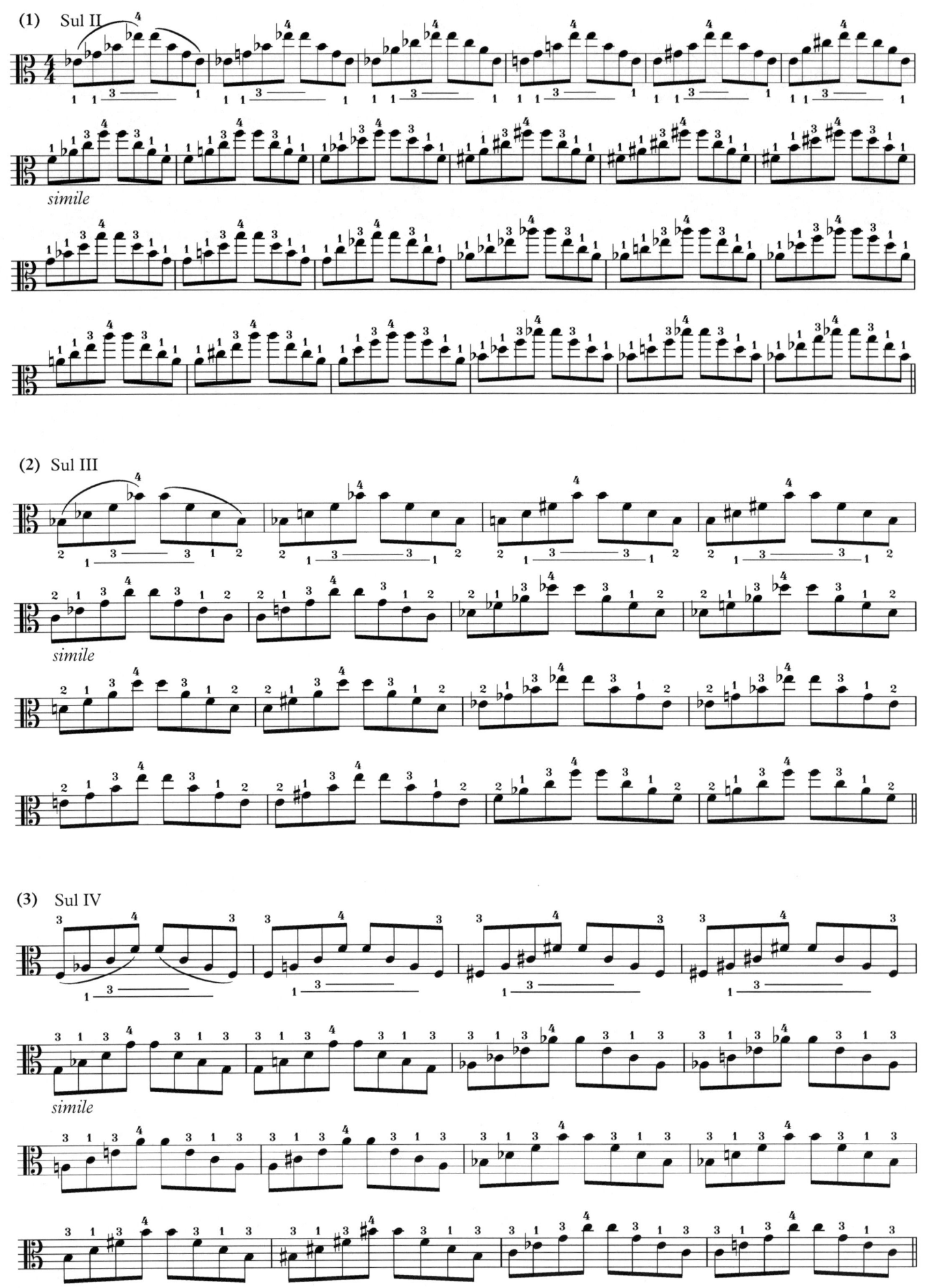

Arpeggios: shifting exercise

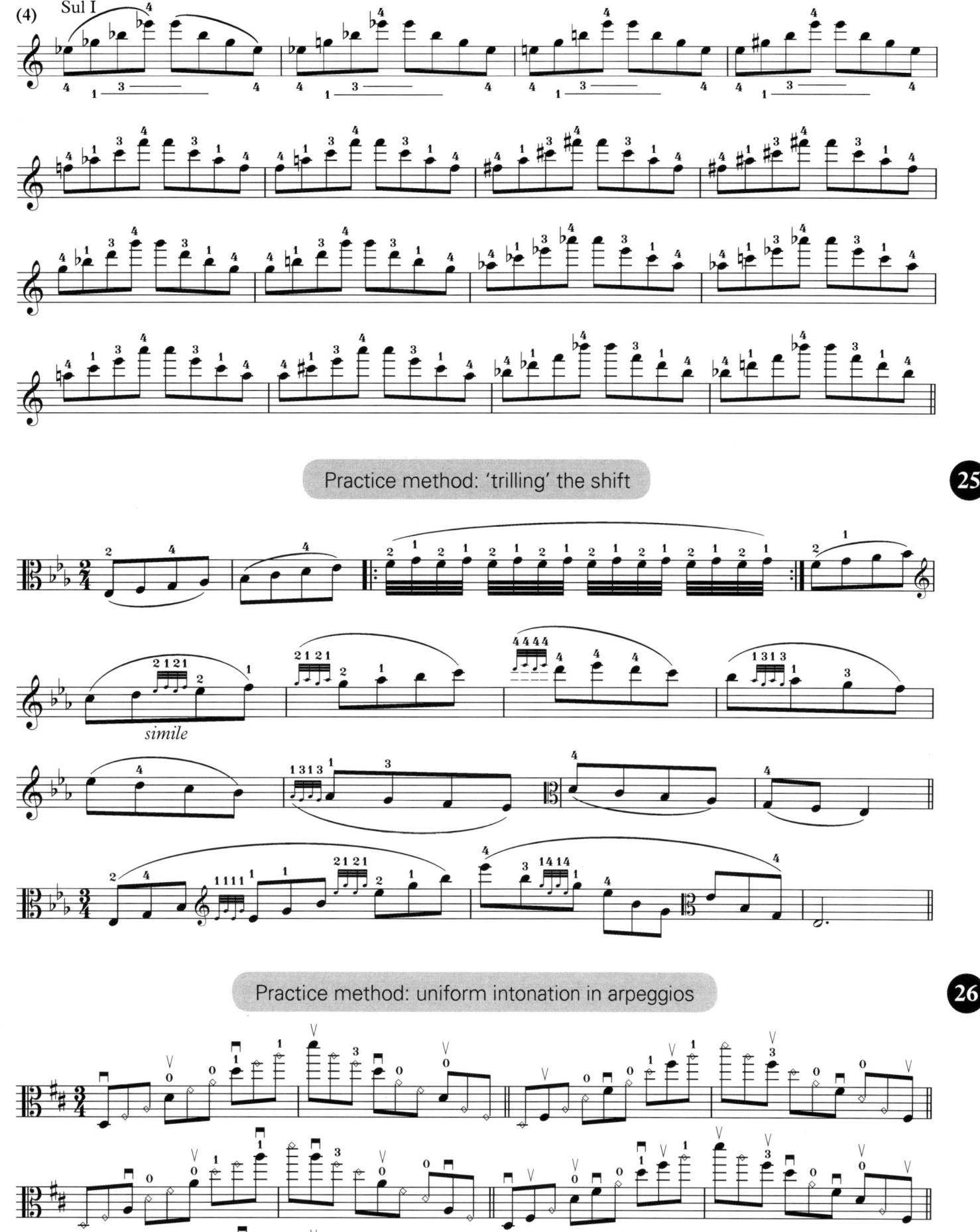

Practice method: 'trilling' the shift

Practice method: uniform intonation in arpeggios

Part 2: Three-octave scales and arpeggios: preparatory practice   See notes, page 48

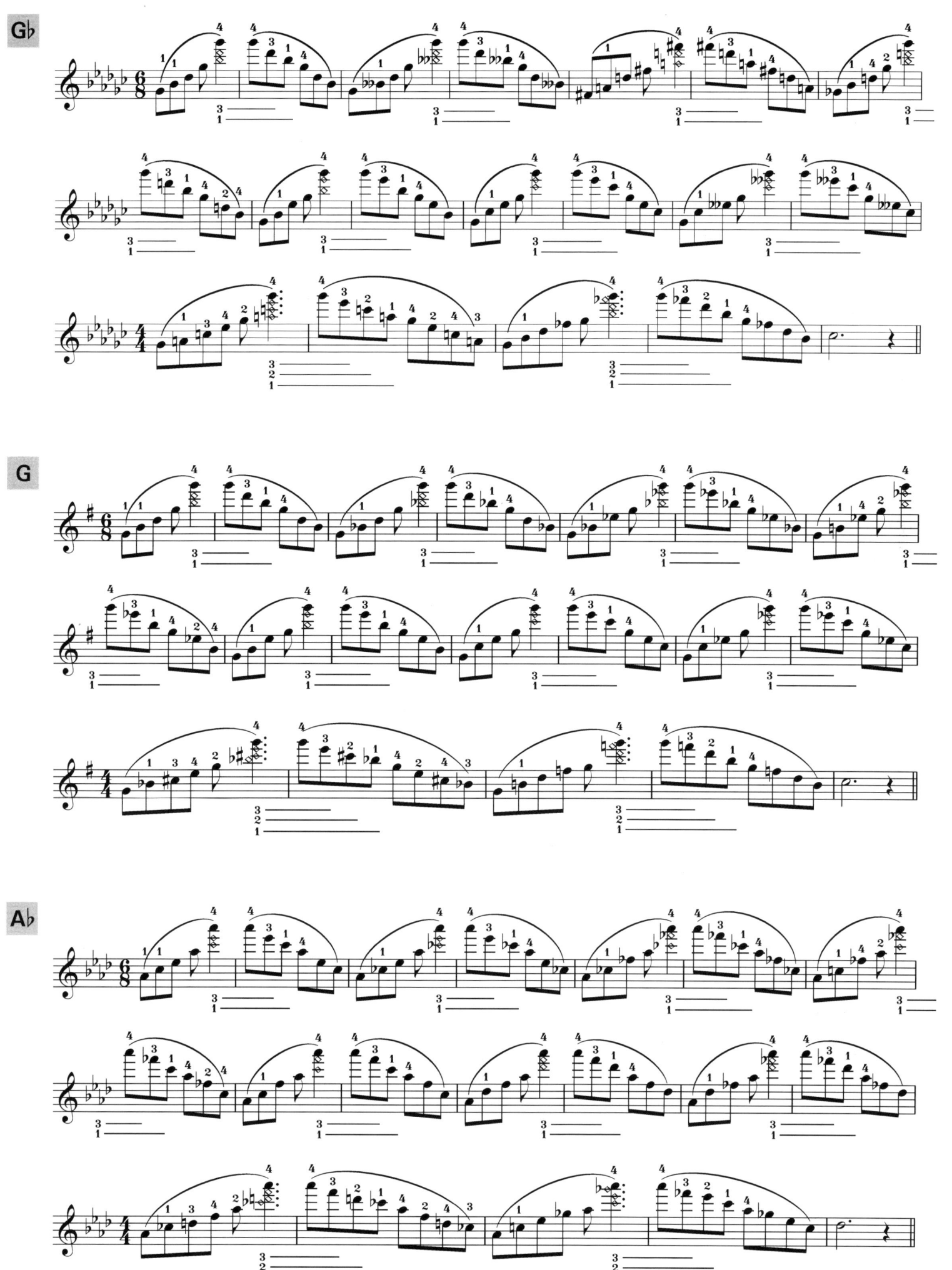

Arpeggios: placing fingers in blocks

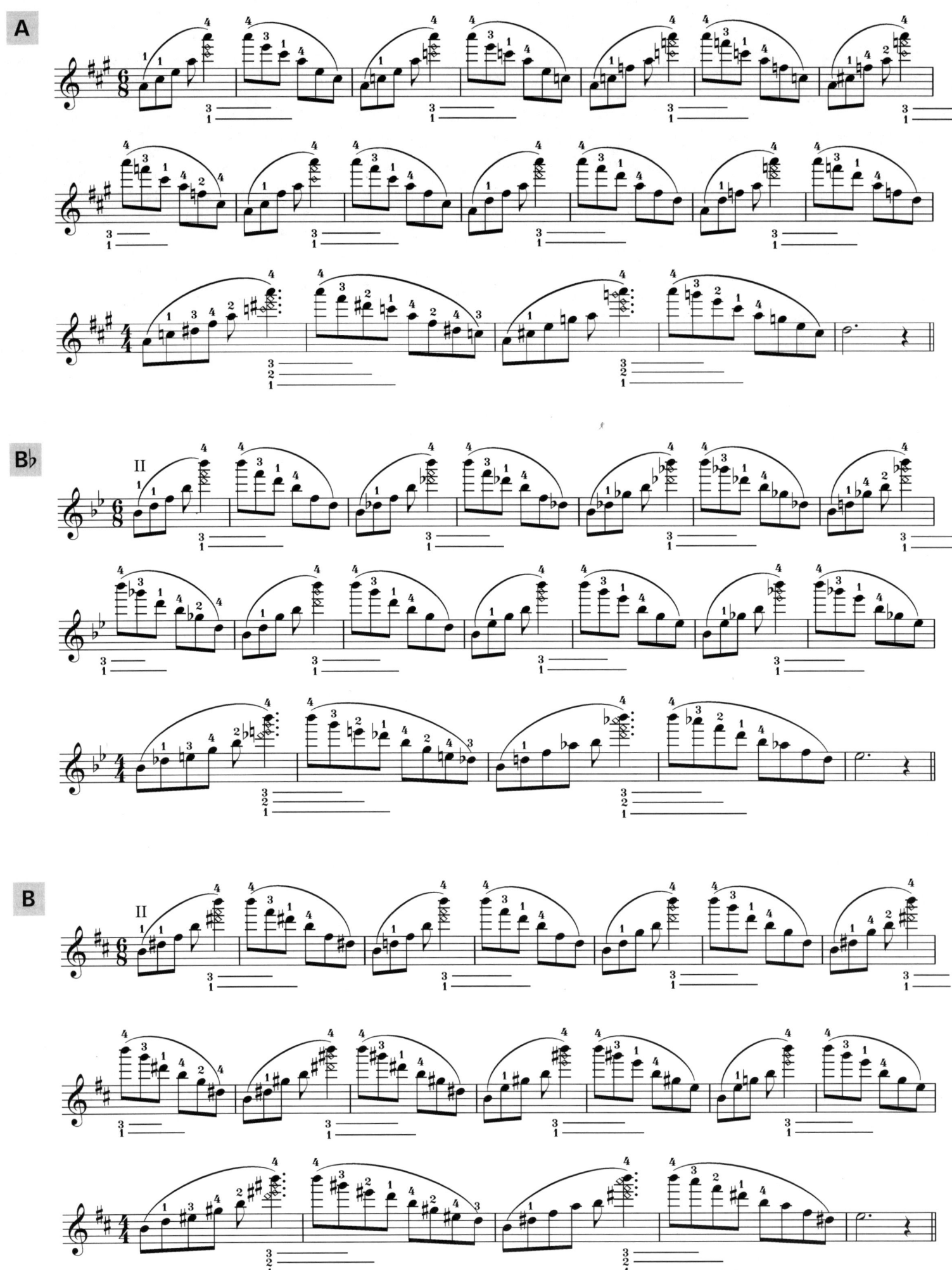

Part 2: Three-octave scales and arpeggios: preparatory practice   See notes, page 48

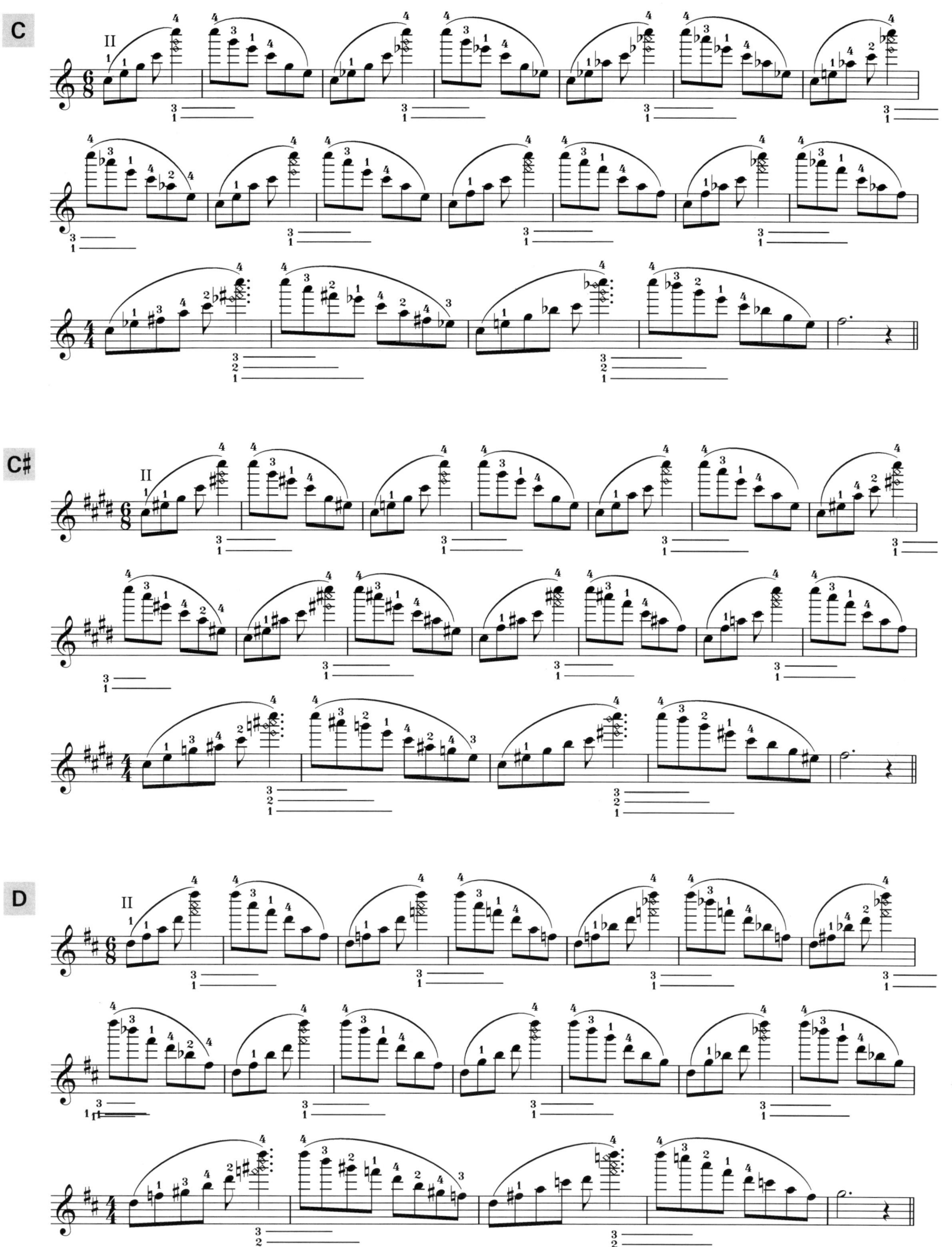

28 Chromatic scales: exercise for 321 or 123 fingering

Part 3

Three-octave scales, arpeggios and chromatic scales

Notes

part 3

29 — Rhythm, accent, bowing and dynamic patterns *Page 122*

Apply rhythm and accent patterns to all scales and arpeggios. These are powerful practice methods which produce the greatest improvement in the shortest time.

By learning how to play the patterns, you discover and repair all the weak areas where you do not really know what to tell the fingers or bow to do, or the places where the fingers do not respond quickly enough. The normal, even, legato scale seems much easier to play after practising in rhythms and accents.

The application of bowing patterns to scales and arpeggios is one of the standard and logical ways to build mastery of all strokes in all parts of the bow. Practise bowing patterns using little bow near the point, at the middle, and at the heel; using more bow in the upper half, lower half and in the middle of the bow; and using whole bows. Separate bow strokes can include every type of stroke, e.g. *spiccato, martelé* and *sautillé*.

At first, practise rhythm, accent and bowing patterns separately so that you can focus on one thing at a time. Later, combine rhythms and accents; finally apply all three at the same time for the most interesting, creative and rewarding practice.

Dynamic variations train great control of the bow. There are naturally many combinations of crescendos and diminuendos that can be applied to scales and arpeggios. Start by playing dynamic variations either between the bottom and top of the scale or arpeggio, or within the compass of one group or octave.

For actual performance of scales or arpeggios, either in an examination or when they appear in a passage in a piece or concerto, a crescendo to the top is usually desirable (unless you are seeking a different effect).

30 — Speeding up with the metronome *Page 124*

Speeding up with the metronome is another central practice method, and a natural next step after work using rhythms and accents. A medium tempo is 60 per beat.

31 Three-octave scales, arpeggios and chromatic scales

This arpeggio sequence, widely used throughout Eastern Europe, is an alternative to the Ševčík pattern. The augmented arpeggio has been added to the sequence but may be omitted if preferred.

1. Major
2. Minor
3. Flattened sub-mediant, first inversion
4. Augmented
5. Relative minor, 1st inversion
6. Sub-dominant major, 2nd inversion
7. Sub-dominant minor, 2nd inversion
8. Diminished seventh
9. Dominant seventh

Rhythm, accent, bowing and dynamic patterns

Rhythm patterns

Apply two-, three- and four-note rhythm patterns to all scales and arpeggios:

Two-note patterns

You can also think of (2) as being the same as (1) but beginning on the second note.
Play all rhythms with separate bows as well as slurred.

Three-note patterns

Begin three-note patterns on the first note of the scale; then on the second note, playing the first note as an upbeat; and on the third note, playing the first two notes as an upbeat:

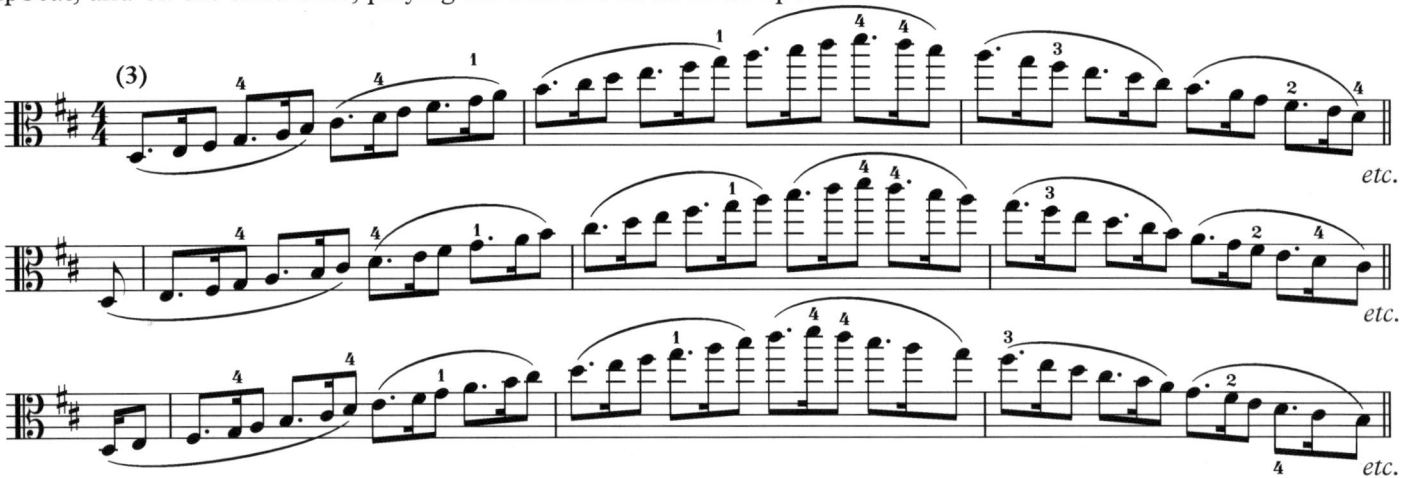

Apply the following three-note dotted patterns in the same way, starting on the first, second and third notes of the scale:

The non-dotted three-note group of one long and two short is another key pattern. Play without upbeats:

Four-note patterns

Begin four-note patterns on the first, second, third and fourth notes of the scale:

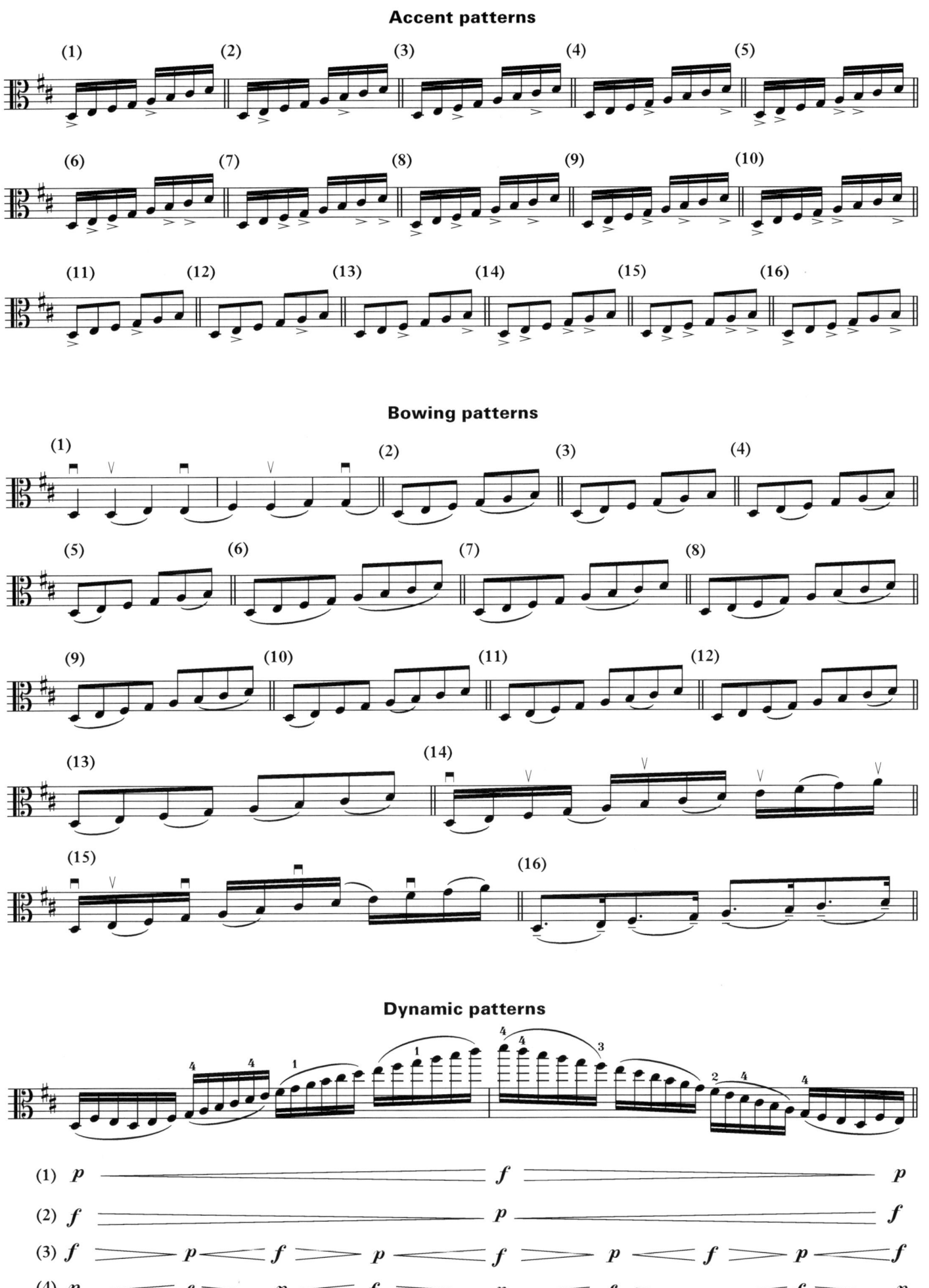

30 Speeding up with the metronome

Three-octave scales

Acceleration pattern 1

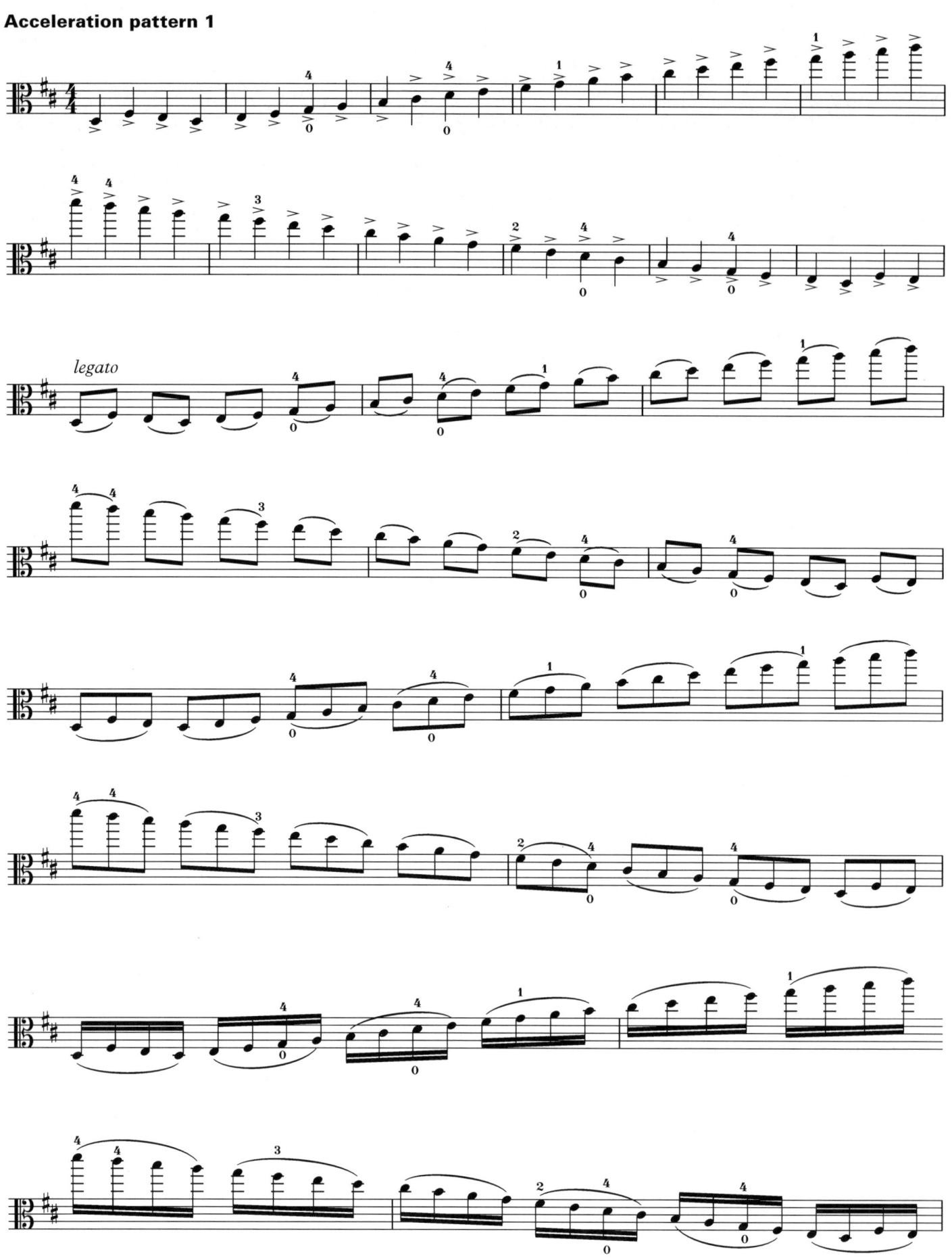

Speeding up with the metronome

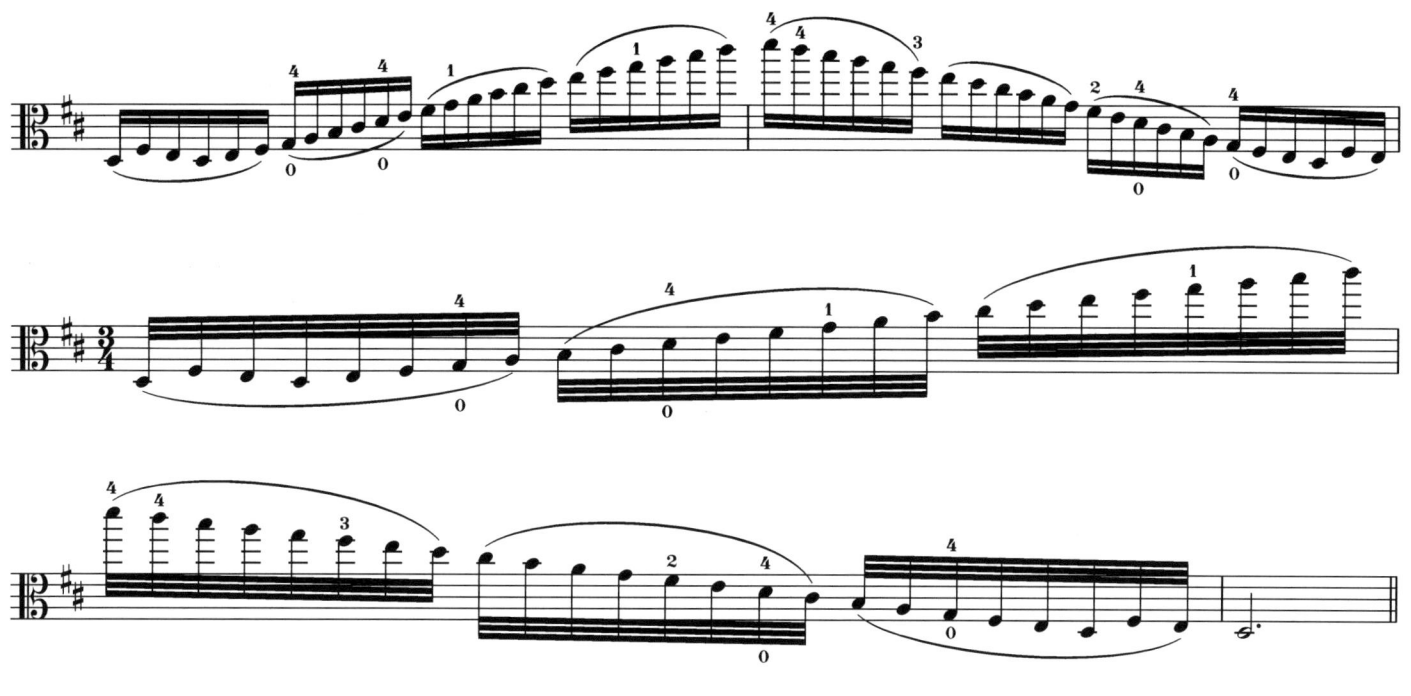

Acceleration pattern 2

Acceleration pattern 3

Building the final stage of eights

If it seems difficult to keep up with the metronome in the final stage of the acceleration pattern, practise each group separately first. Then join the groups systematically until you have assembled the entire scale:

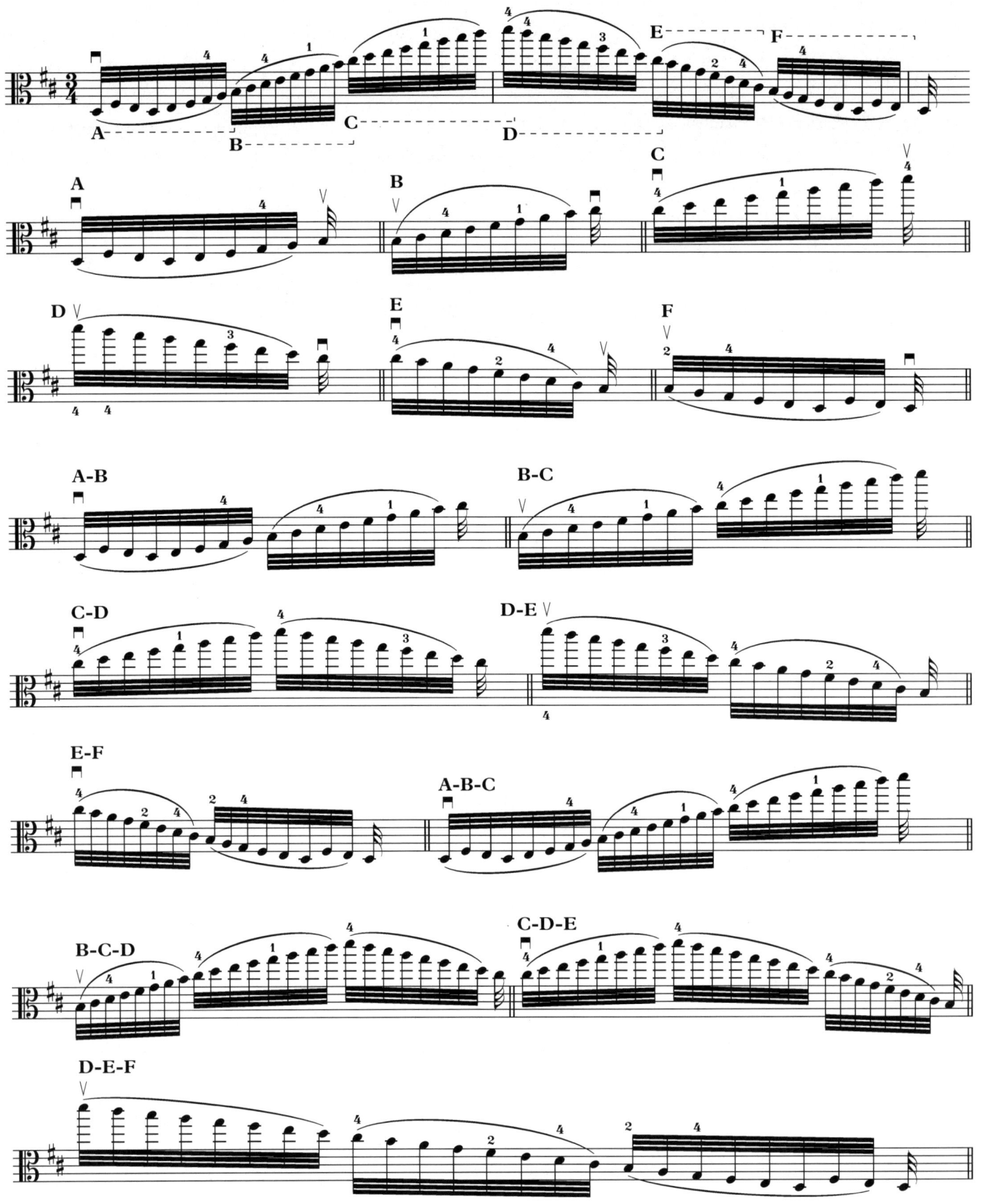

Speeding up with the metronome

Three-octave arpeggios

Three-octave dominant and diminished sevenths

There is no need to repeat three-octave dominant and diminished sevenths. They total 24 notes, so one, two, three, four, six and eight notes to a beat all arrive back to the tonic on a down bow.

Three-octave chromatic scale

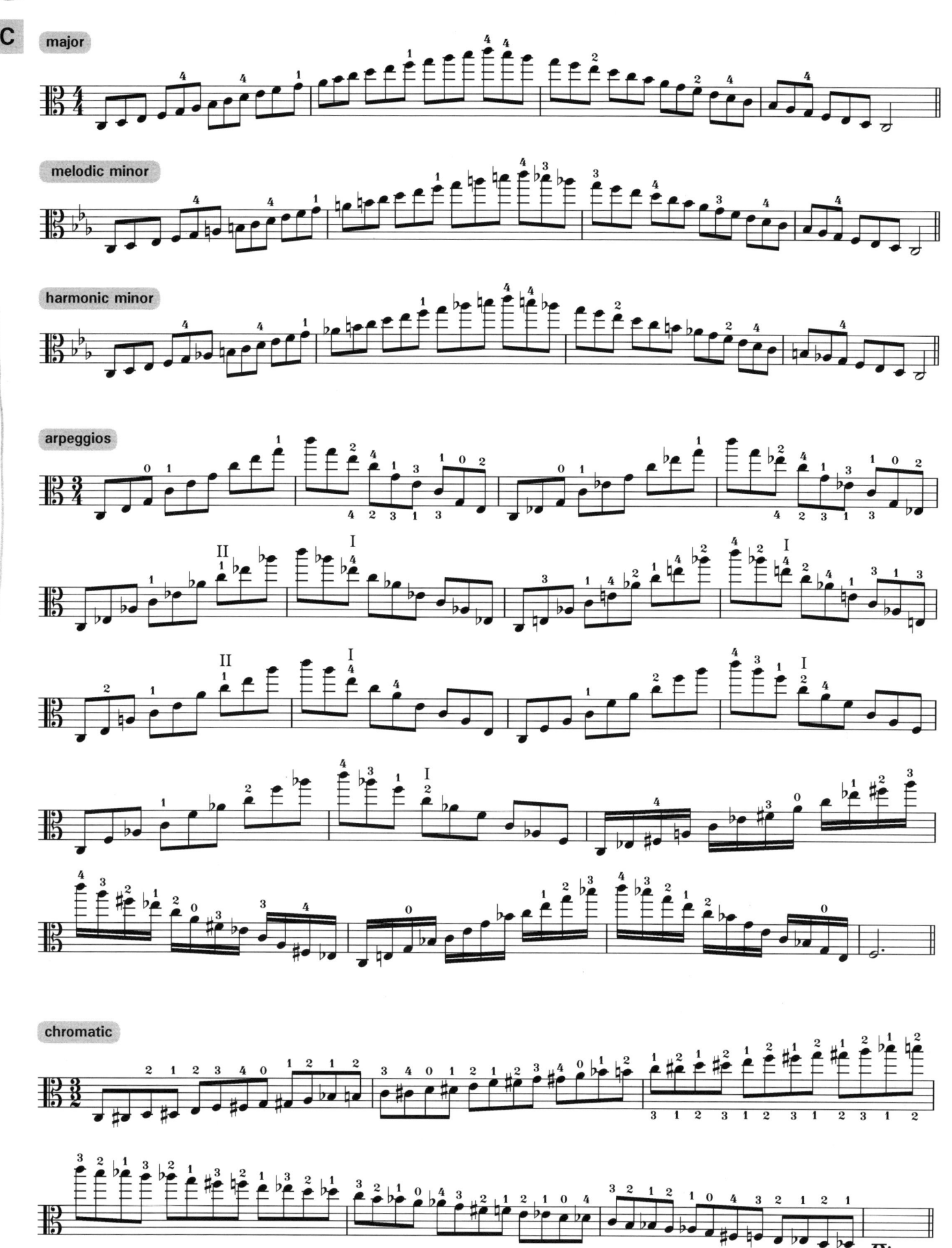

Three-octave scales, arpeggios and chromatic scales

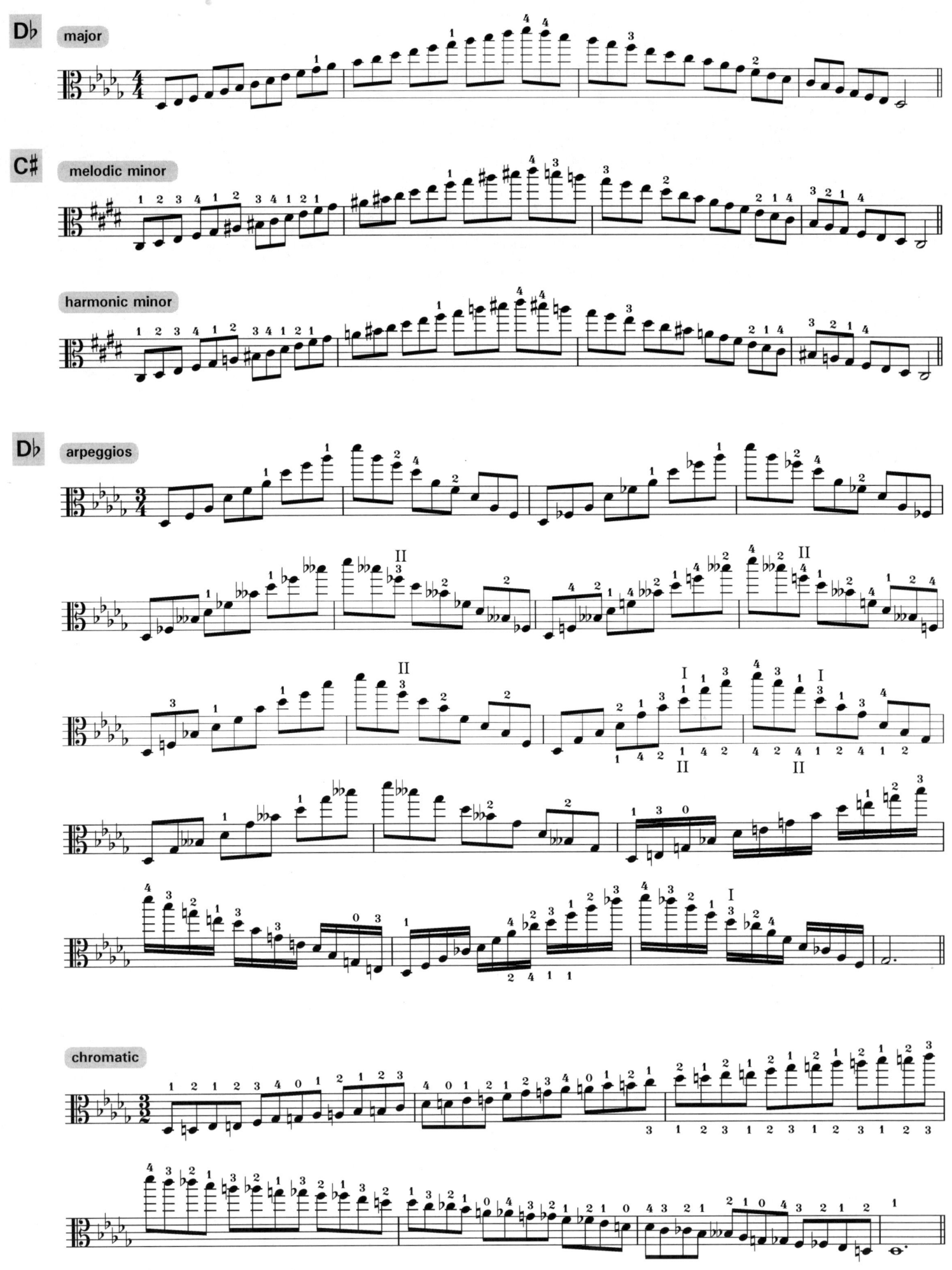

Part 3: Three-octave scales, arpeggios and chromatic scales   See notes, page 120

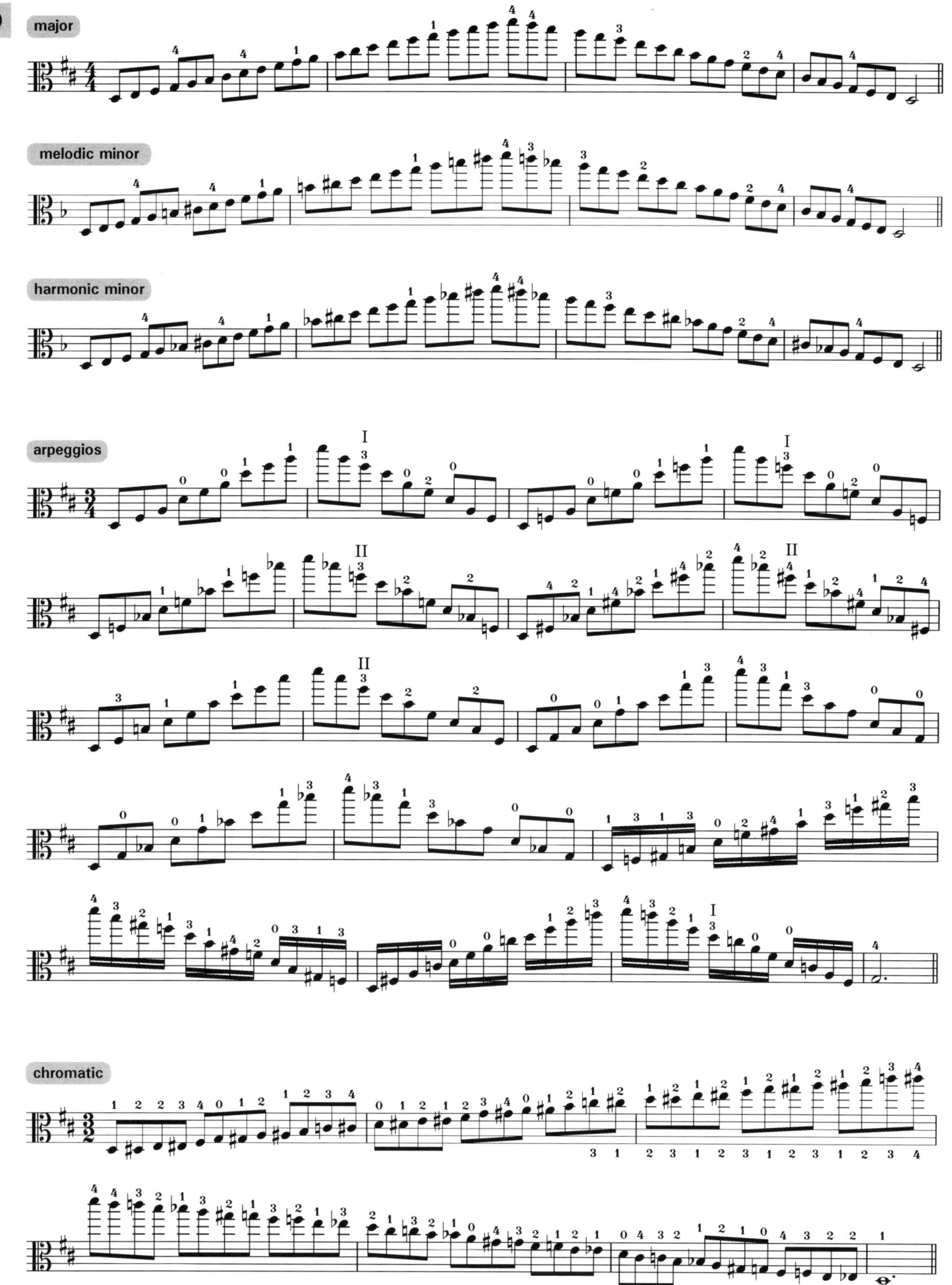

Three-octave scales, arpeggios and chromatic scales

132 Part 3: Three-octave scales, arpeggios and chromatic scales See notes, page 120

Three-octave scales, arpeggios and chromatic scales

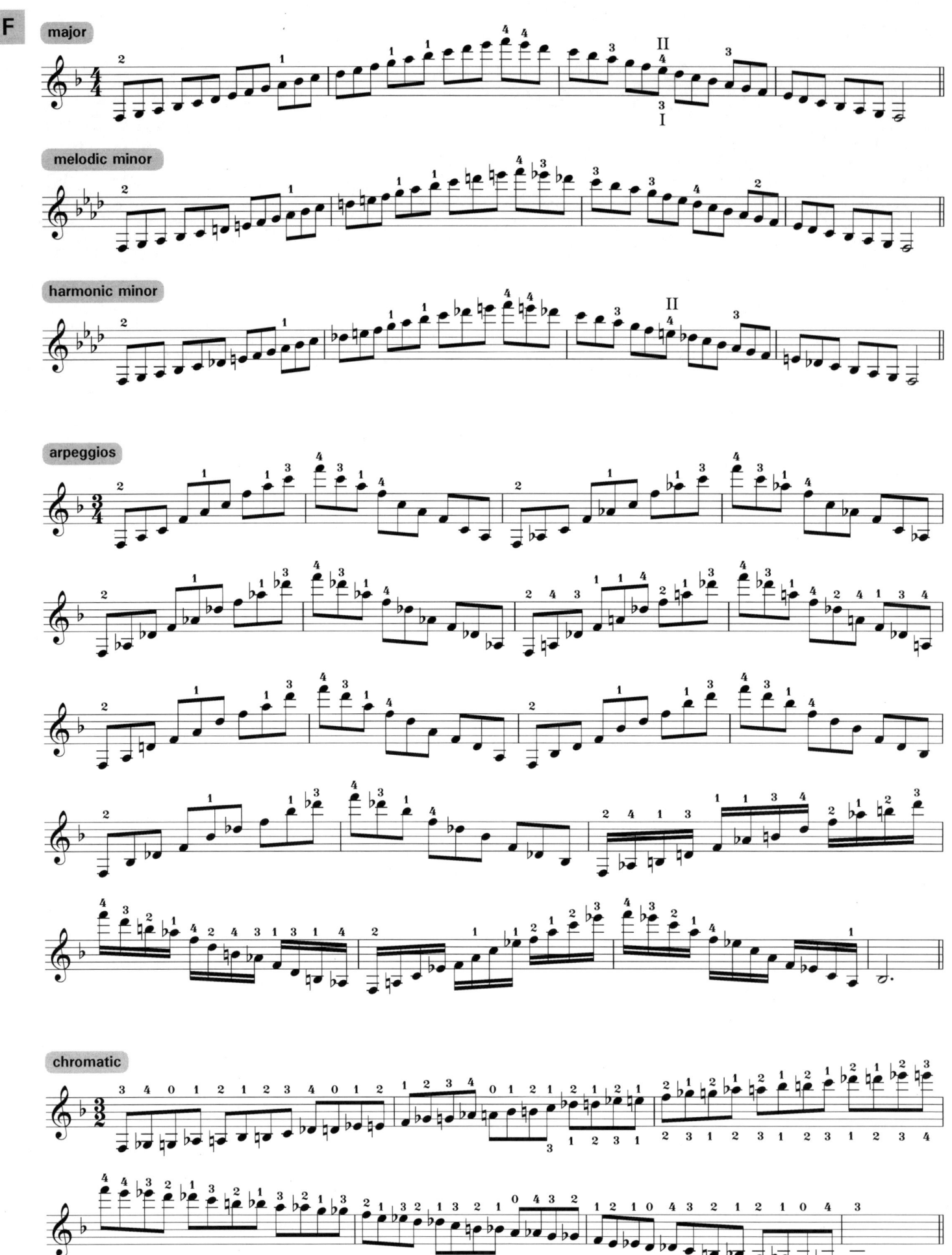

F major

melodic minor

harmonic minor

arpeggios

chromatic

Three-octave scales, arpeggios and chromatic scales

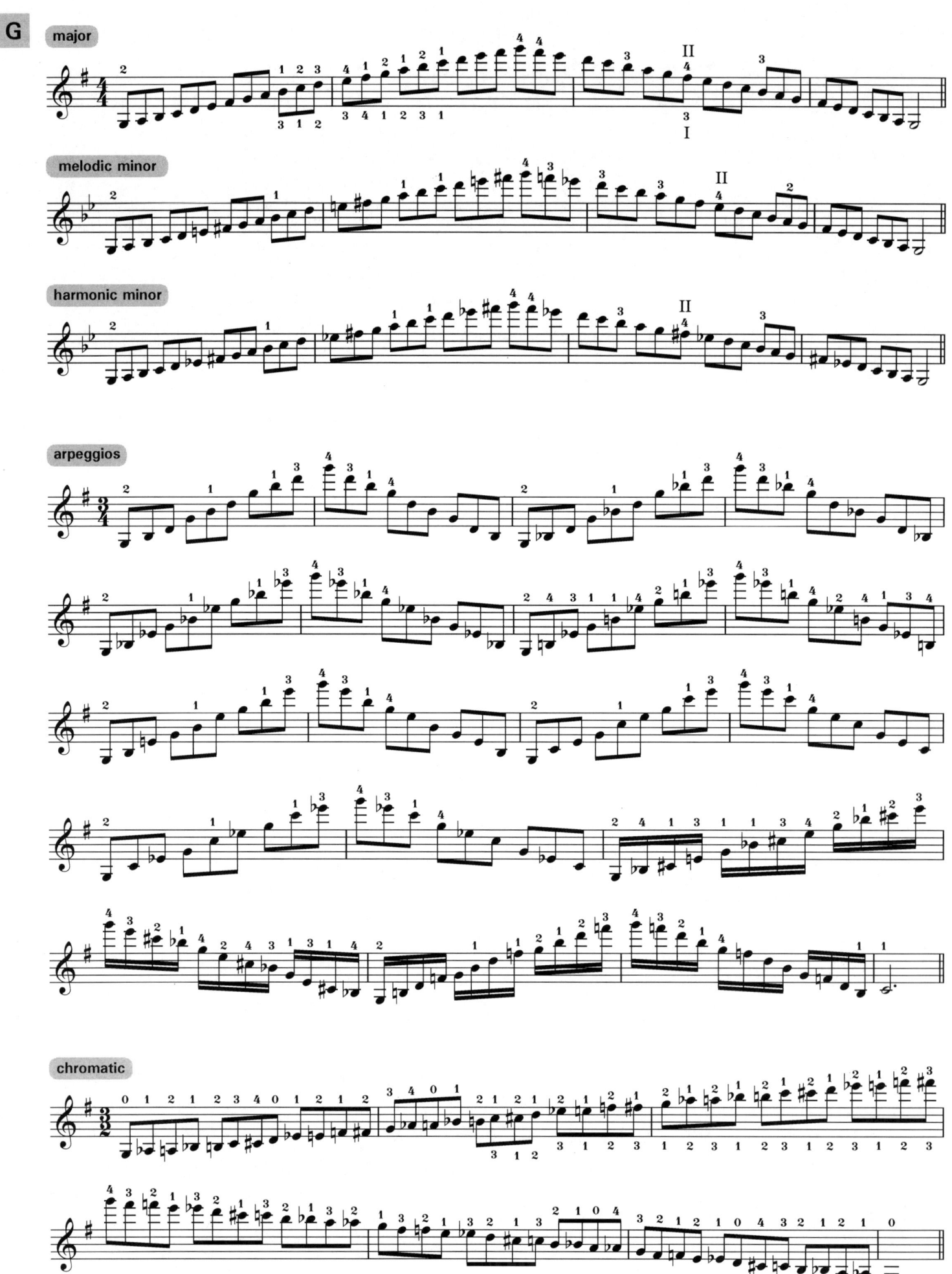

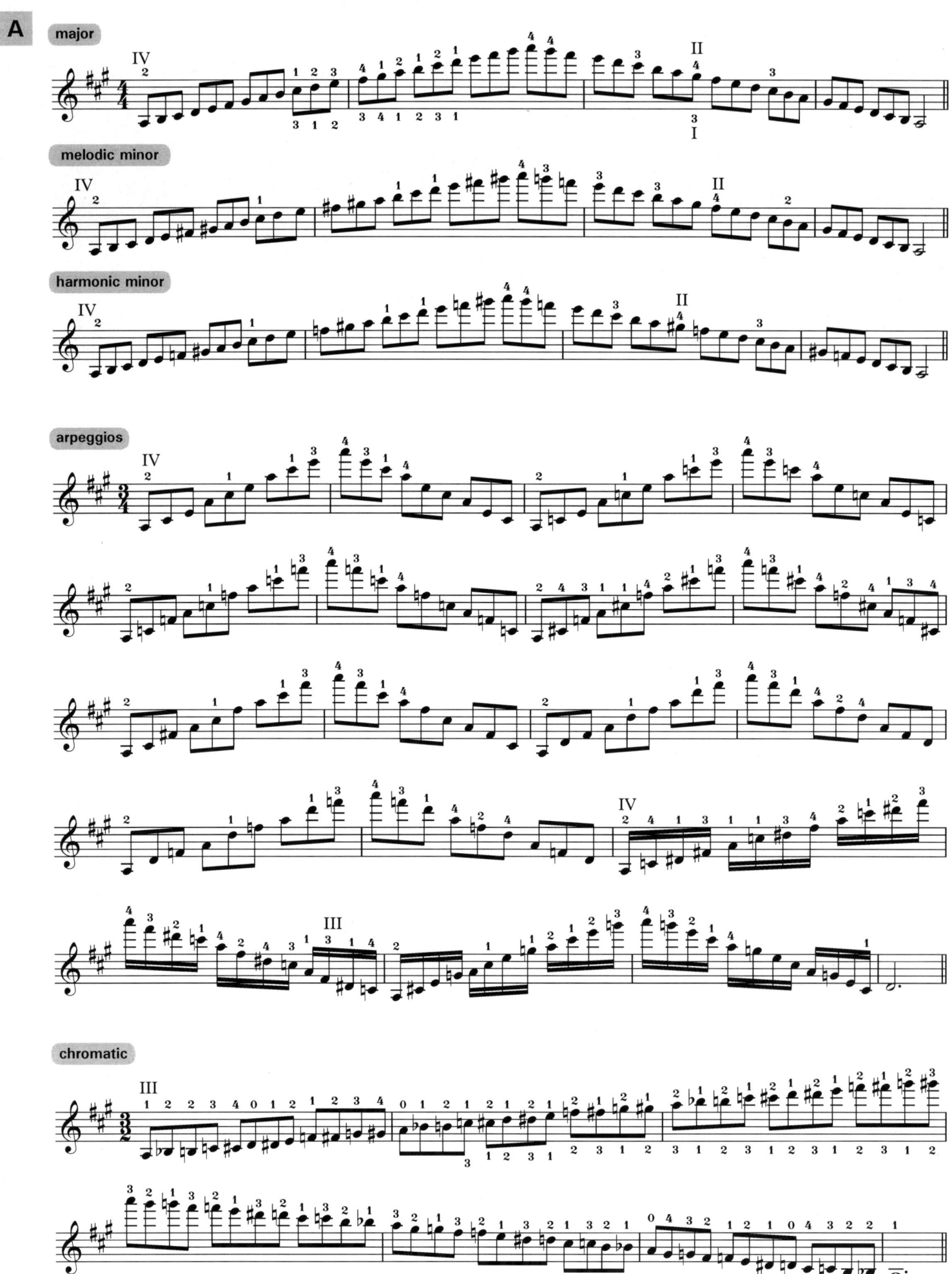

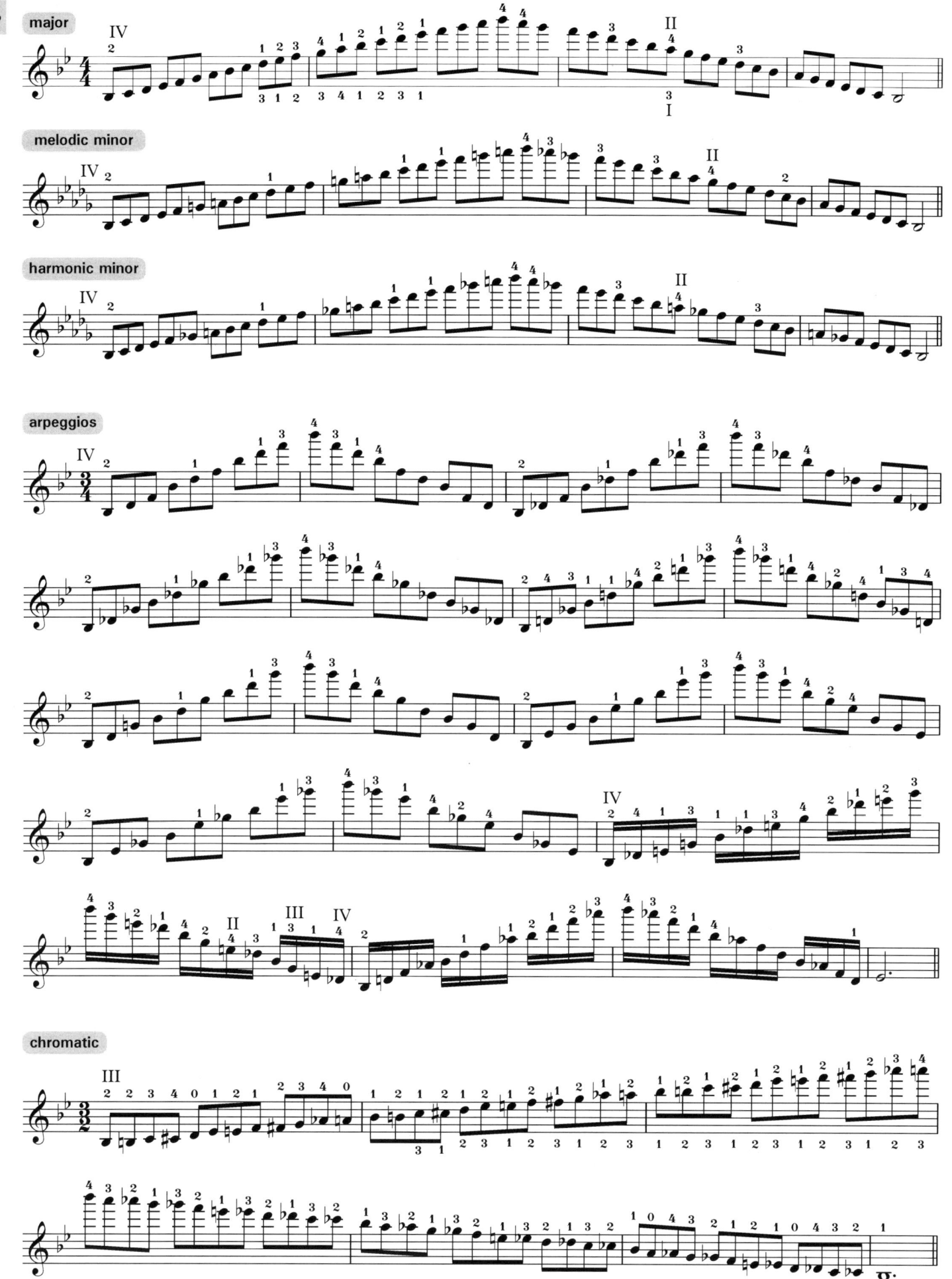

Three-octave scales, arpeggios and chromatic scales

B

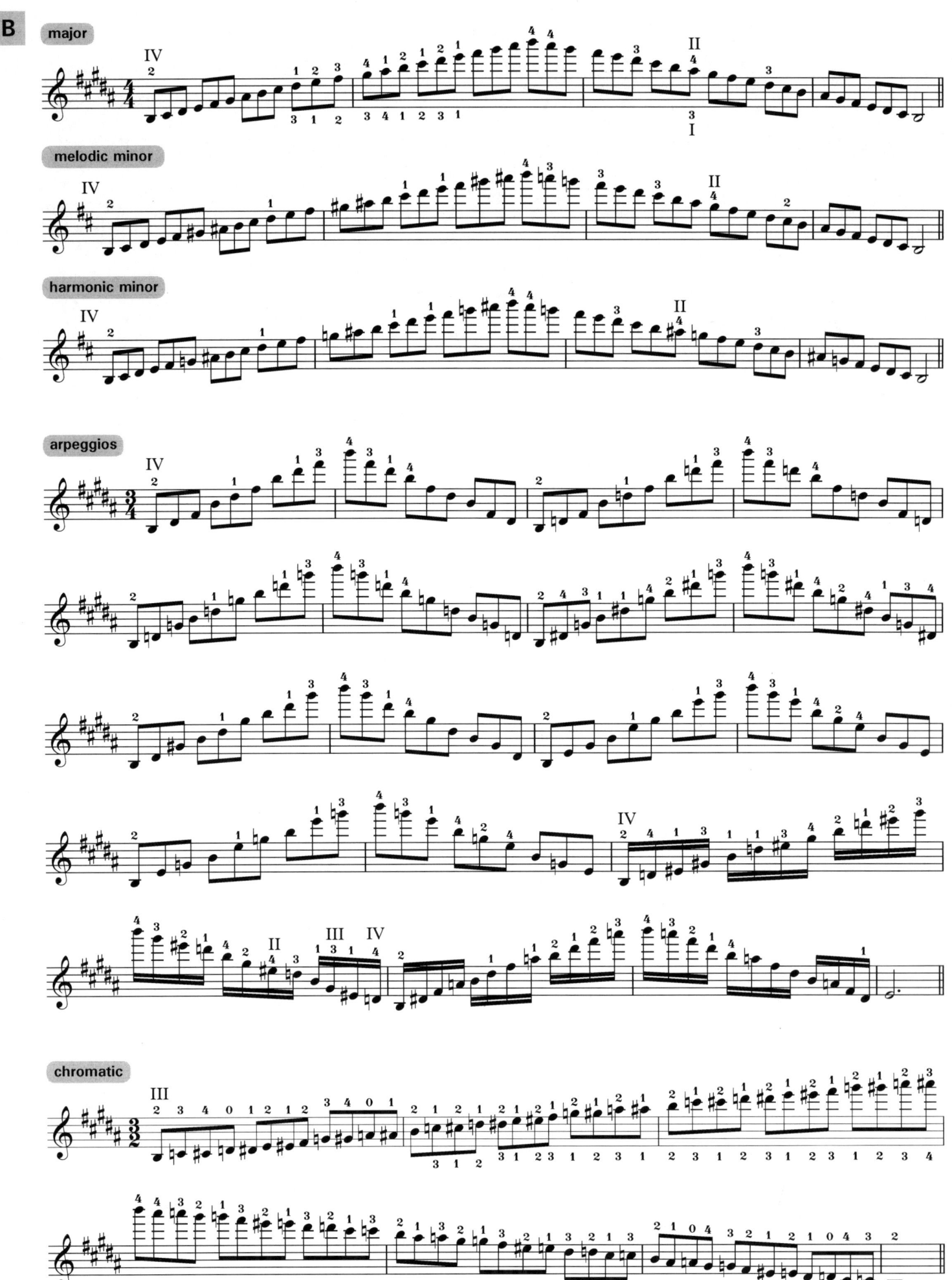

Part 4

Scales and arpeggios on one string

Notes

part 4

32 Single-finger scales and arpeggios   *Page 144*

Keep a good hand position when practising single-finger scales, with the other three fingers hovering near the string in the same playing shape and position as would be the case if you were just about to play them.

As an added practice method, when playing these scales with the first or second fingers, keep the fourth finger lightly on the next string, stopping the octave or seventh. This will help maintain a good hand position.

1. Semitones
2. Whole tones
3. Minor thirds (diminished)
4. Major thirds (augmented)
5. Perfect fourths
6. Major scale
7. Melodic minor scale
8. Harmonic minor scale
9. Minor arpeggio
10. Major arpeggio

33 Two-finger scales   *Page 152*

1. Isolating the first finger
2. Measuring the distance of the shift from the previous position of the finger
3. Shifting using substitutions
4. Play repeated separate strokes to force precise timing of the shifts. (This should sound the same as if playing without shifting – see page 90.)
5. The complete scale

These practice routines use 'ghost' notes, shown as x-notes. Play them by releasing the left finger almost as though to play a harmonic, and at the same time lighten and slow the bow (use very little bow).

To play the harmonic minor, use the major pattern and flatten the third.

34 One-octave scales — Page 156

1. Structuring the scale: I, IV; V, VIII
2. I, III, IV; V, VII, VIII
3. Measuring the distance of the shift from the previous position of the finger
4. Shifting using substitutions
5. Missing out the note before the shift plus fast-fingers
6. The complete one-octave scale on one string

35 One-octave arpeggios — Page 168

1. Shifting using substitutions.
2. Measuring the distance of the shift from the previous position of the finger. This variation is also an exercise for slow arrival-speed: shift quickly to just below the arrival note, and then glide into it slowly.
3. Missing out the note before the shift plus fast-fingers. Also play this without the repeated notes, slurred in minims and crotchets (half and quarter notes).
4. This practice method produces an immediate feeling of ease and accuracy, and perfect timing, in each shift. Play the groups of chromatics strictly in time so that the pulse is not disturbed. Shift with the whole hand, not just by sliding the finger. Practise with a metronome.
5. The complete sequence.

36 Broken thirds on the A string — Page 180

See no. 35 (4)

37 Arpeggios: strengthening the top octave — Page 182

Keep all the fingers down on the string, lifting only when necessary. Crescendo to the top, and then keep that dynamic during the descending pattern.

Play the same pattern on the C string, and also on the G and D strings.

38 Two-octave scales and arpeggios — Page 183

The real final test and goal in the mastery of scales is not in playing four-octave scales across the strings, but two octaves on one string. Four-octave scales can use no more than the two-octave range of the fingerboard, so they go no higher than two-octave scales anyway.

To play two octaves on one string is naturally more challenging than playing across the strings, so any work on these scales forms the perfect basis and preparation for four-octave scales, which feel much easier afterwards.

But even if two octaves on one string seem overly difficult, and you do not yet play four-octave scales, the point is that three-octave scales and arpeggios feel very straightforward after tackling two octaves on one string (as does everything else in your general repertoire). They are worth practising for that reason alone, even if you do not yet play up to the top of the fingerboard in your normal playing.

Single-finger scales and arpeggios

D string

Part 4: Scales and arpeggios on one string   See notes, page 142

Single-finger scales and arpeggios

Second finger

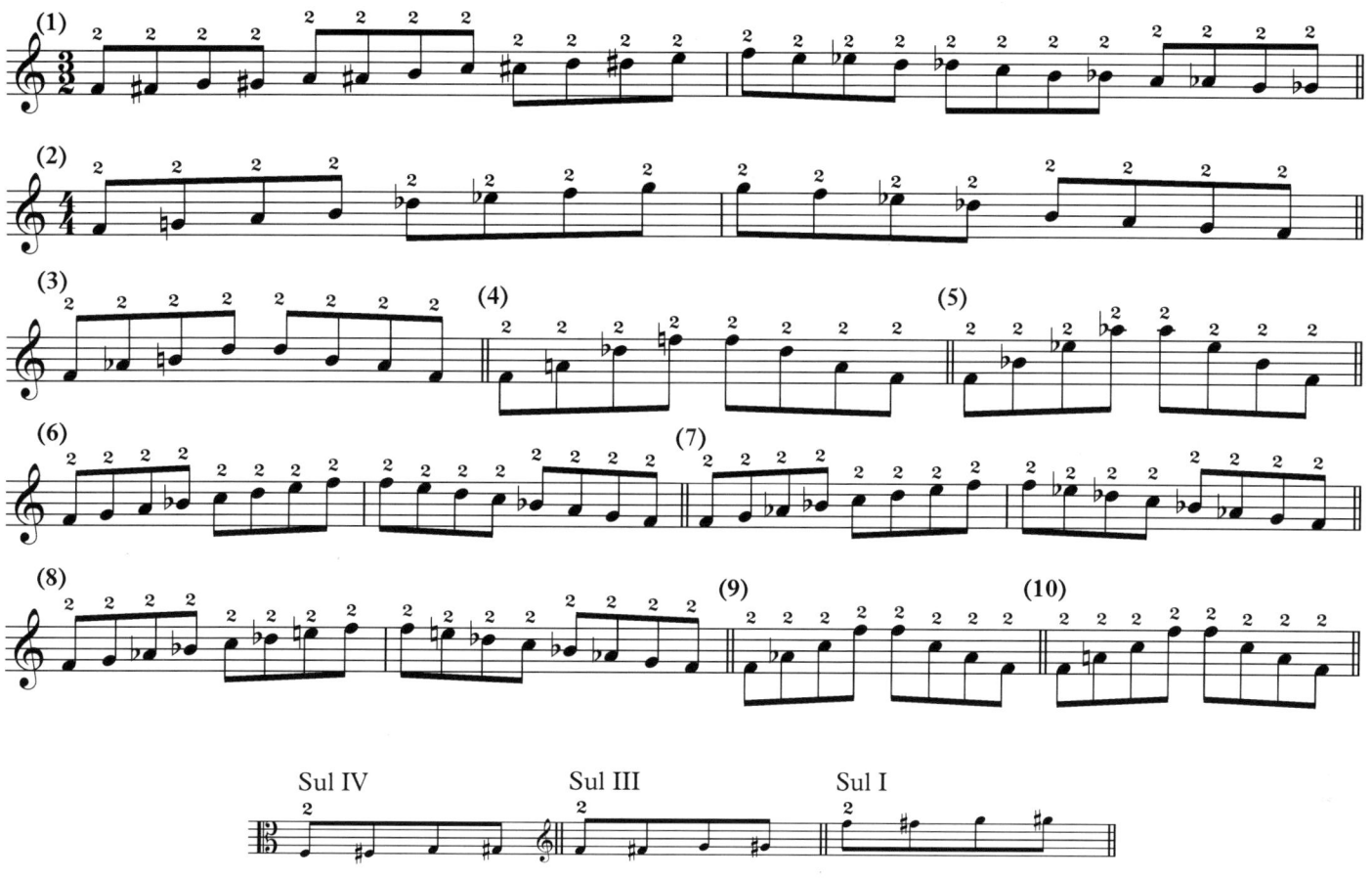

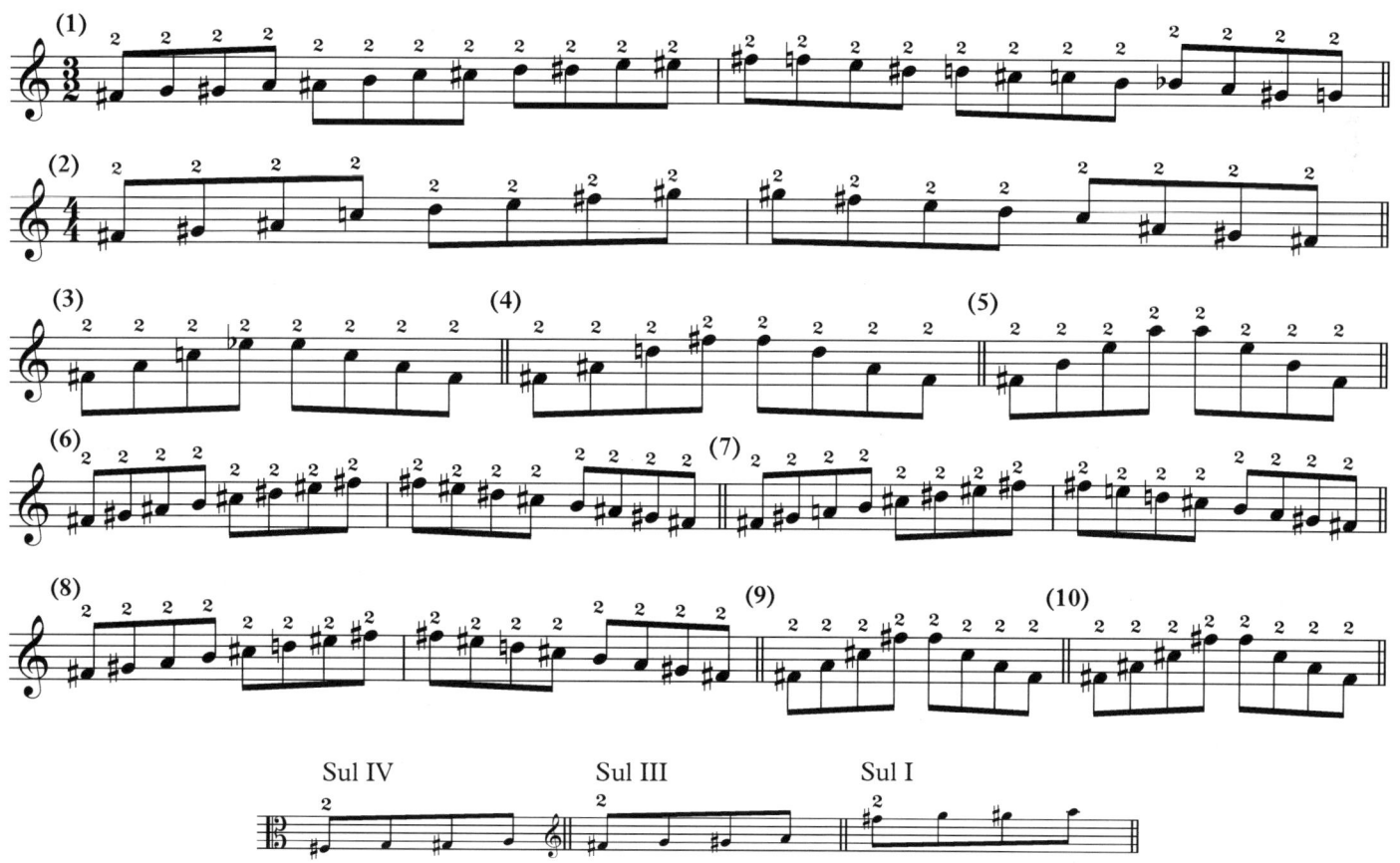

Single-finger scales and arpeggios

Third finger

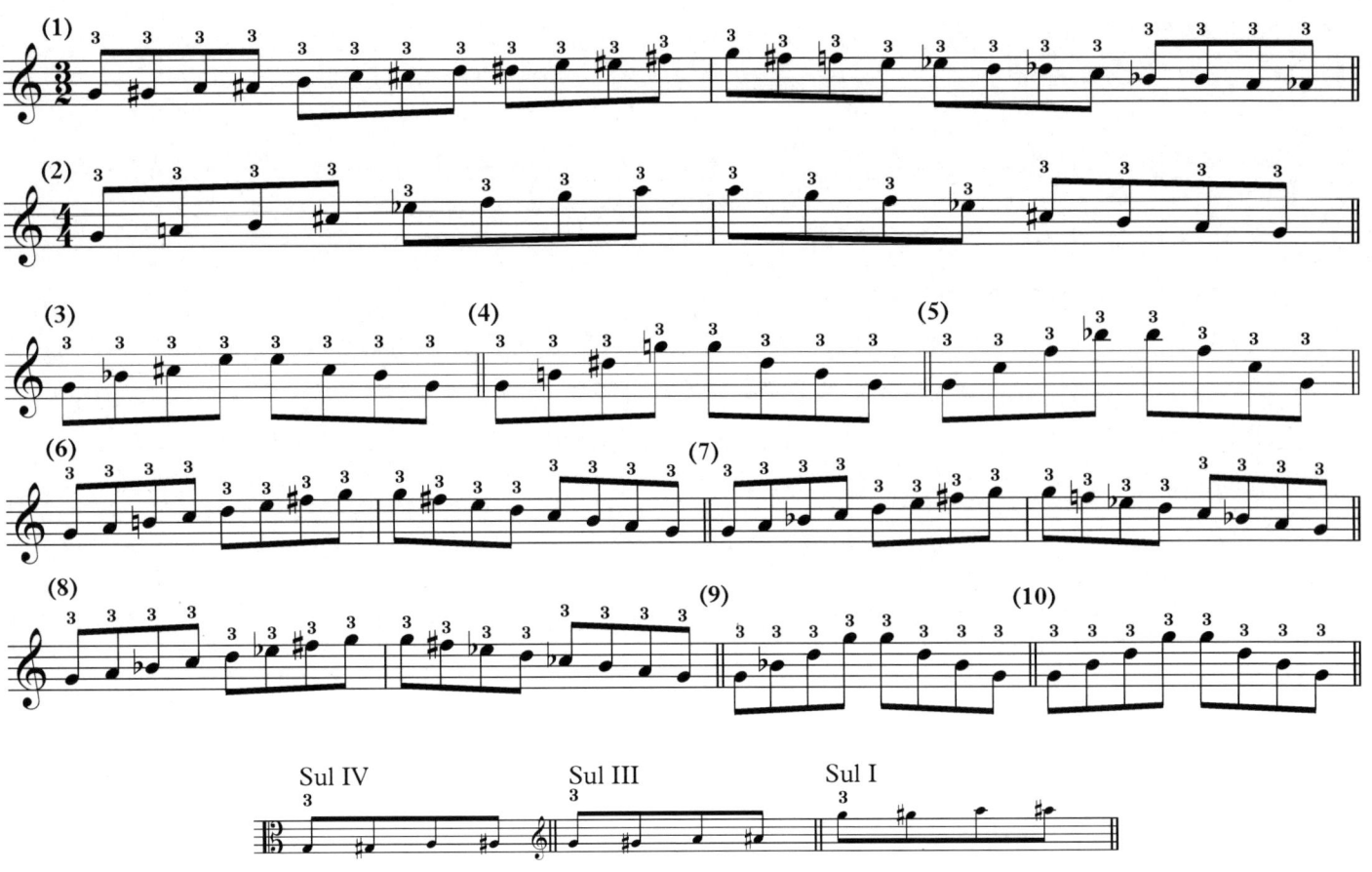

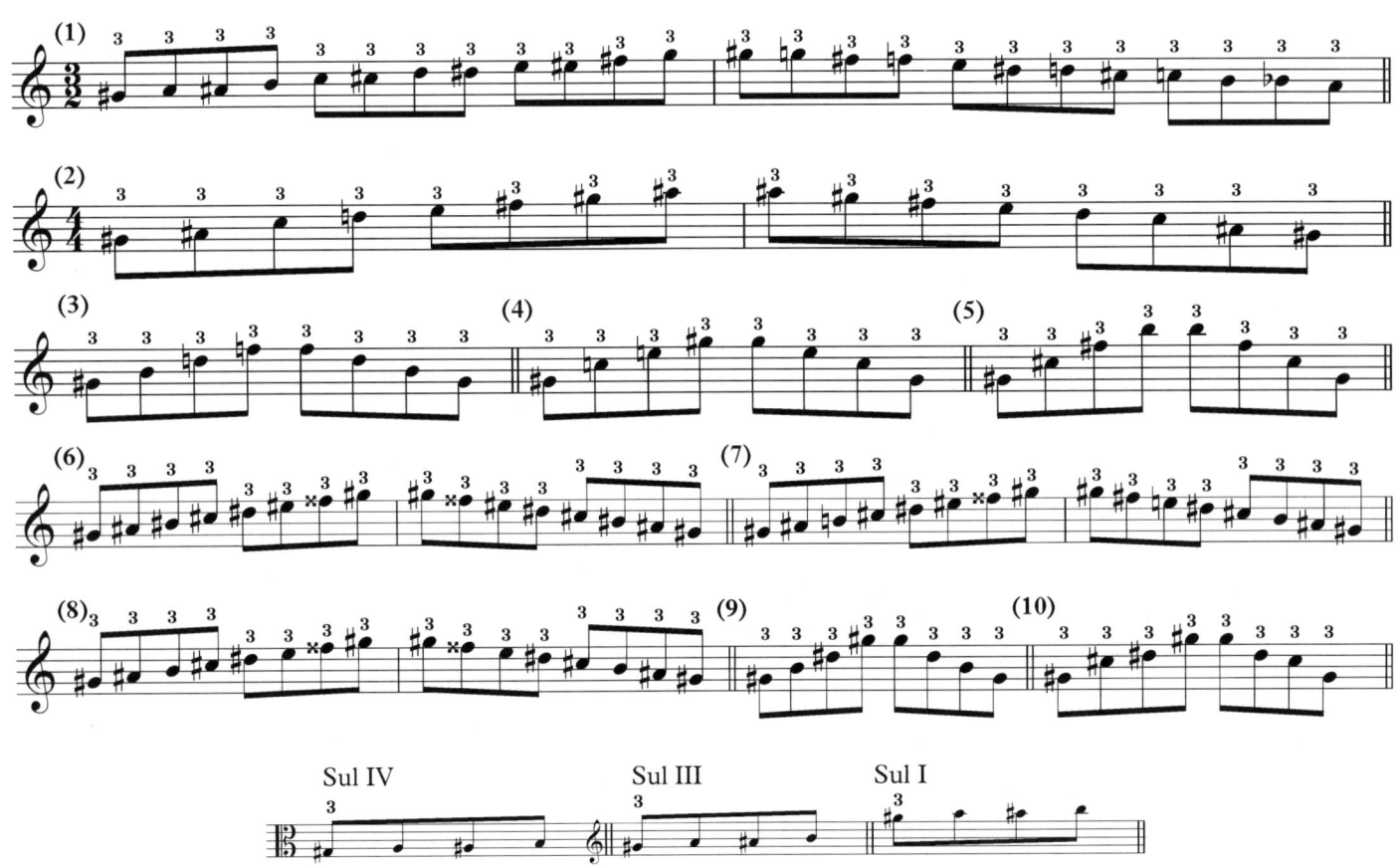

Fourth finger

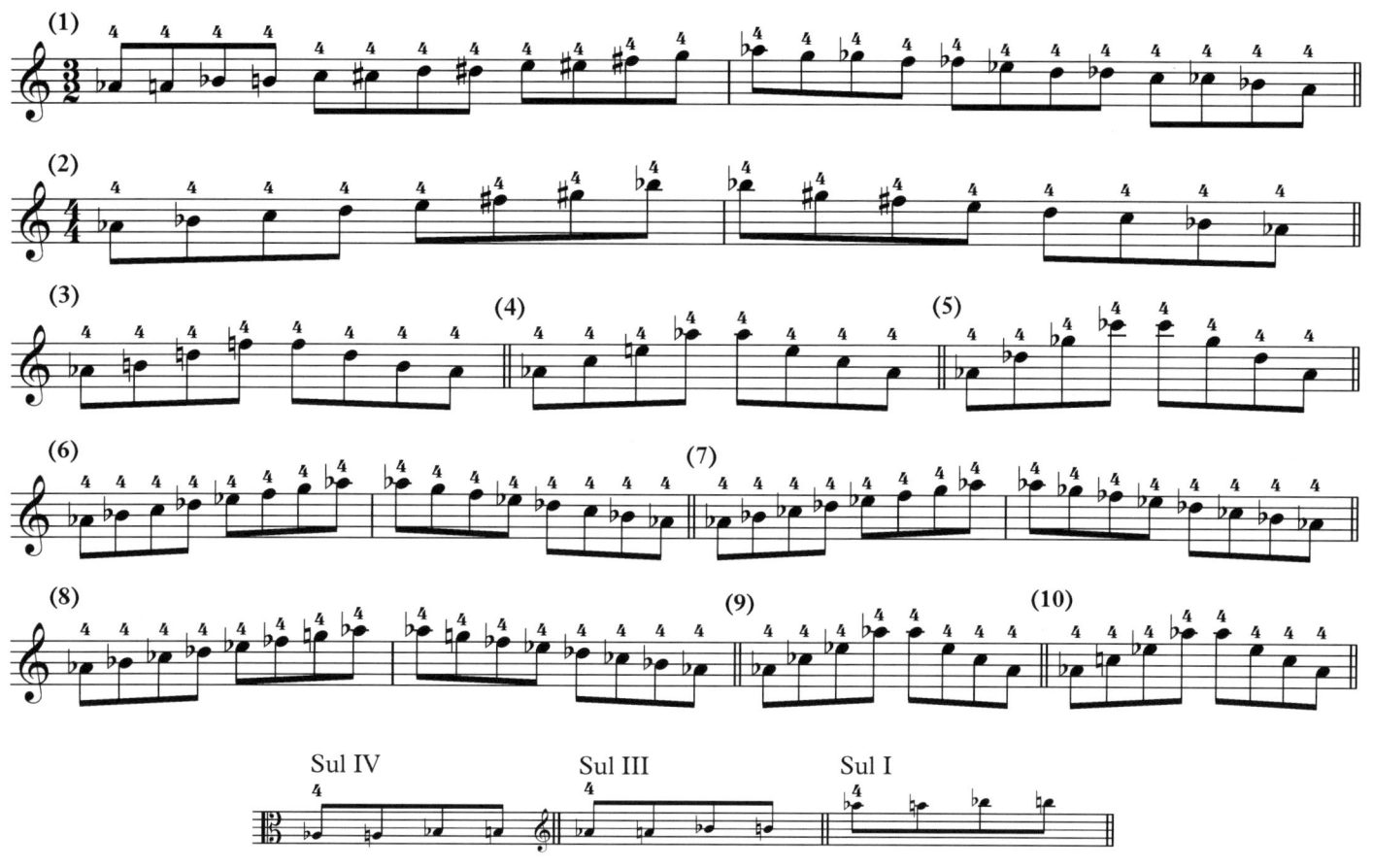

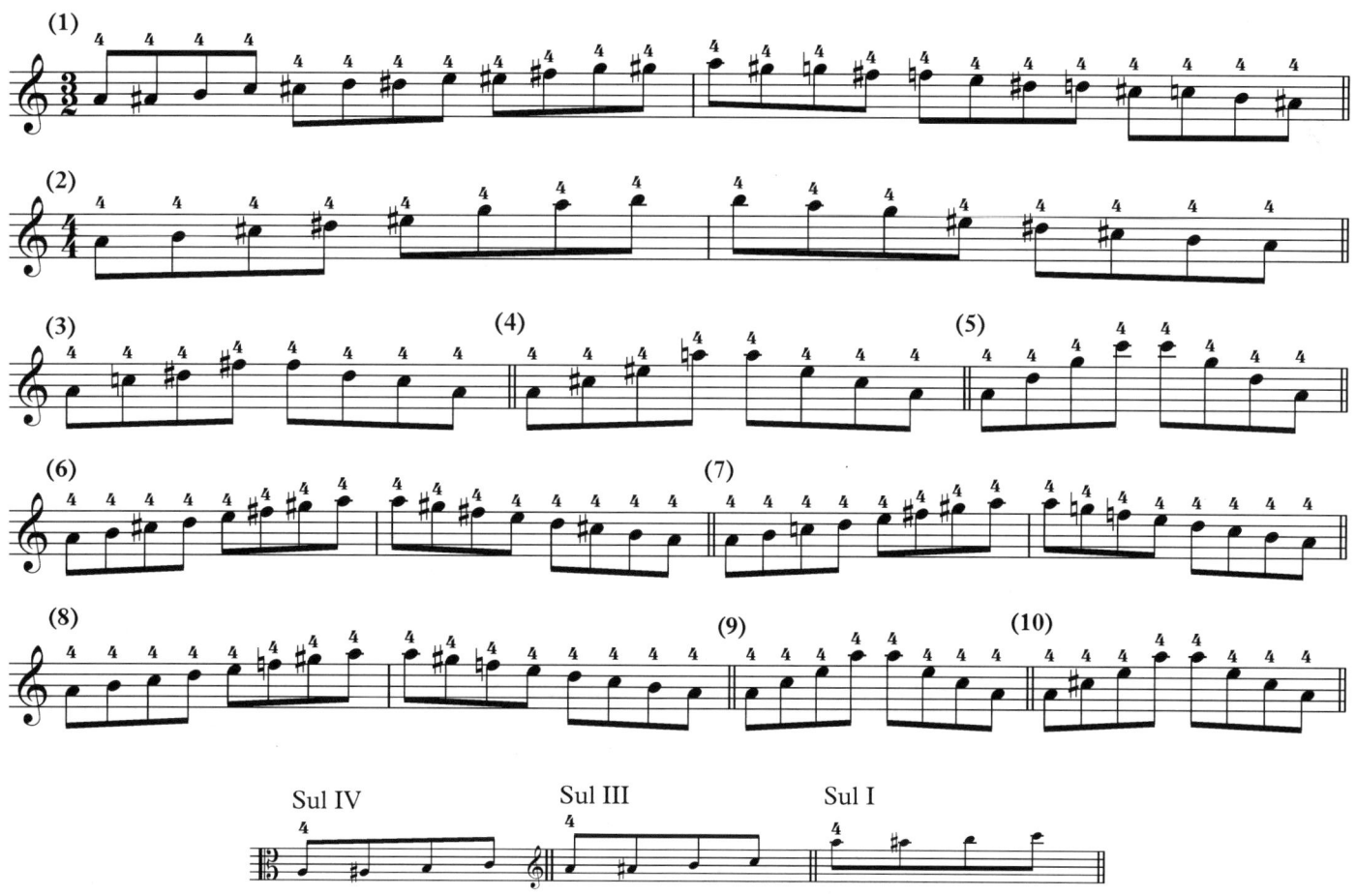

Part 4: Scales and arpeggios on one string   See notes, page 142

Single-finger scales and arpeggios

A string

First finger

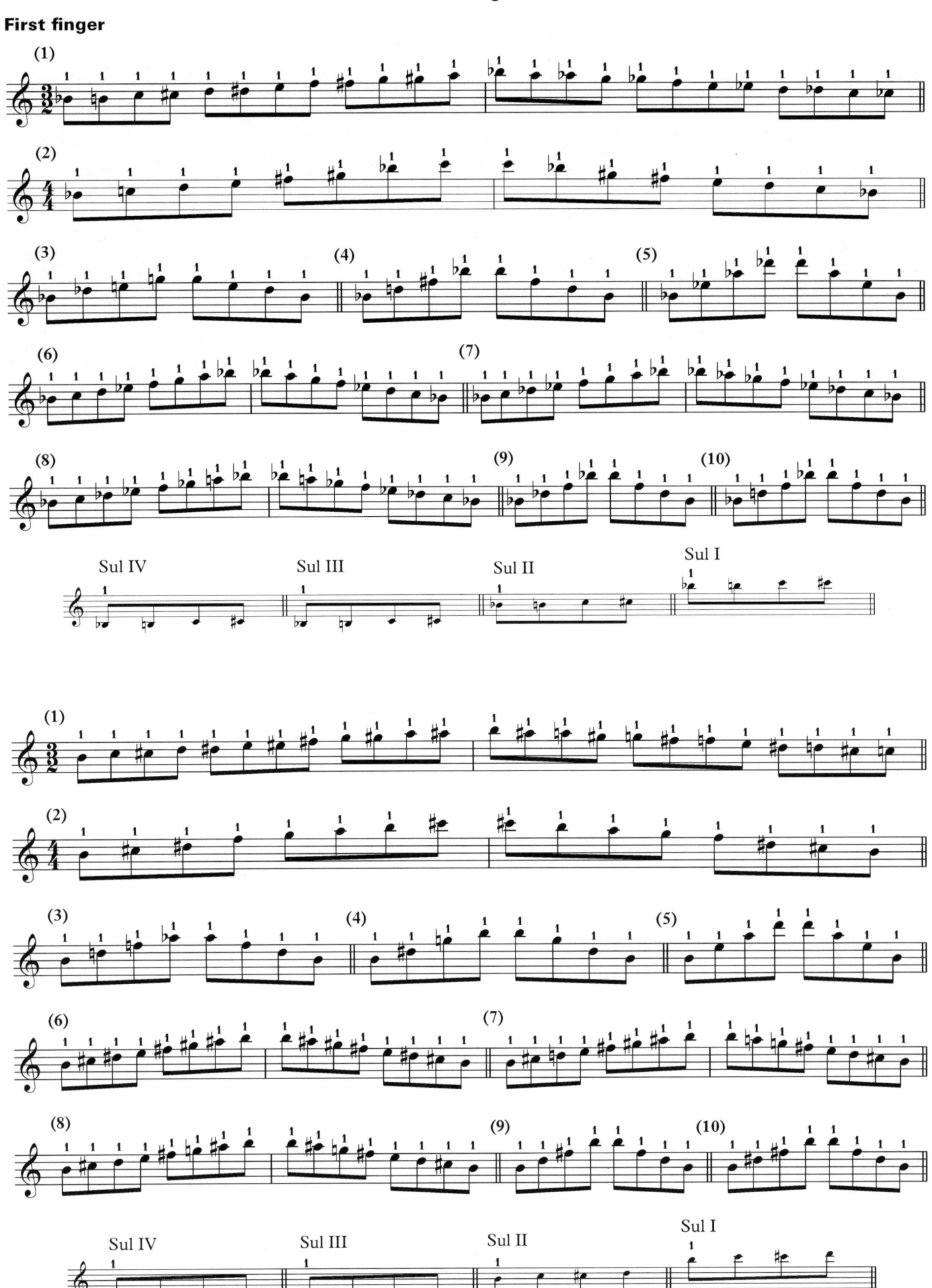

148 Part 4: Scales and arpeggios on one string   See notes, page 142

Single-finger scales and arpeggios

Second finger

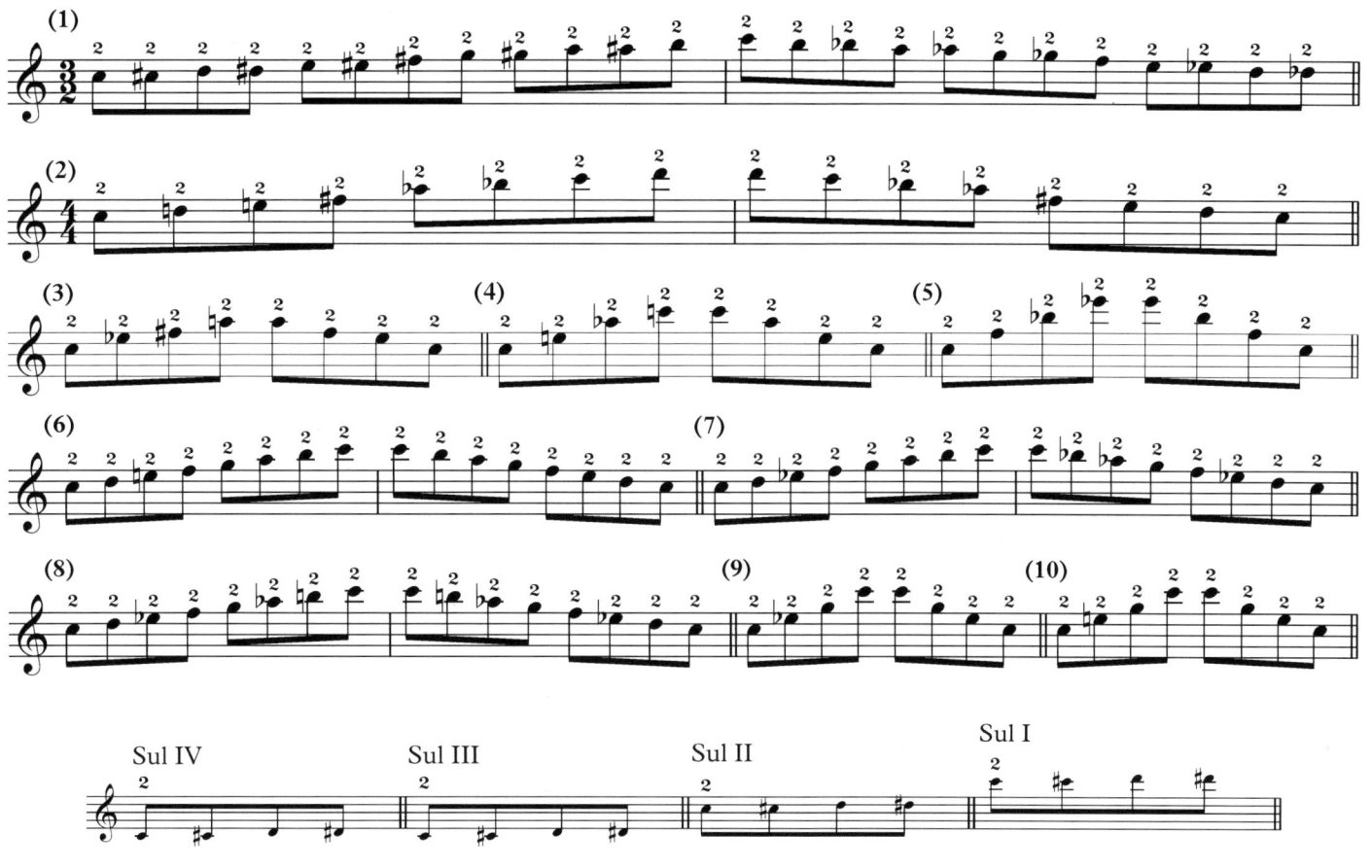

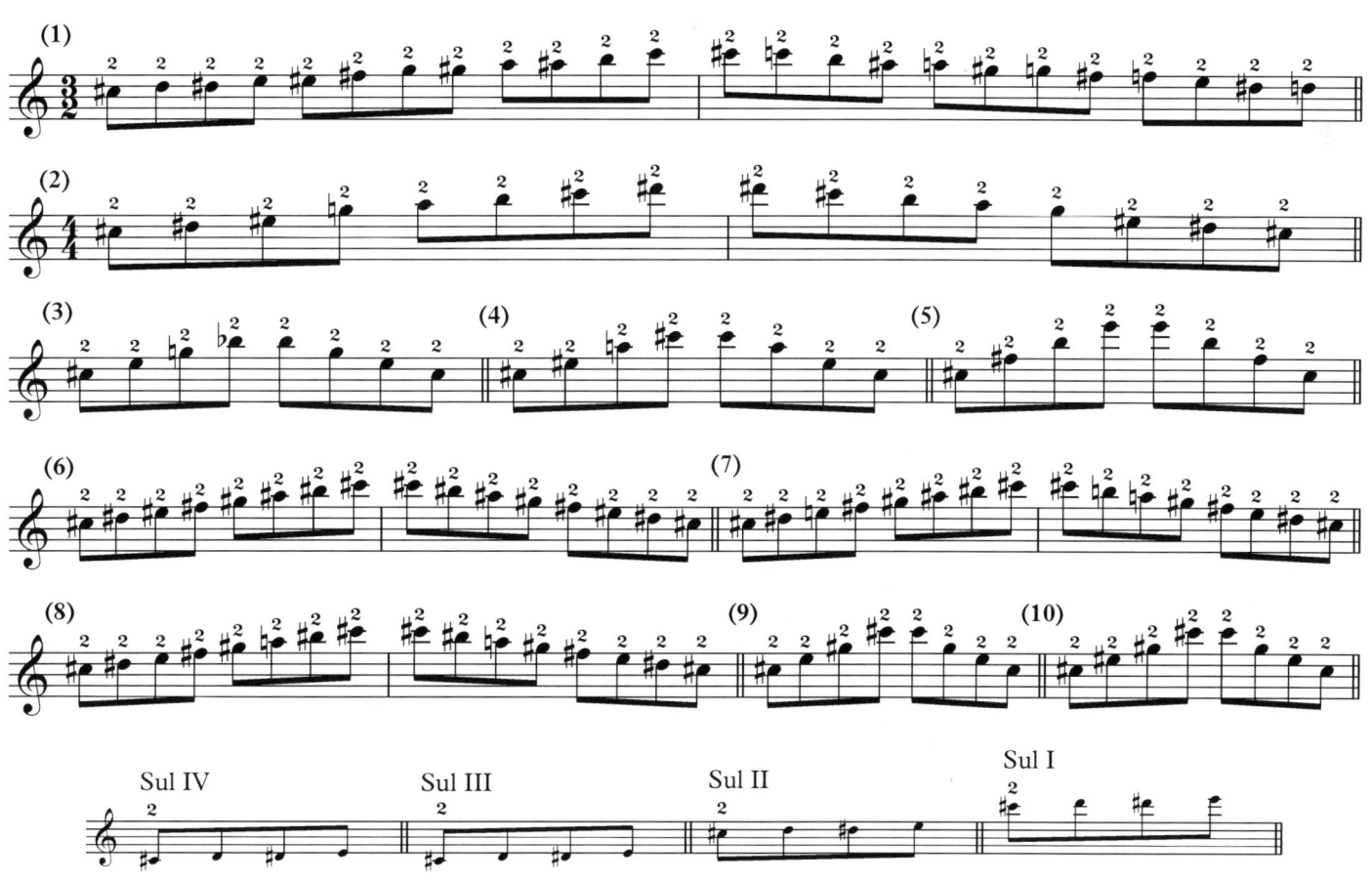

Part 4: Scales and arpeggios on one string   See notes, page 142

Single-finger scales and arpeggios

Third finger

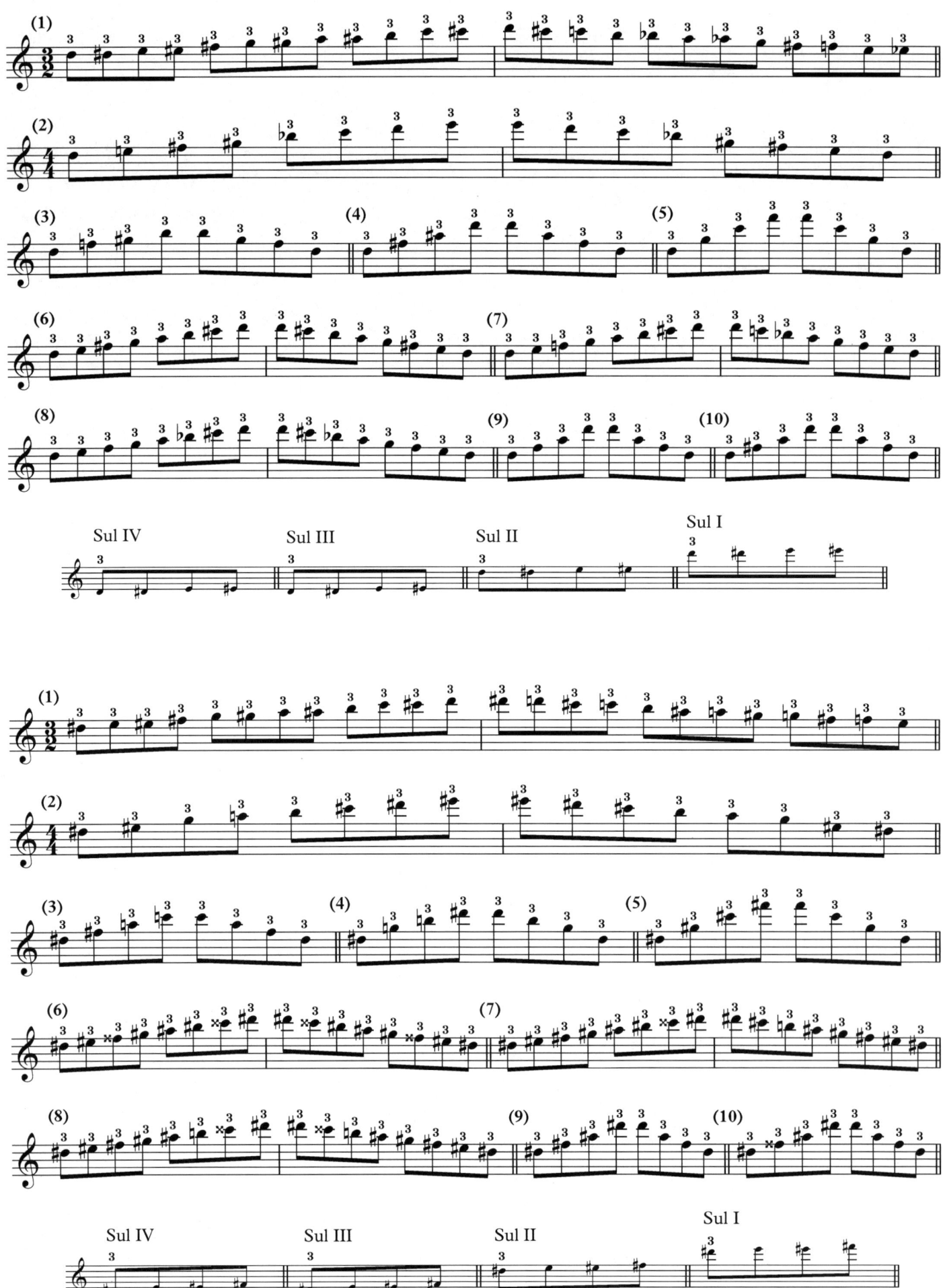

Part 4: Scales and arpeggios on one string   See notes, page 142

Single-finger scales and arpeggios

Fourth finger

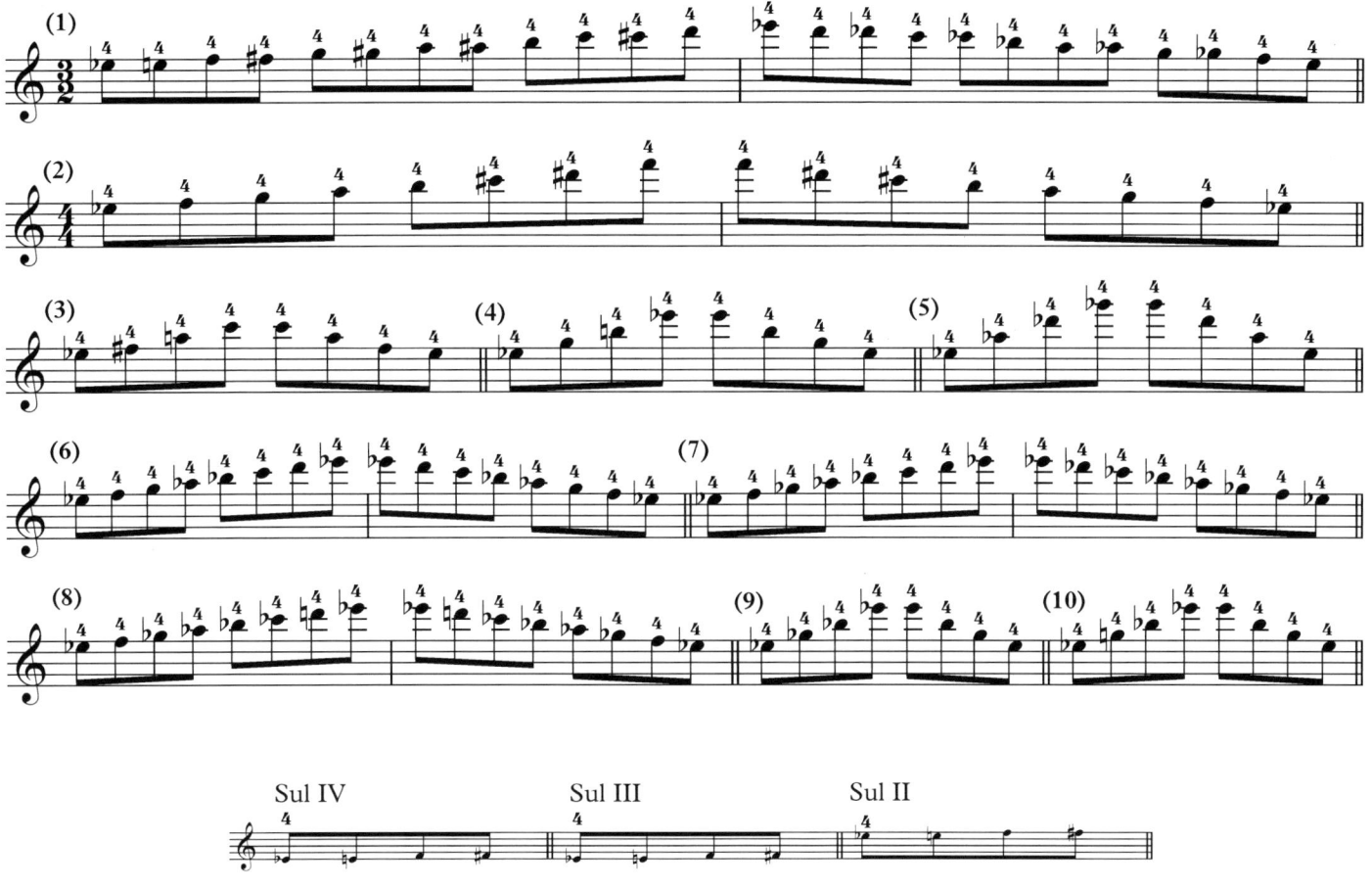

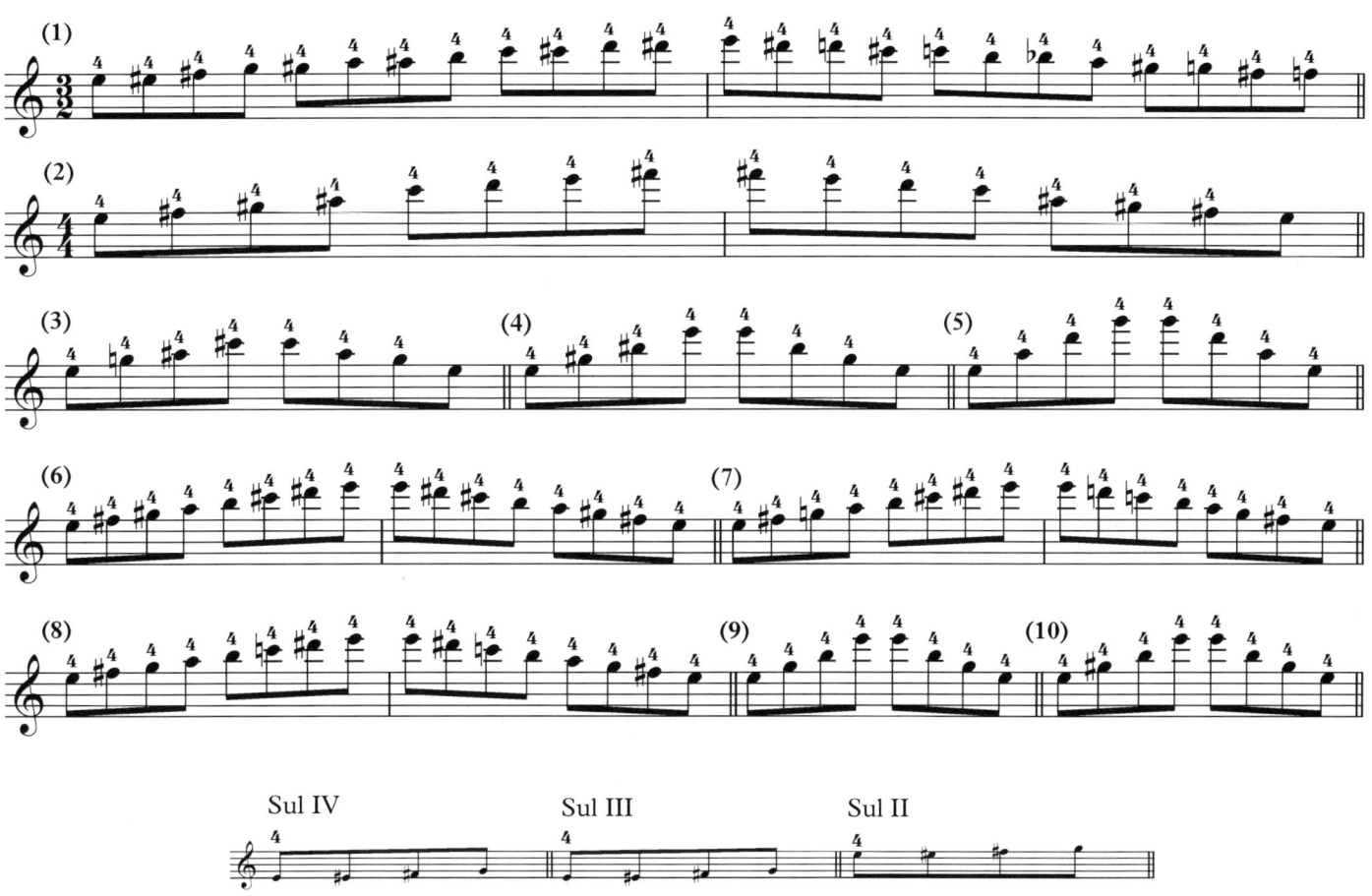

Part 4: Scales and arpeggios on one string   See notes, page 142

Two-finger scales

C string

First and second fingers

D *major*

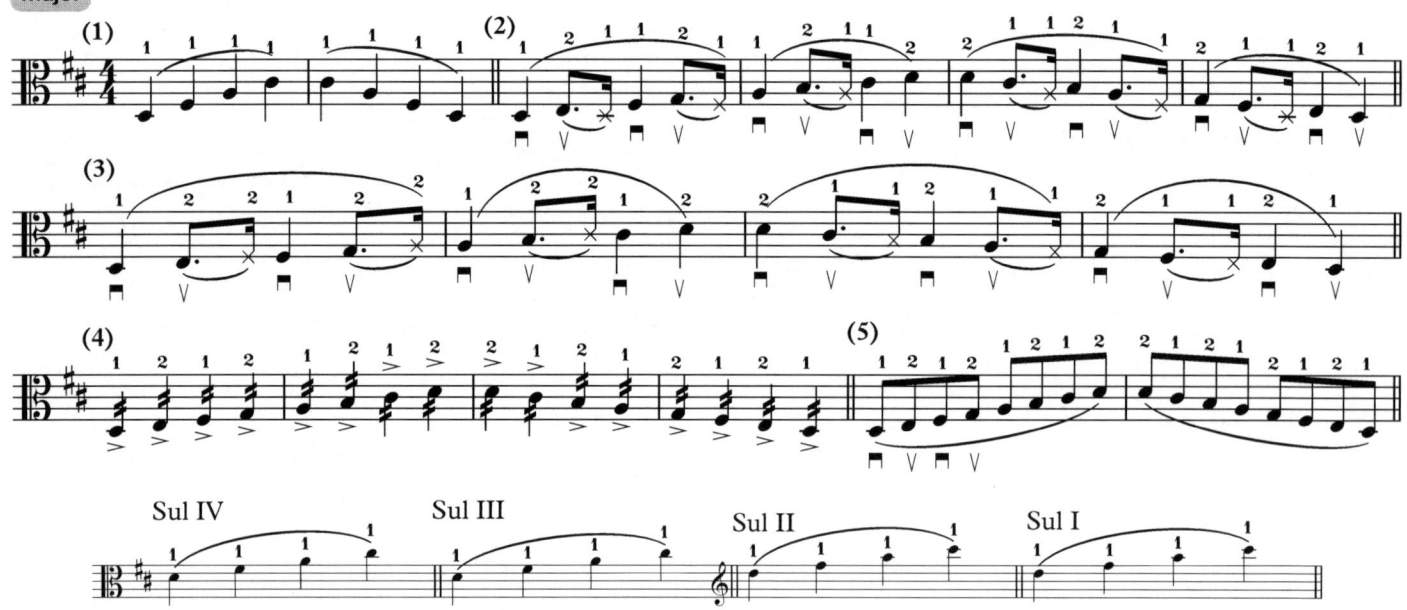

melodic minor

Second and third fingers

E *major*

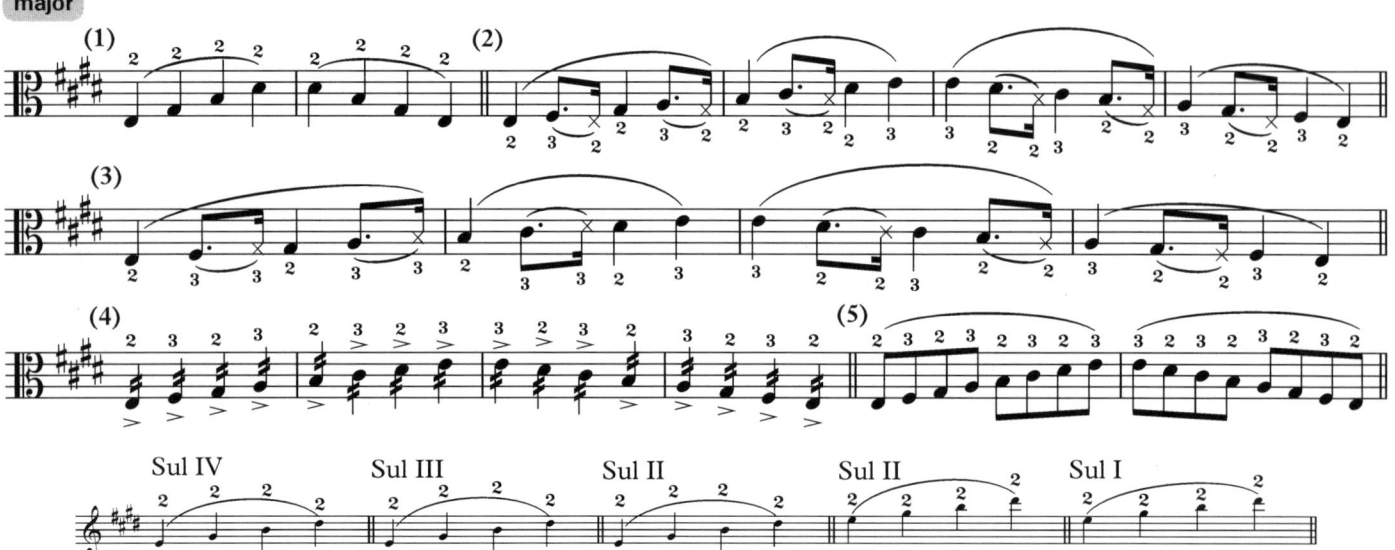

Part 4: Scales and arpeggios on one string   See notes, page 142

Two-finger scales

melodic minor

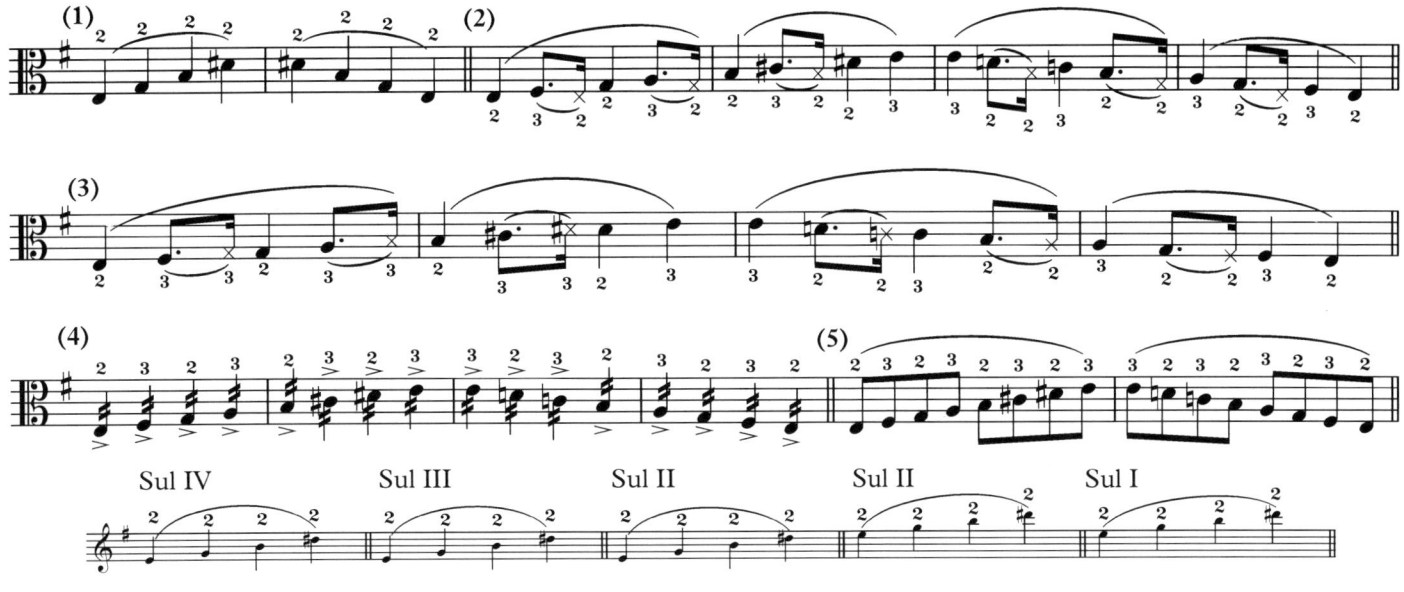

Third and fourth fingers

F major

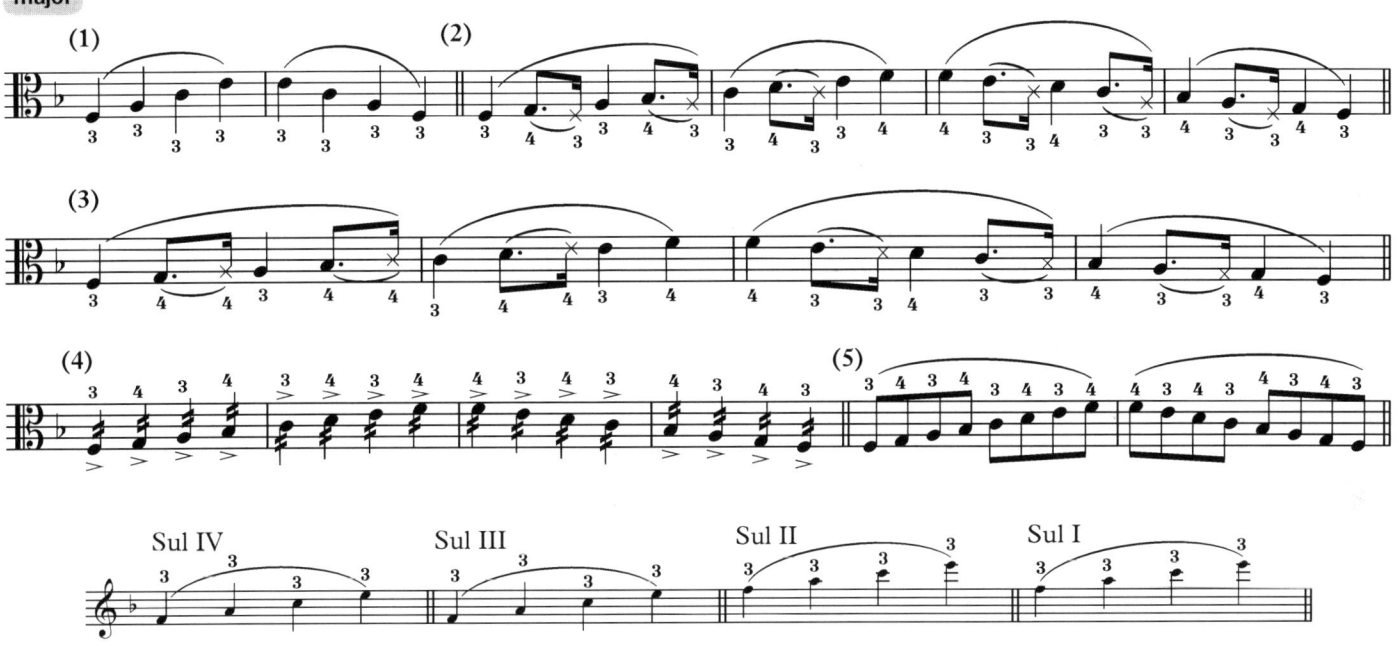

melodic minor

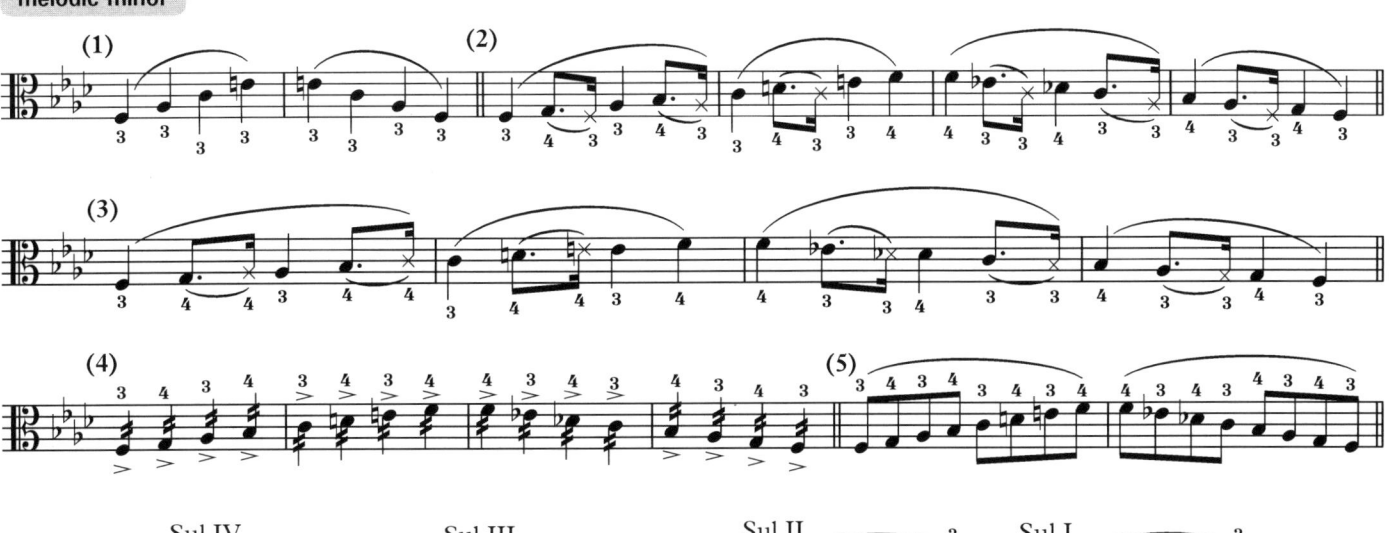

Two-finger scales

First and second fingers

A string

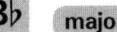 **B♭ major**

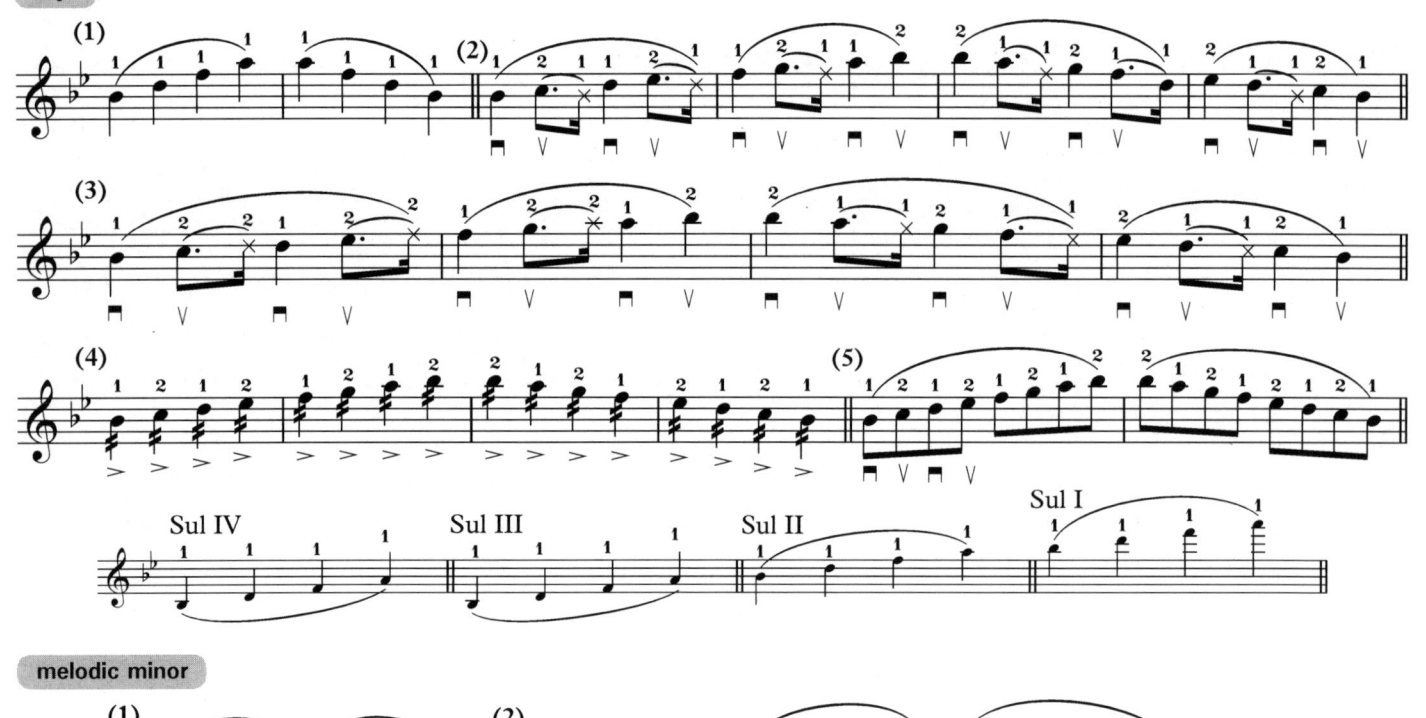

melodic minor

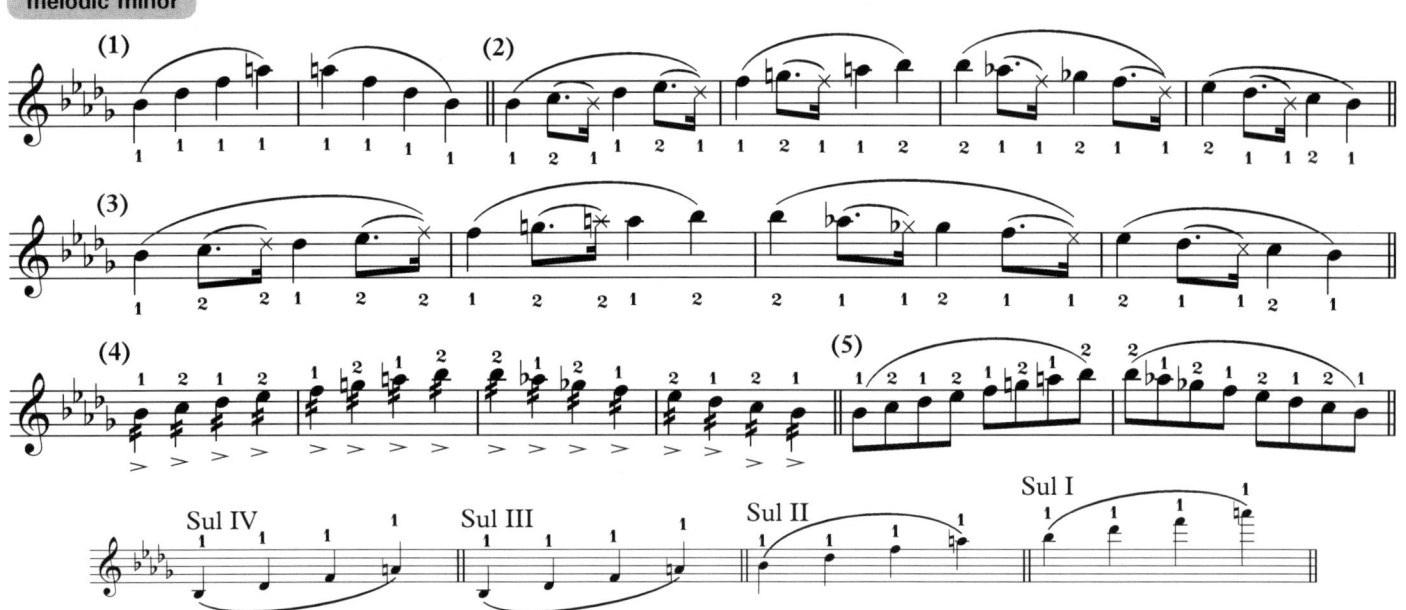

Second and third fingers

 **C major**

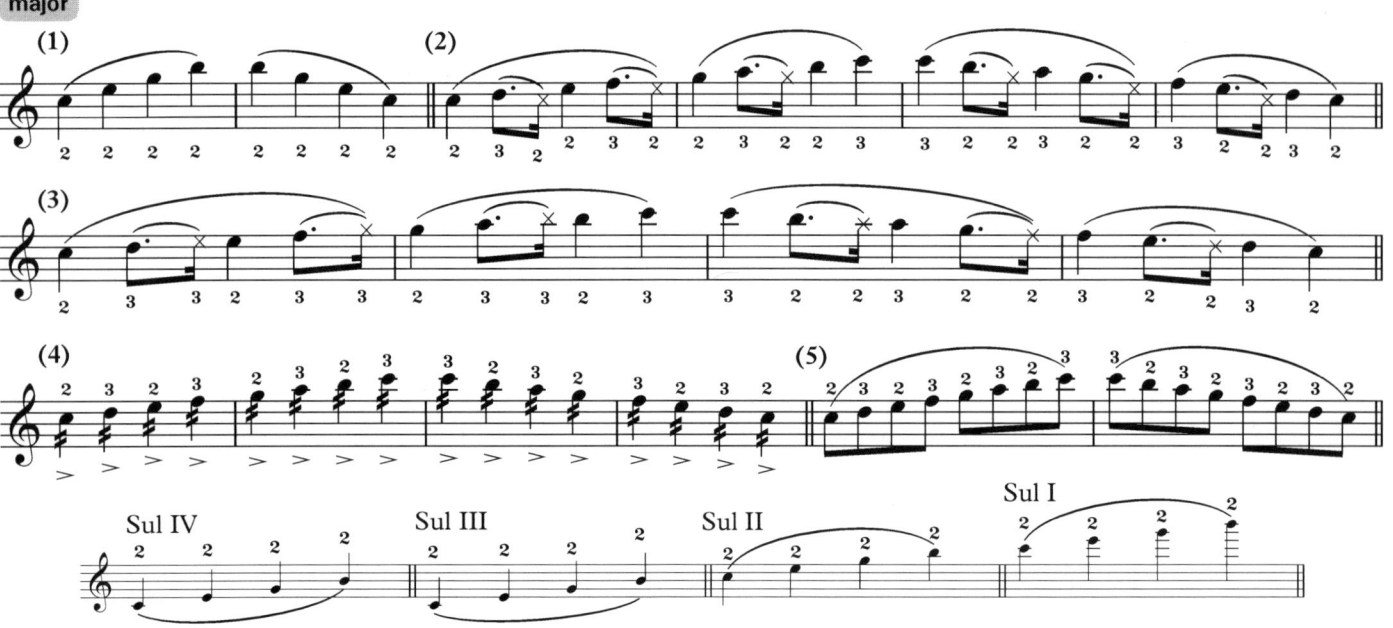

Two-finger scales

melodic minor

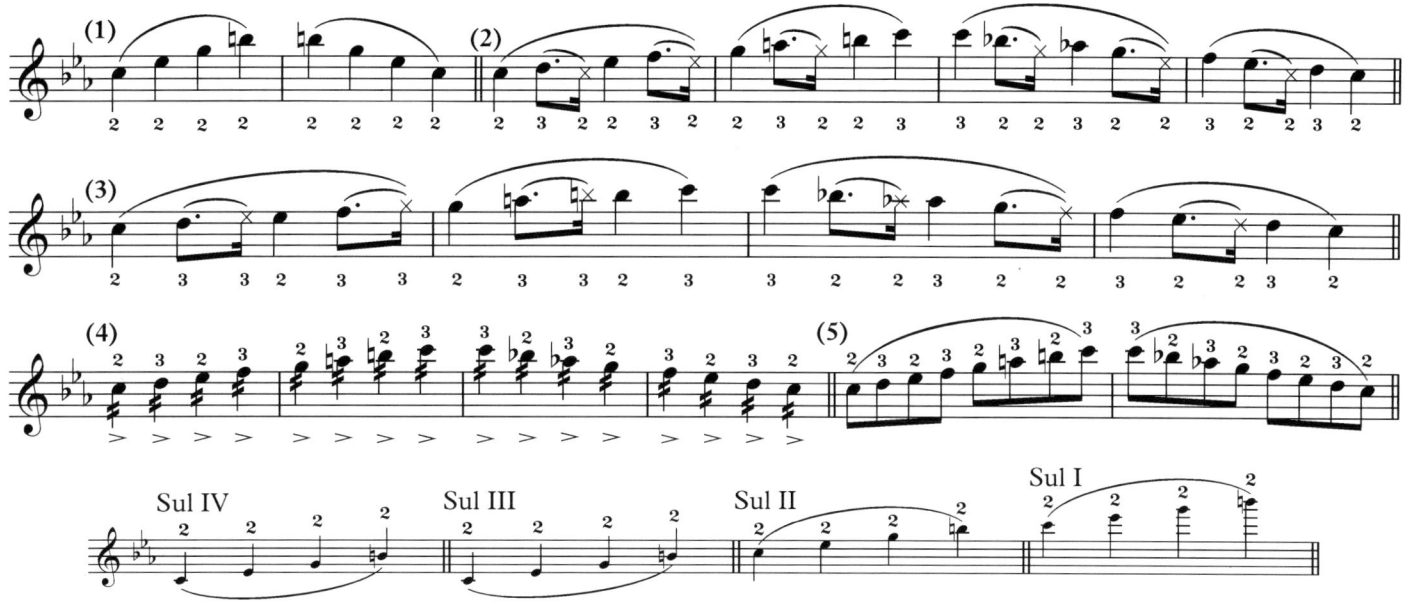

Third and fourth fingers

D♭ major

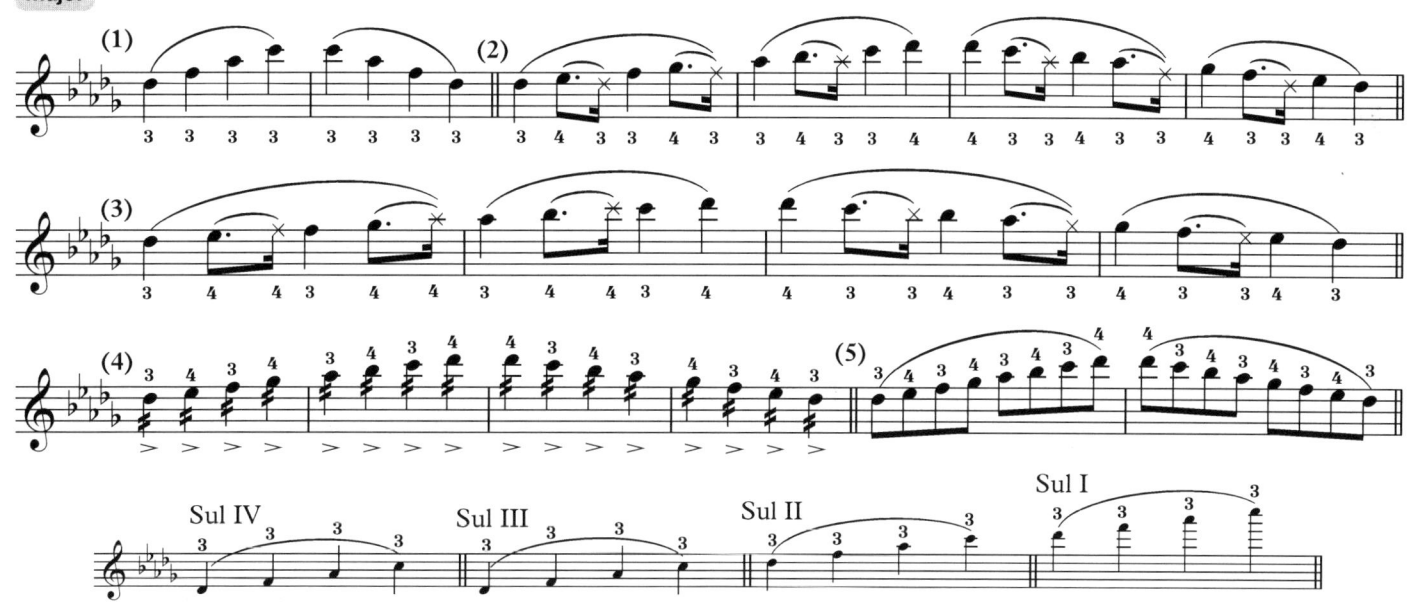

C♯ melodic minor

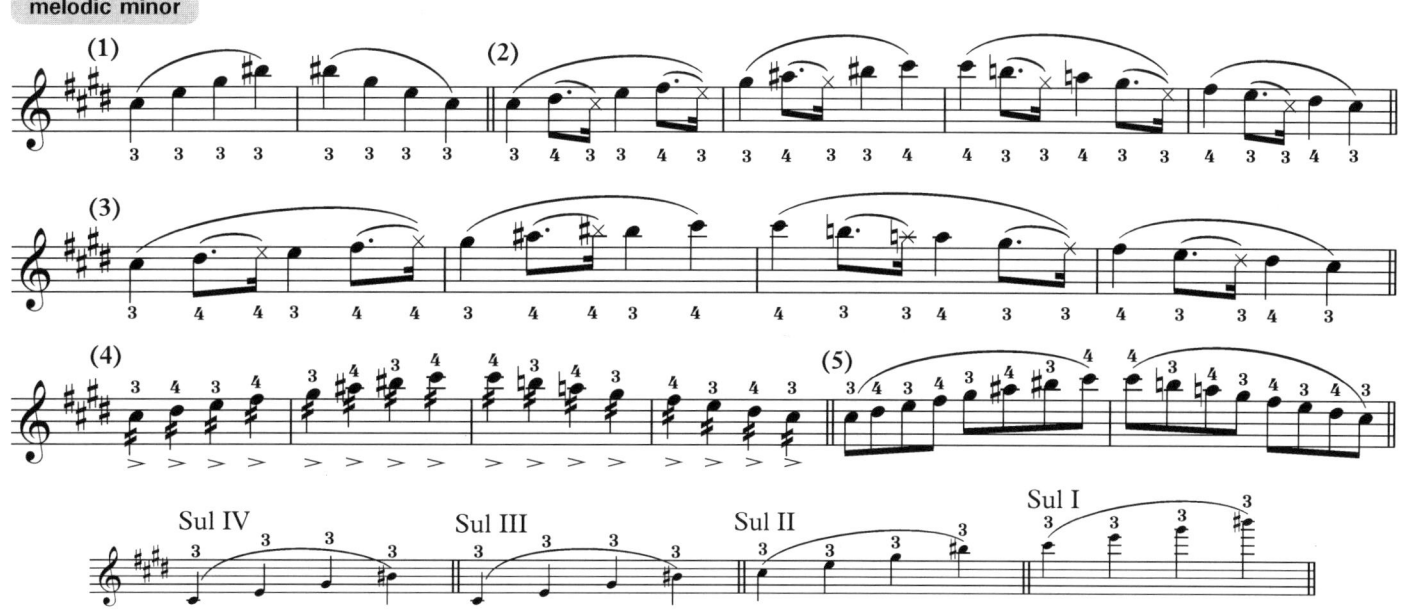

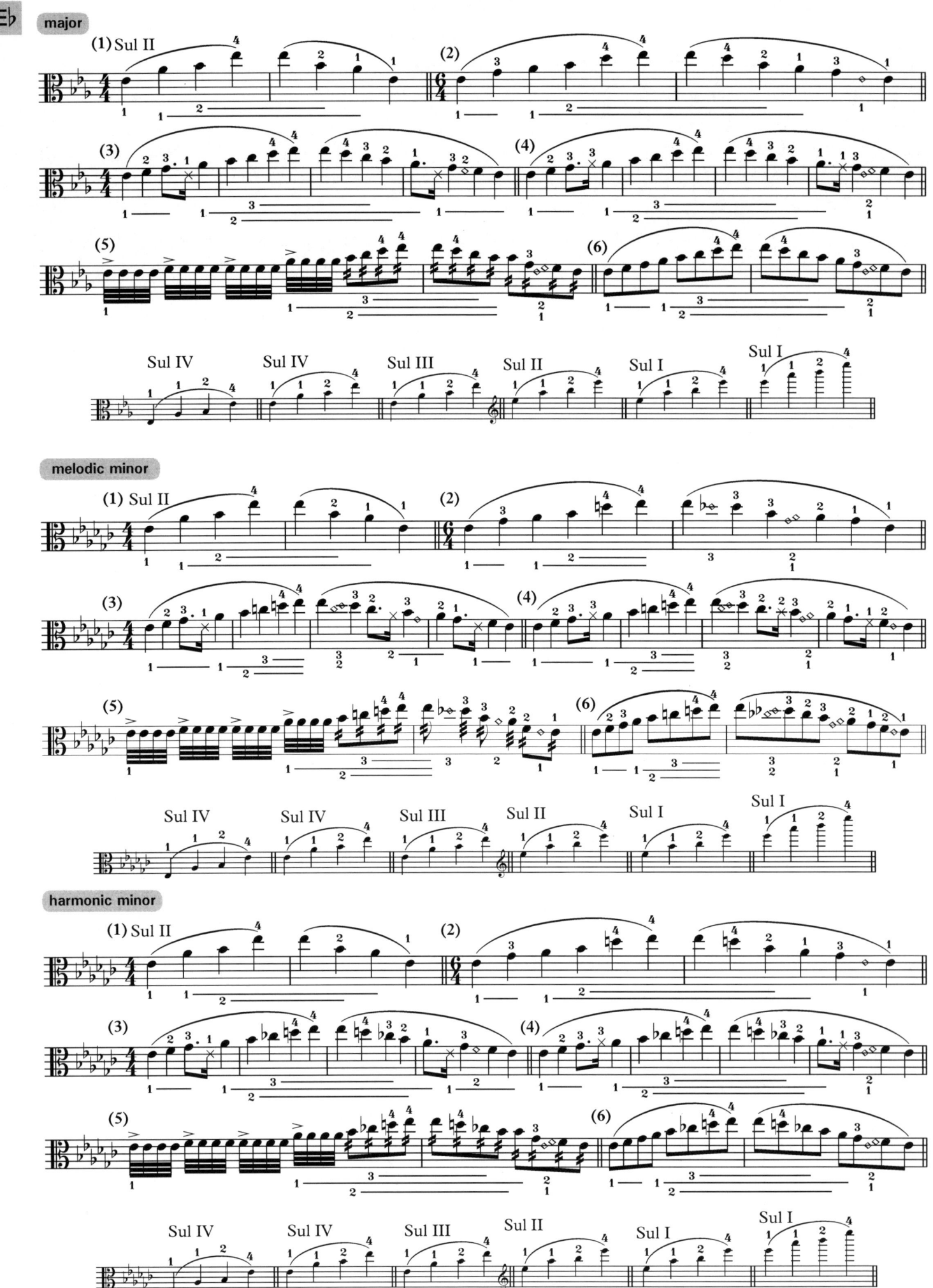

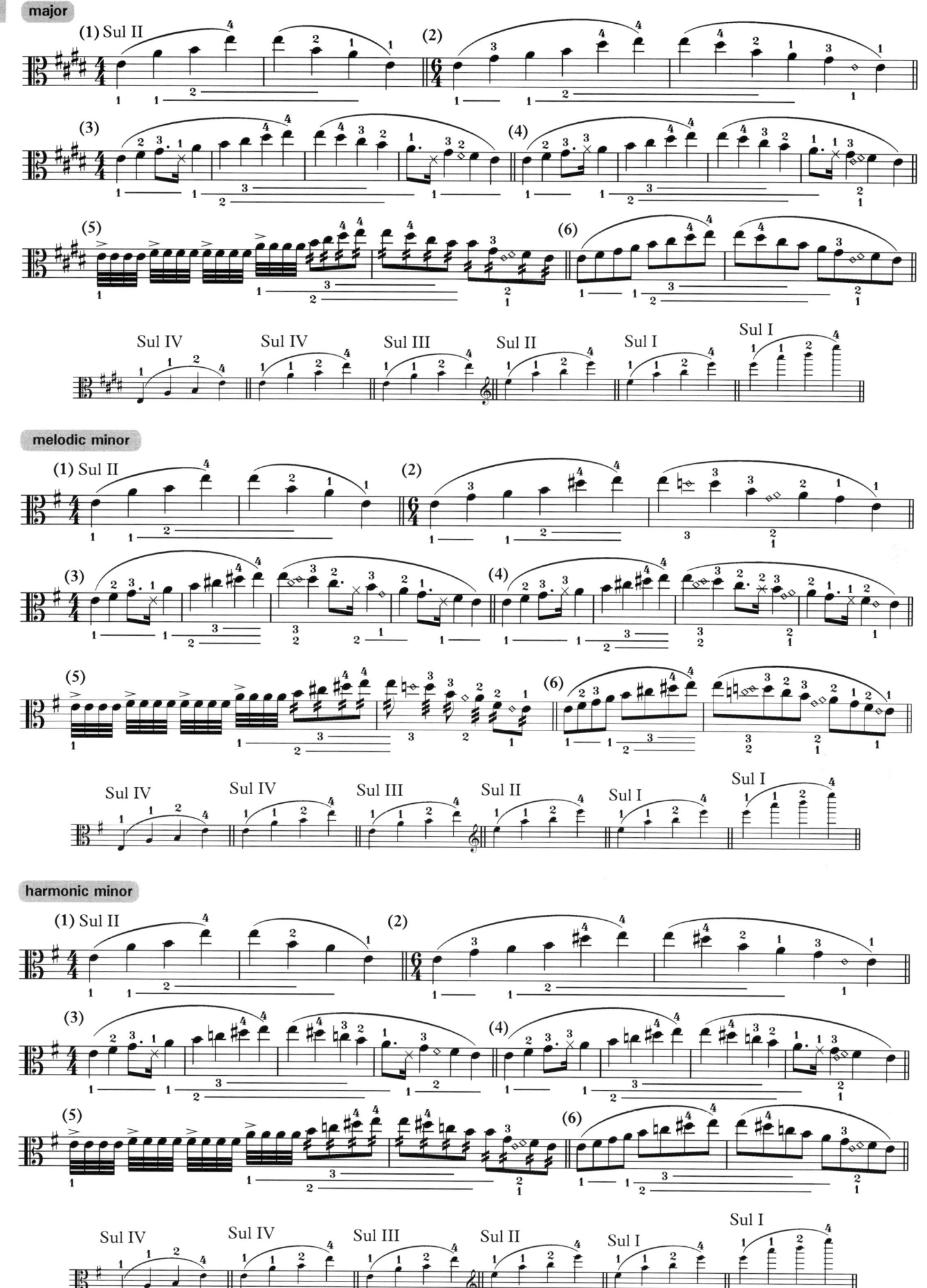

One-octave scales

F major

melodic minor

harmonic minor

Part 4: Scales and arpeggios on one string   See notes, page 142

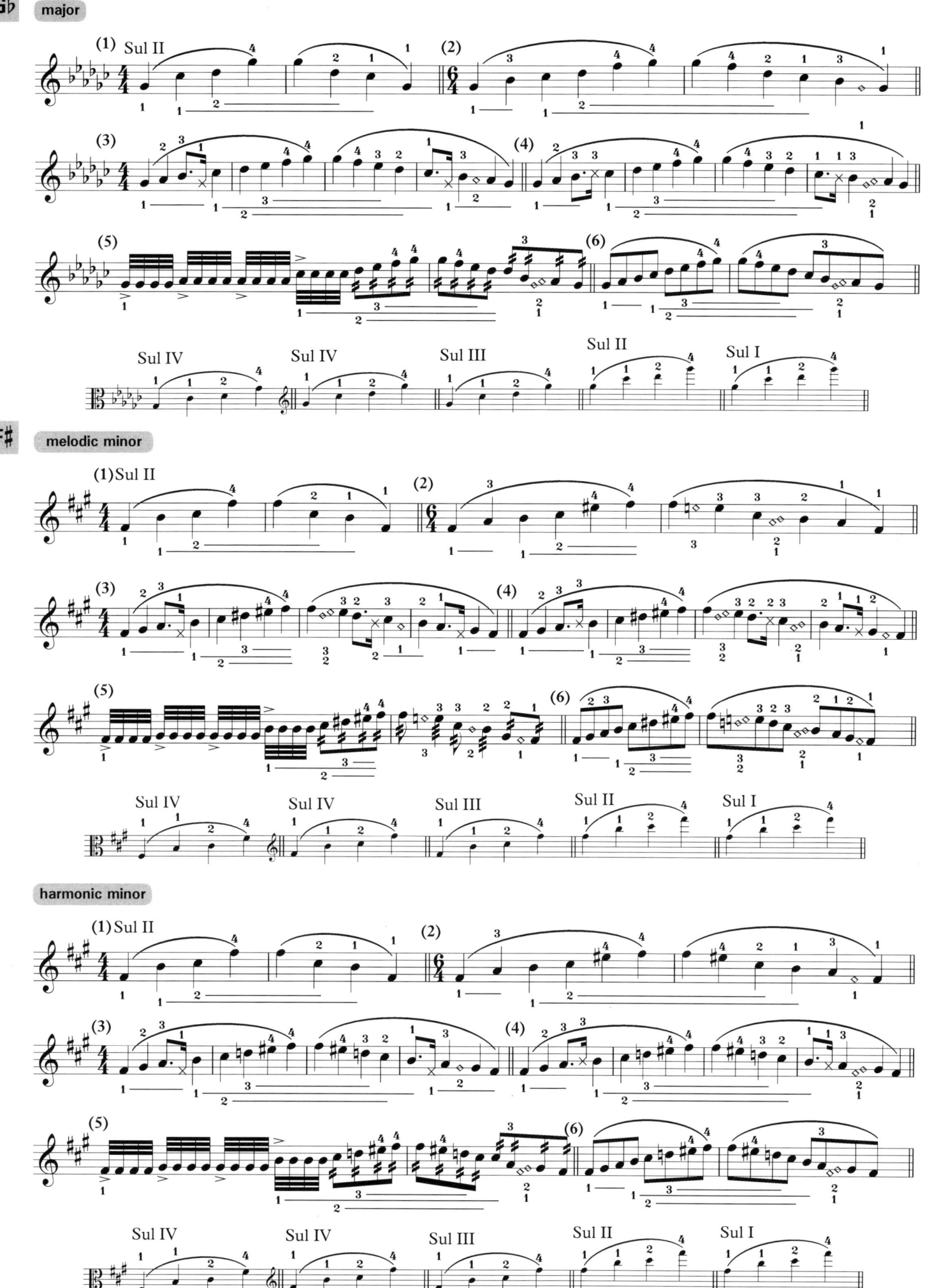

One-octave scales

G major

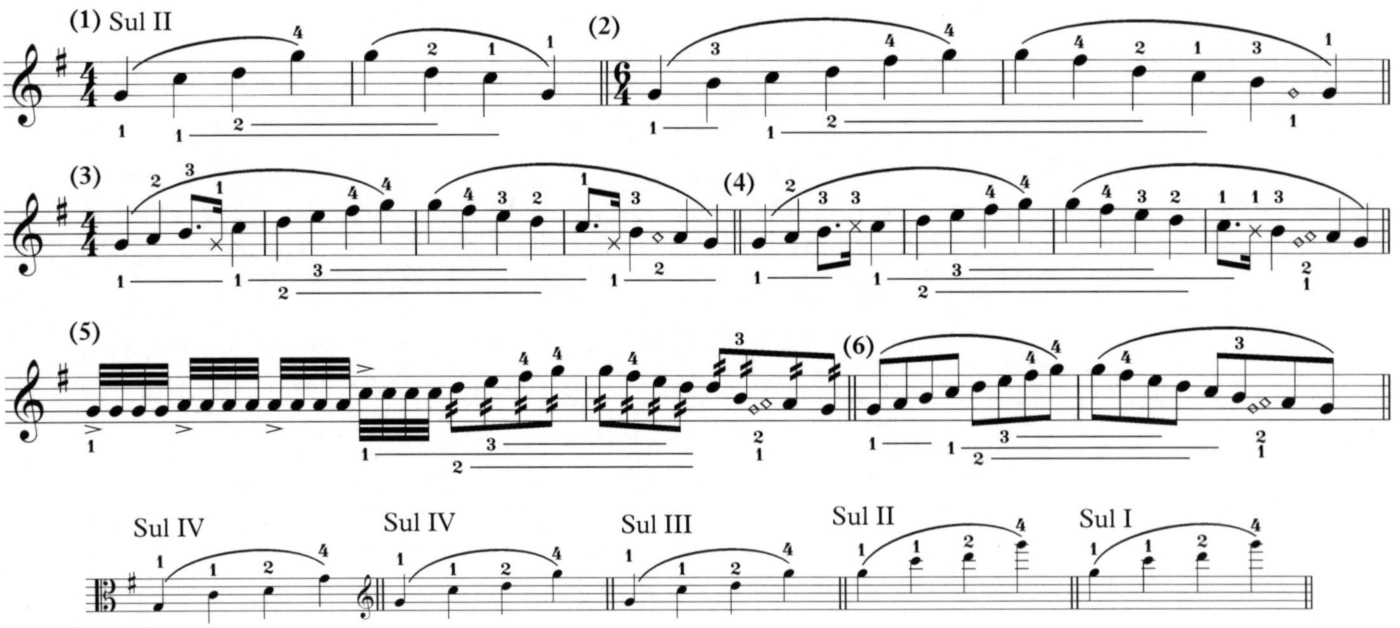

melodic minor

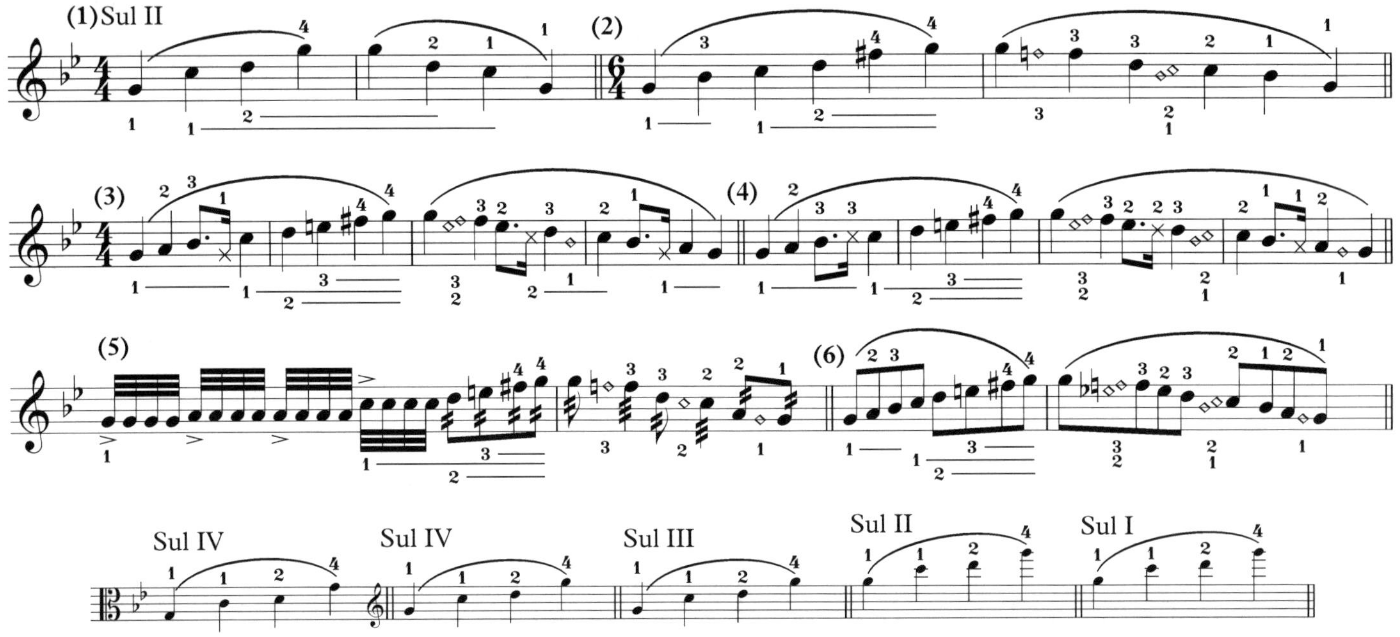

harmonic minor

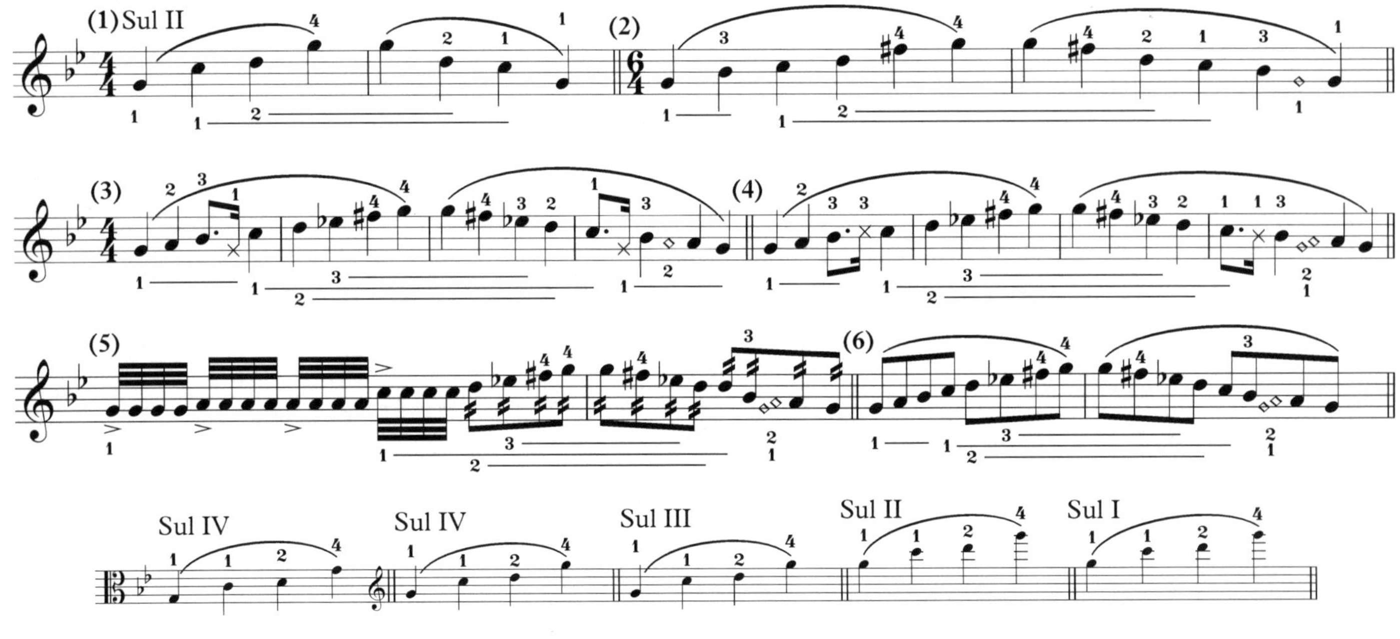

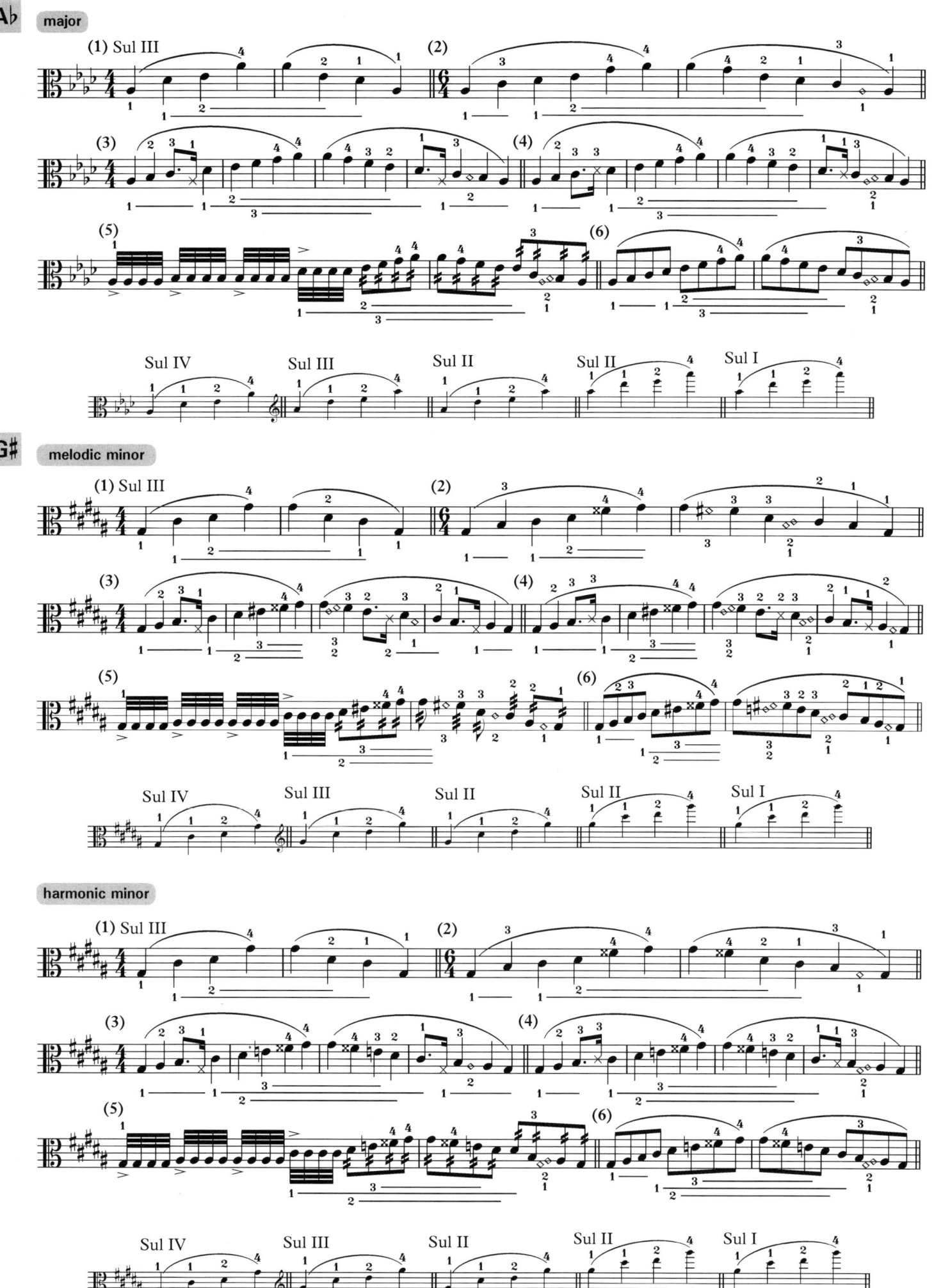

One-octave scales

A major

162 Part 4: Scales and arpeggios on one string   See notes, page 142

One-octave scales

B

Part 4: Scales and arpeggios on one string   See notes, page 142

One-octave scales

C major
melodic minor
harmonic minor

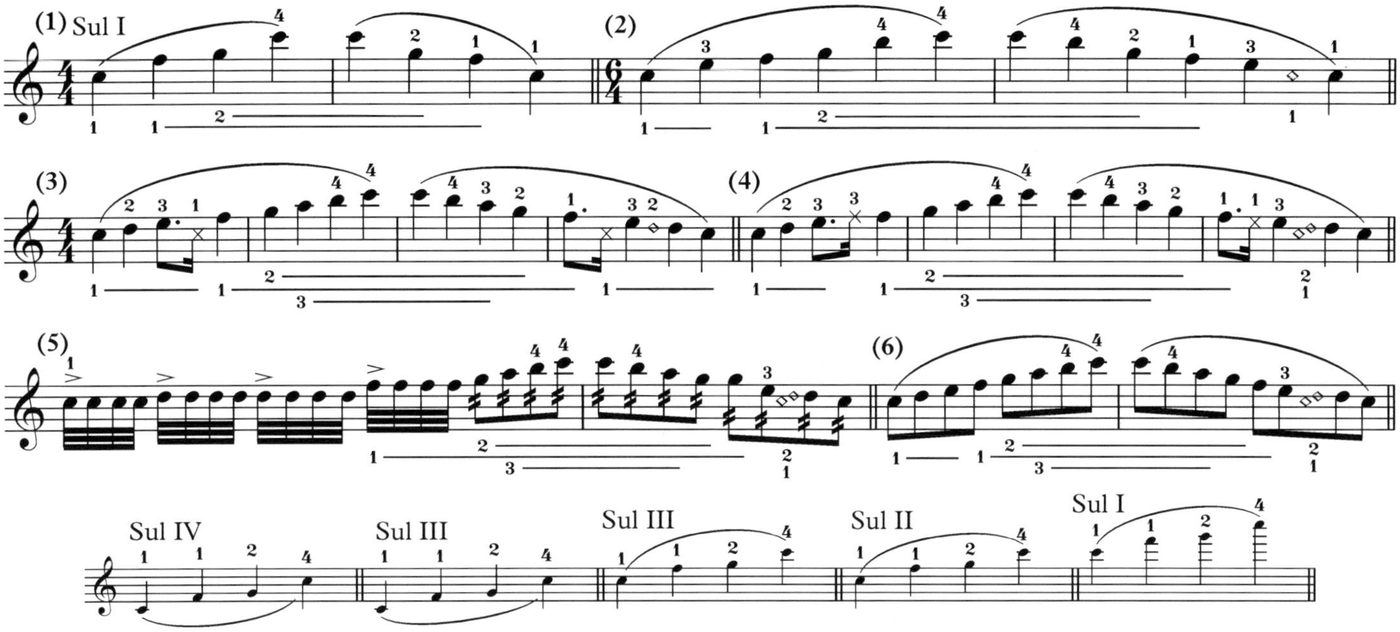

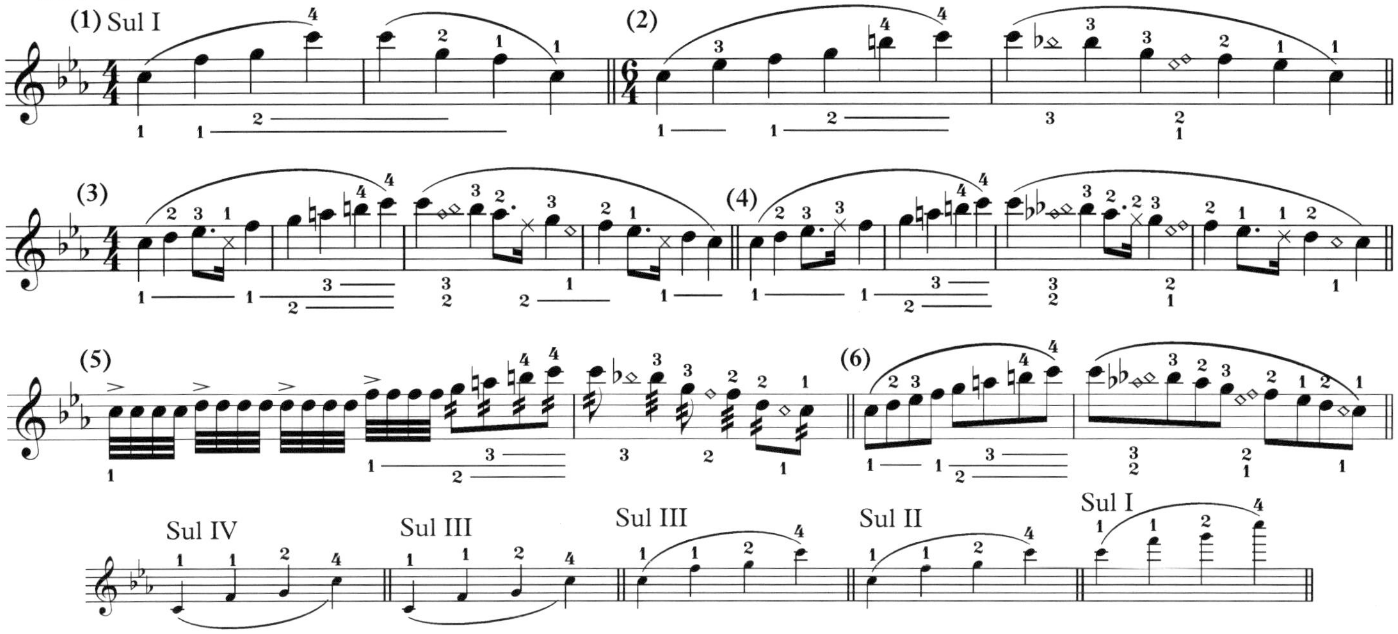

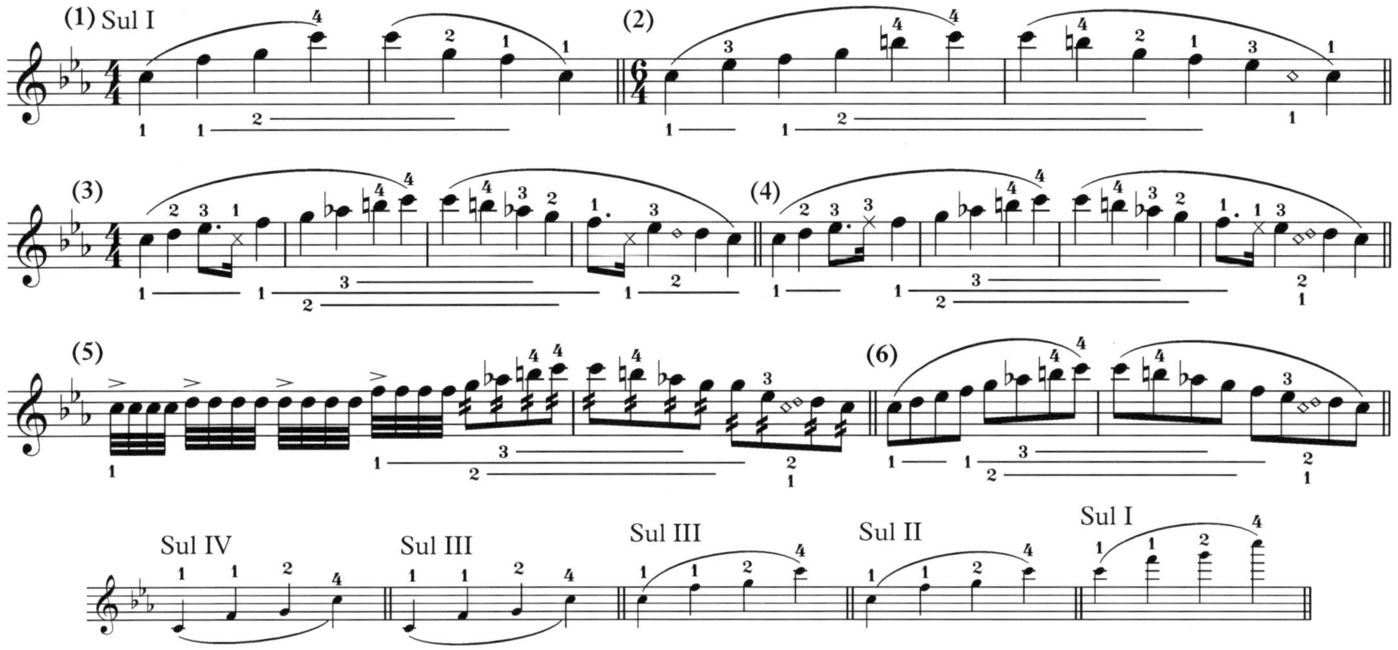

One-octave scales

Part 4: Scales and arpeggios on one string   See notes, page 142

One-octave scales

D major

melodic minor

harmonic minor

Part 4: Scales and arpeggios on one string   See notes, page 142

One-octave arpeggios

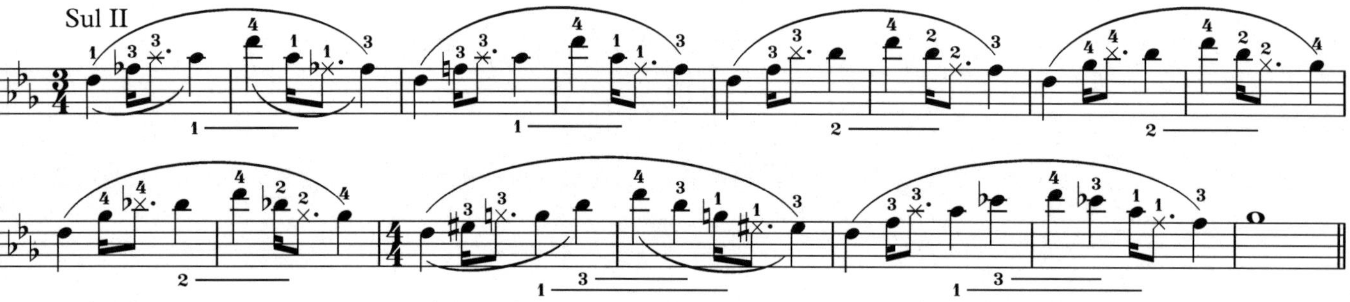

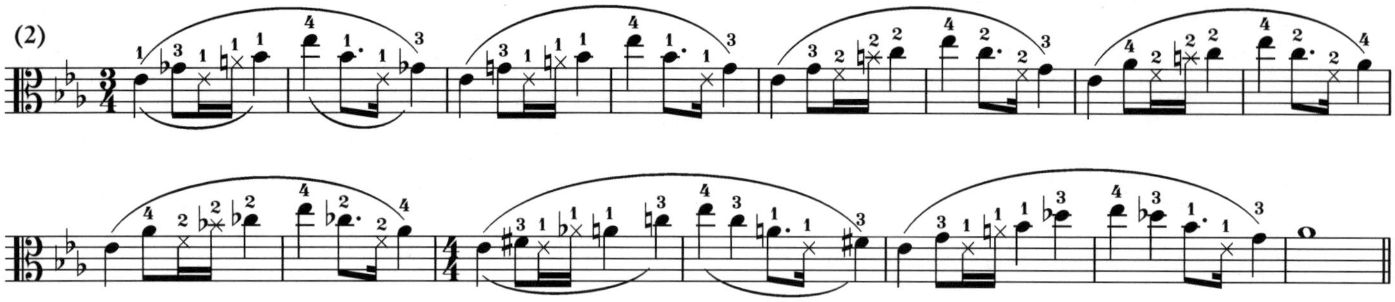

E♭

Part 4: Scales and arpeggios on one string See notes, page 142

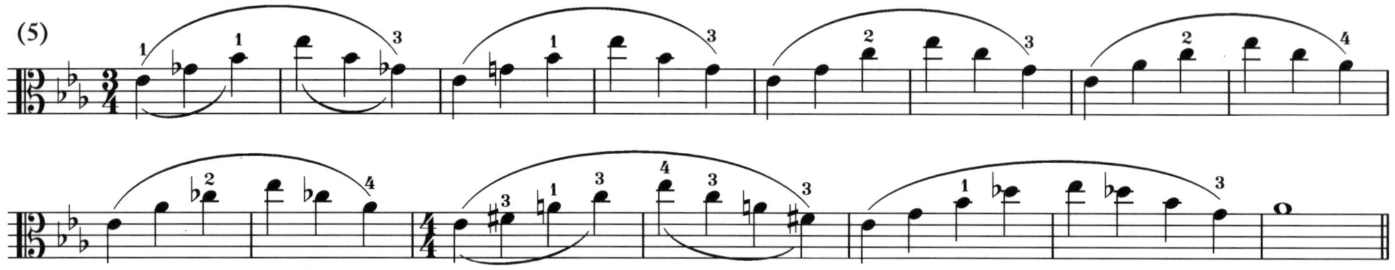

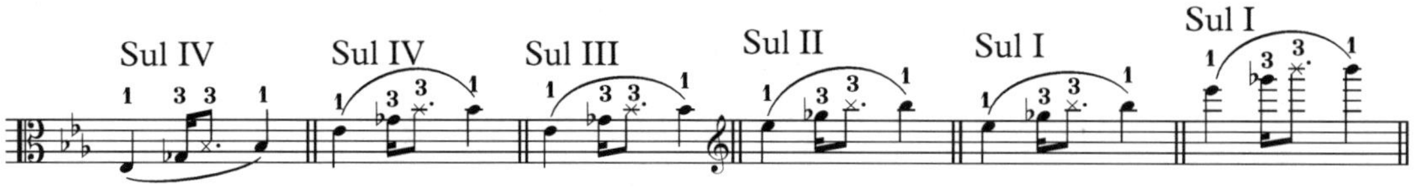

One-octave arpeggios

Part 4: Scales and arpeggios on one string   See notes, page 142

F#

One-octave arpeggios

One-octave arpeggios

G

Part 4: Scales and arpeggios on one string   See notes, page 142

One-octave arpeggios

A♭

One-octave arpeggios

Part 4: Scales and arpeggios on one string   See notes, page 142

One-octave arpeggios

One-octave arpeggios

One-octave arpeggios

D♭

Part 4: Scales and arpeggios on one string   See notes, page 142

One-octave arpeggios

Part 4: Scales and arpeggios on one string   See notes, page 142

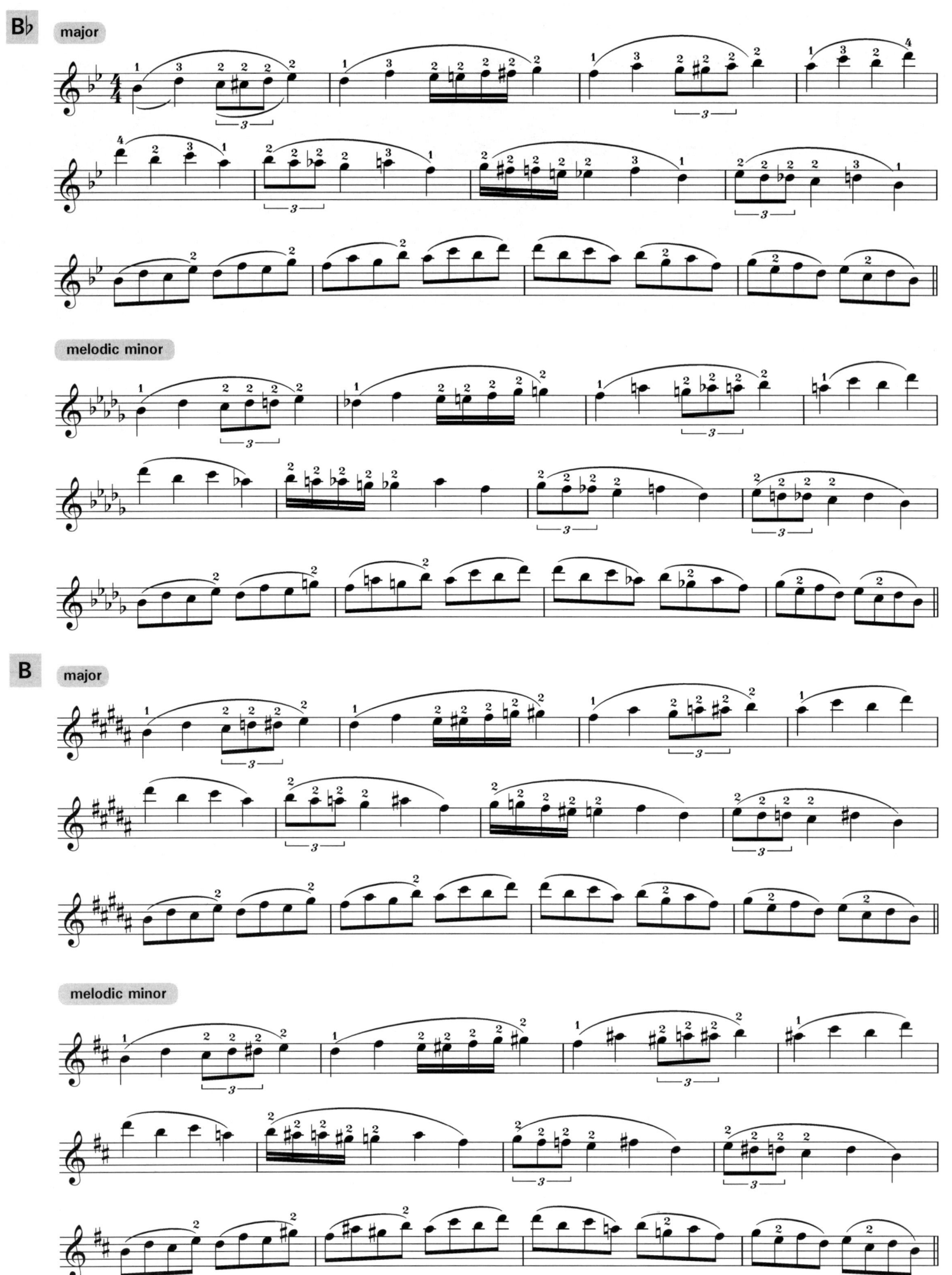

37 Arpeggios: strengthening the top octave

Hold down the fingers throughout, lifting them only when you have to.

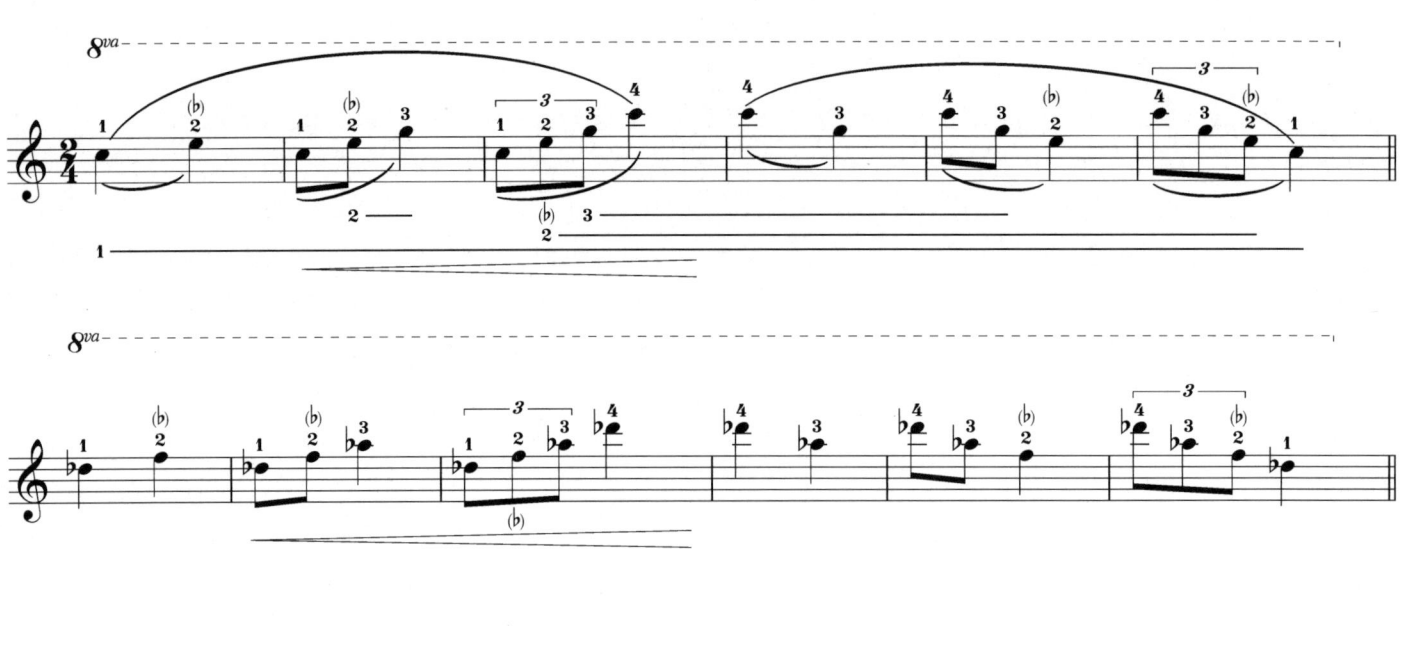
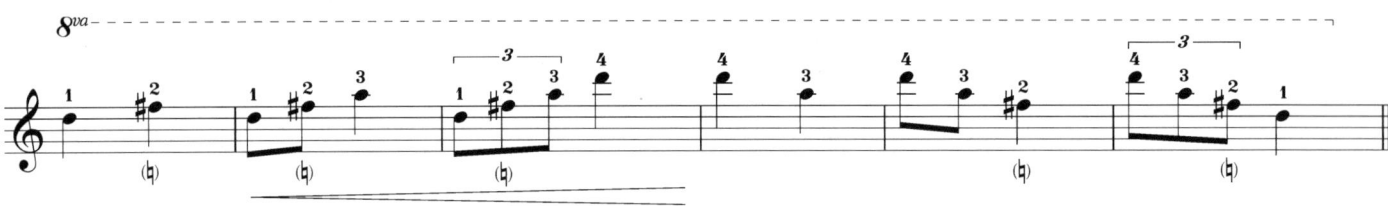
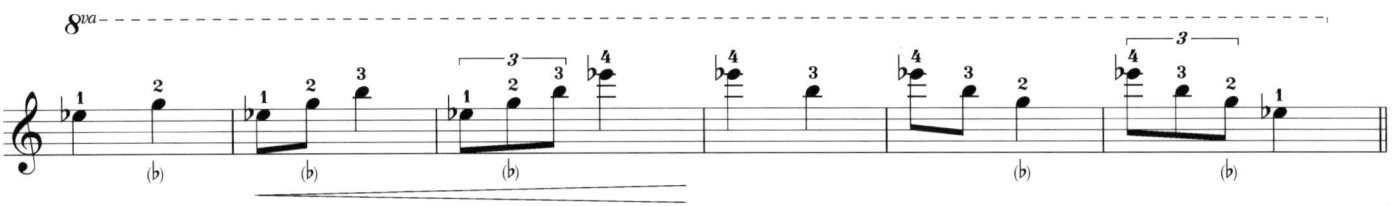
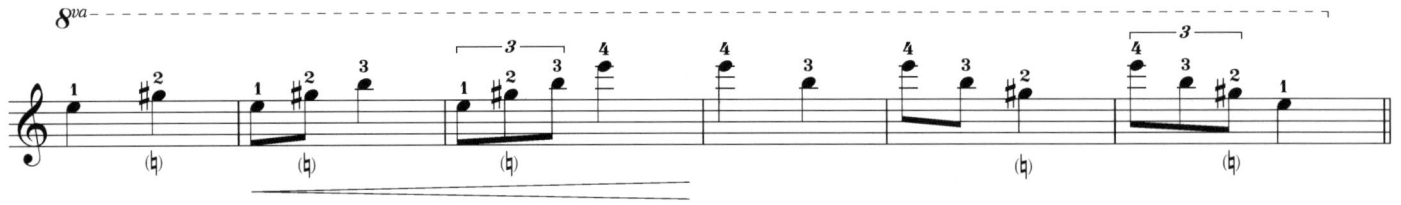
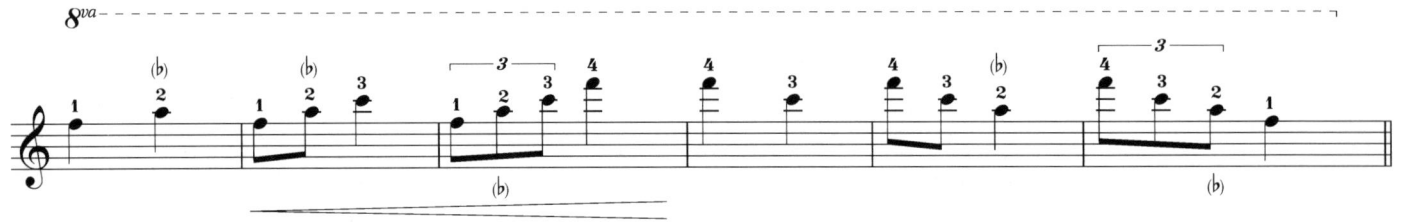

Two-octave scales and arpeggios

184 Part 4: Scales and arpeggios on one string See notes, page 142

Two-octave scales and arpeggios

Part 4: Scales and arpeggios on one string   See notes, page 142

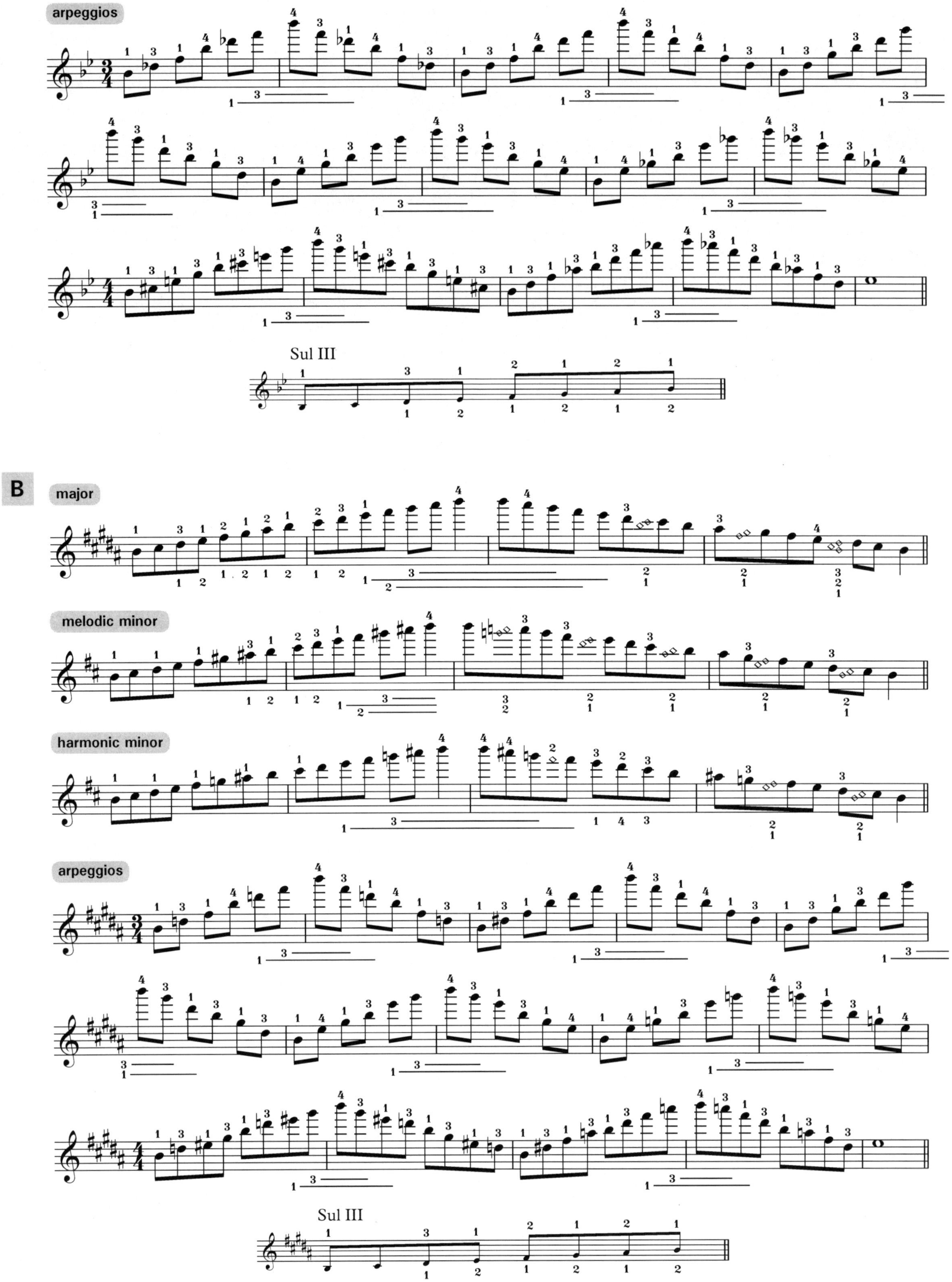

Two-octave scales and arpeggios

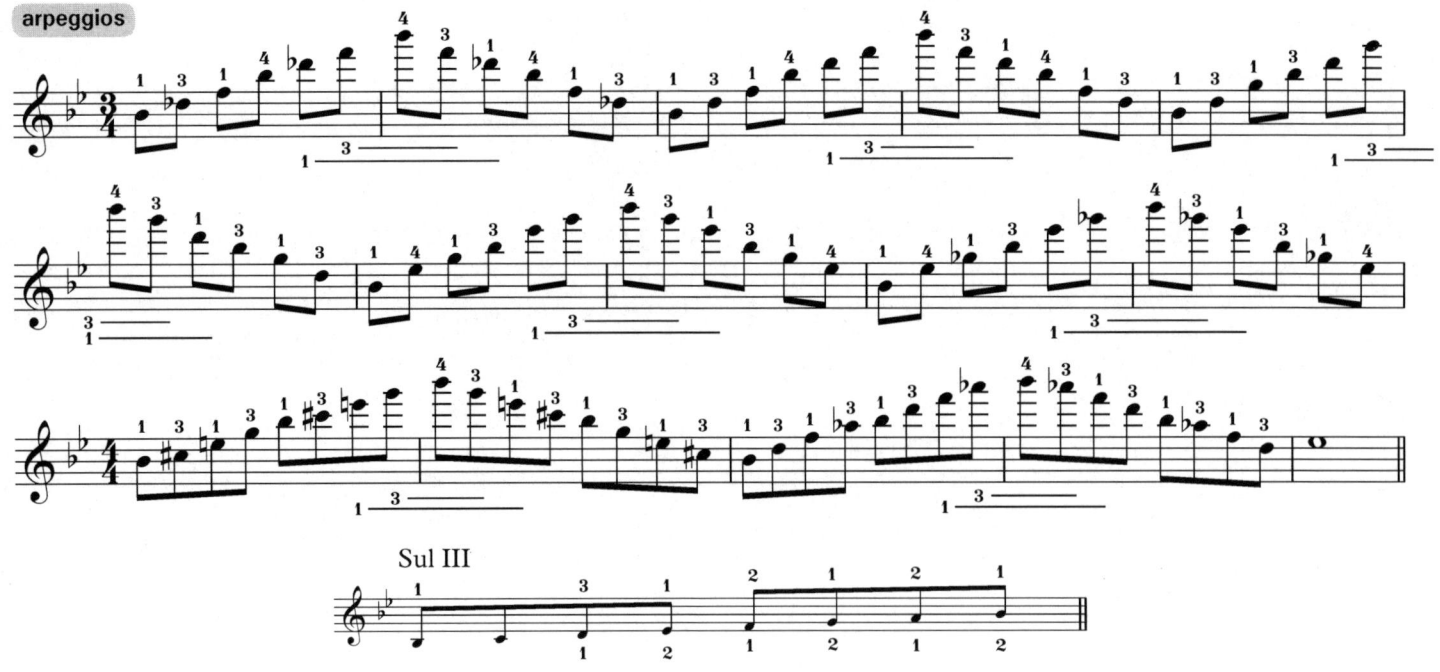

Part 4: Scales and arpeggios on one string   See notes, page 142

Two-octave scales and arpeggios

Part 4: Scales and arpeggios on one string   See notes, page 142

Part 5

Four-octave scales and arpeggios

Notes

part 5

39 Speeding up with the metronome *Page 195*

Unlike three-octave scales (see page 129), there is no single pattern for four-octave scales that divides exactly into groups of 3, 4, 6 or 8 notes; without adding extra notes, groups of 3 or 6 do not arrive back to the tonic on the first beat.

However, it is a simple matter to add extra notes as shown, and in the other groupings simply to play straight up and down without extra notes.

40 Four-octave scales and arpeggios *Page 196*

Speeding up with the metronome

Scales

Arpeggios

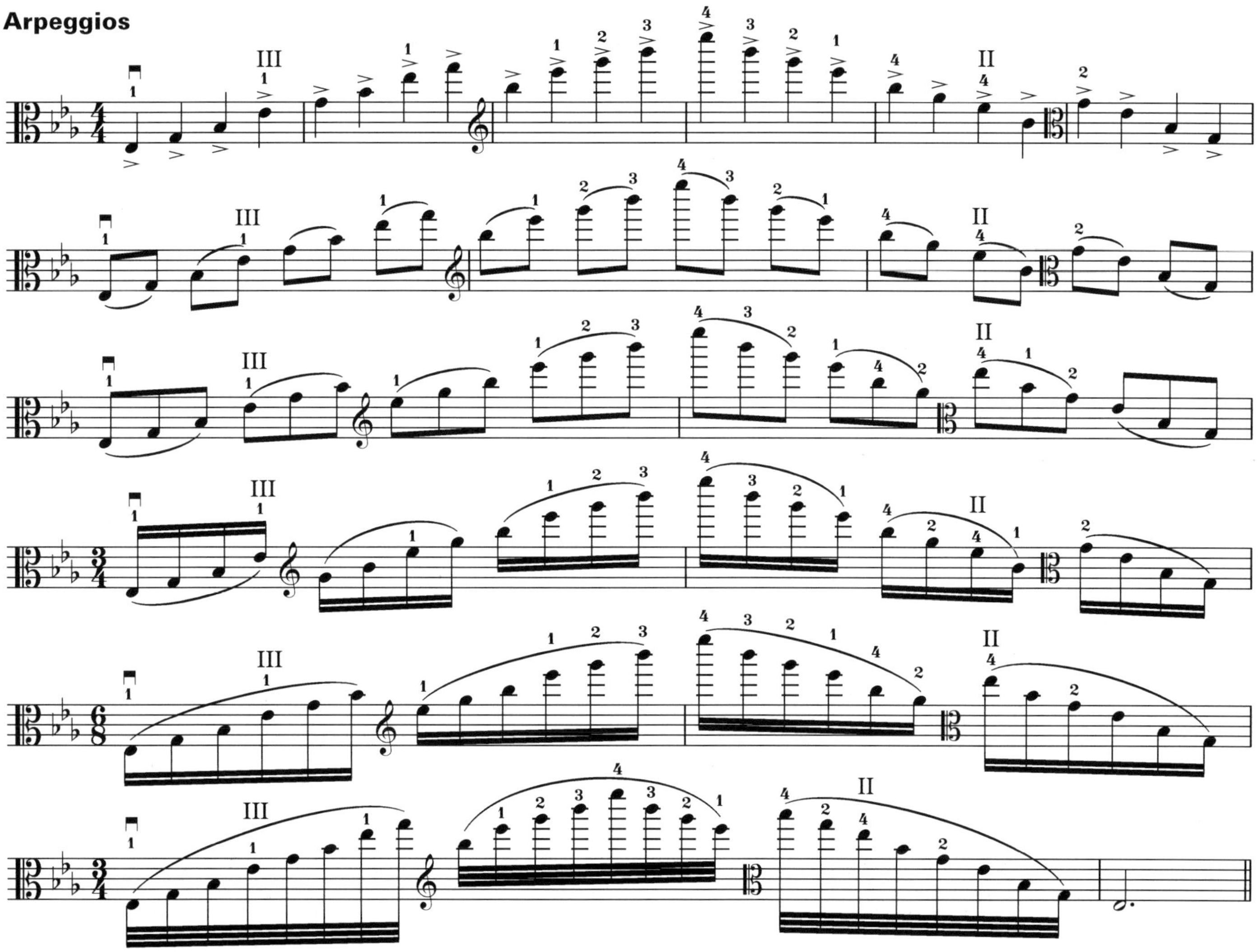

Part 5: Four-octave scales and arpeggios   See notes, page 194

40

Four-octave scales and arpeggios

C major

melodic minor

harmonic minor

arpeggios

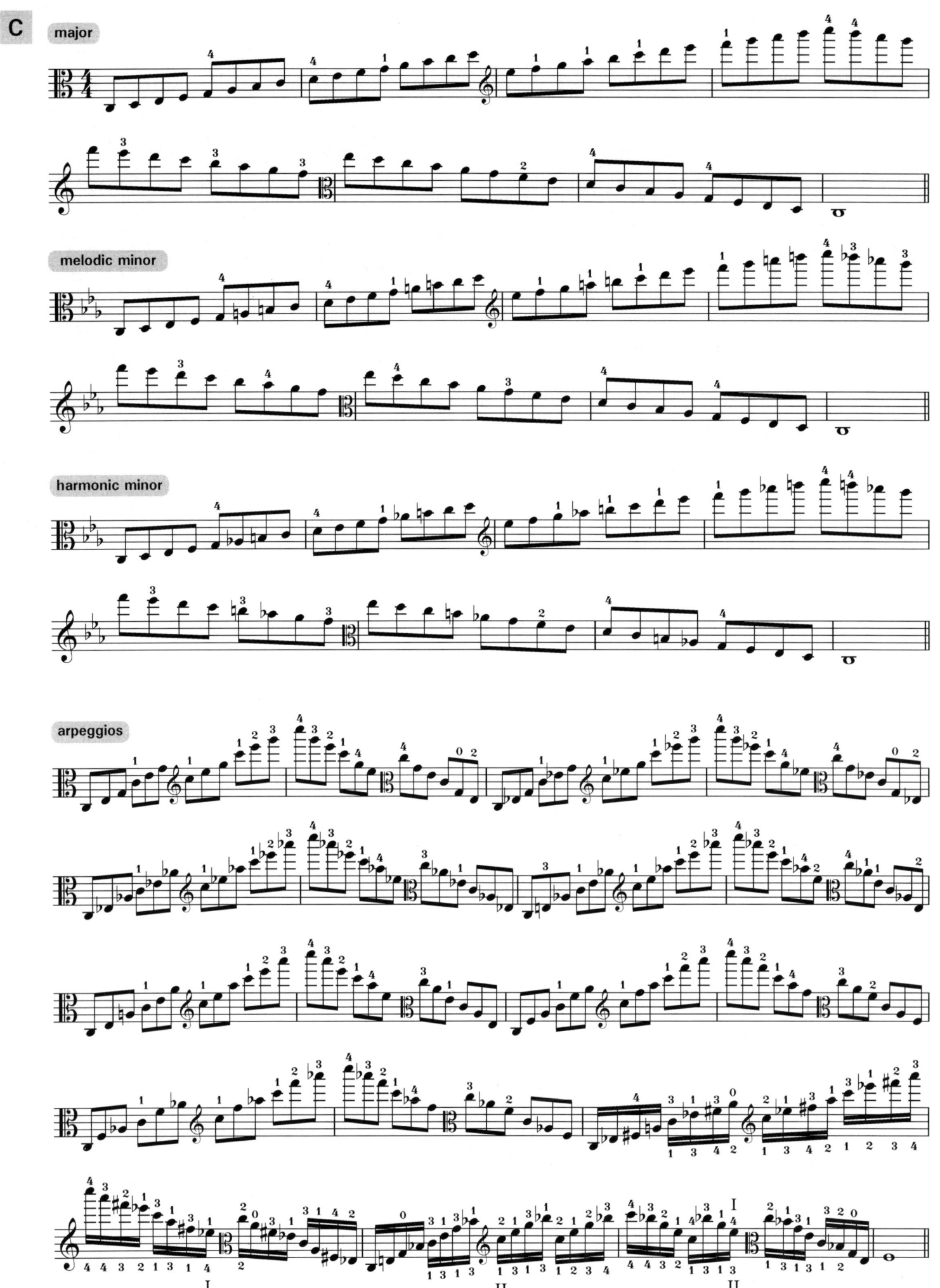

Part 5: Four-octave scales and arpeggios   See notes, page 194

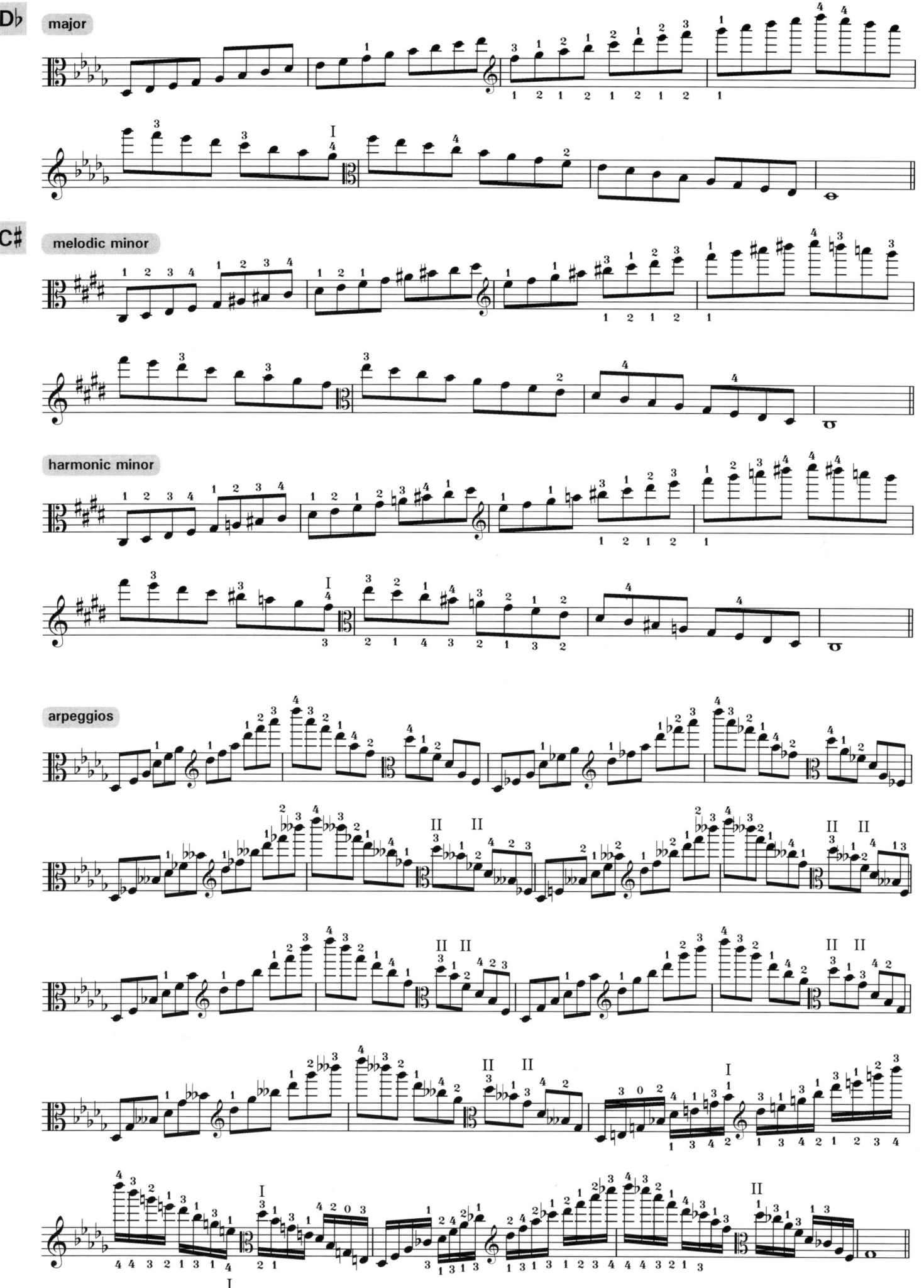

Four-octave scales and arpeggios

D

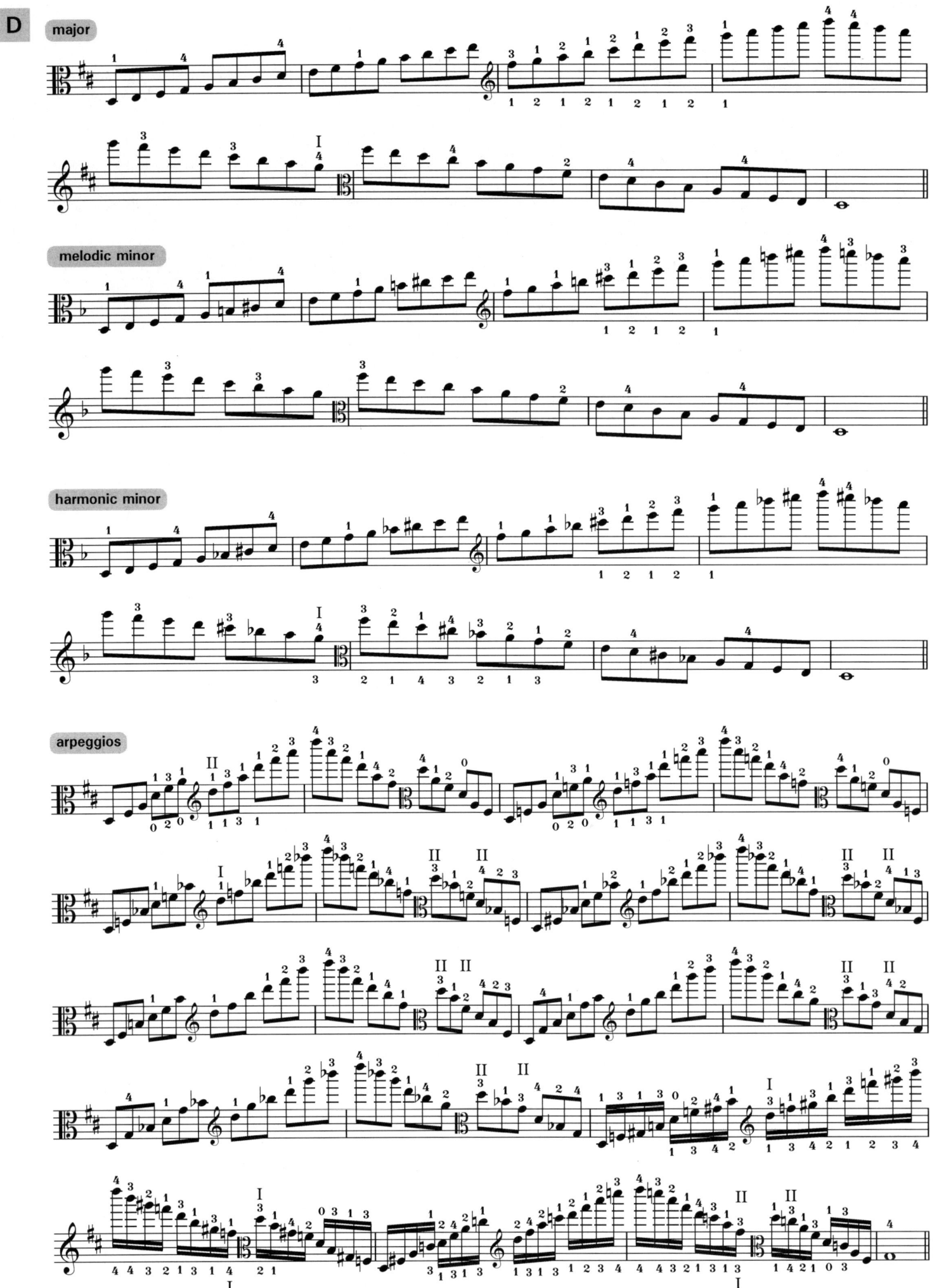

Part 5: Four-octave scales and arpeggios See notes, page 194

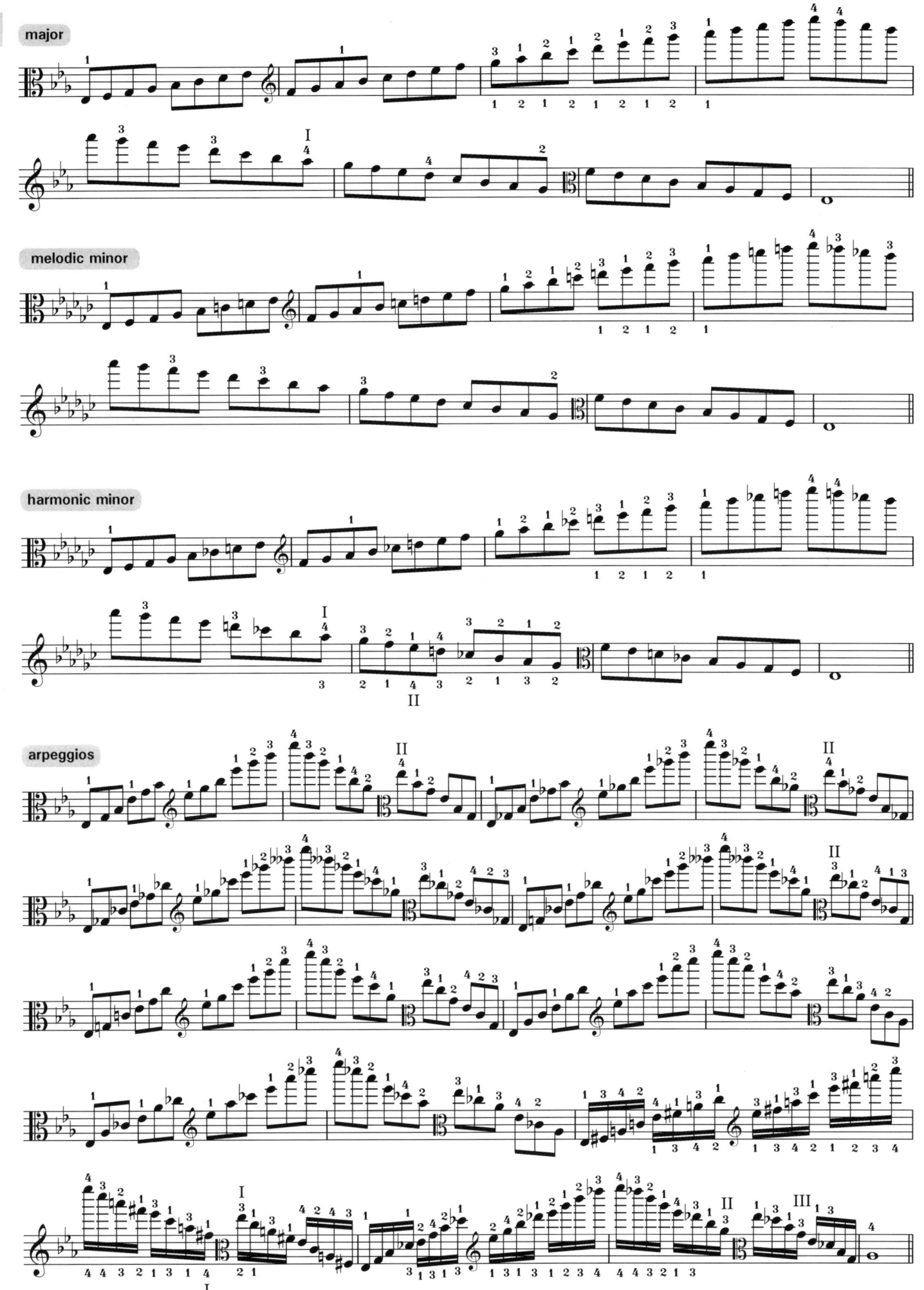

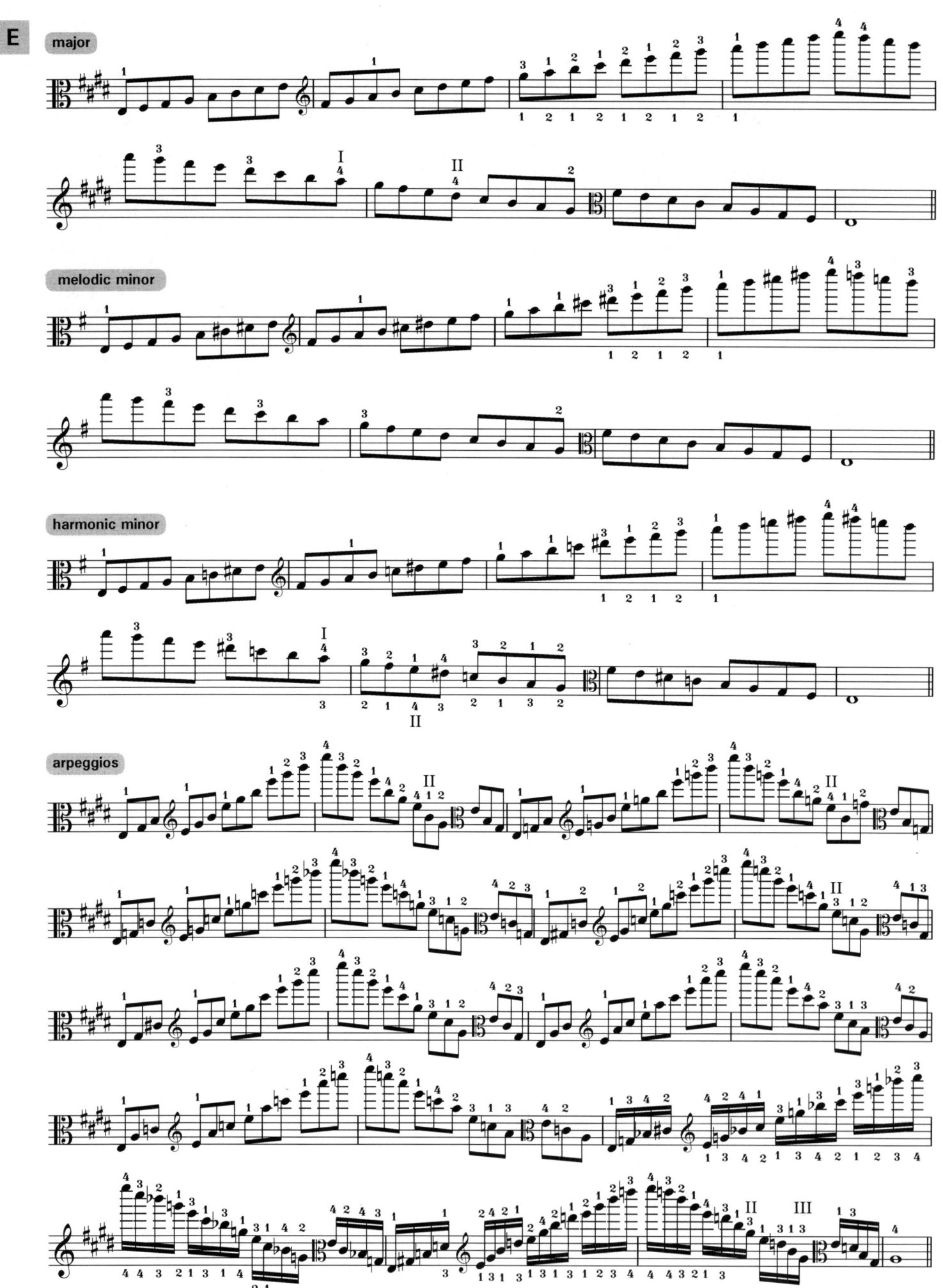

Basics

by Simon Fischer

300 exercises and practice routines for the violin

Basics is the first complete guide to violin technique intended specifically for the music stand rather than the bookshelf. This unique publication covers all the fundamental aspects of playing the instrument. The 300 exercises and practice routines are grouped into seven detailed sections: right arm and hand, tone production, key strokes, left hand, shifting, intonation, vibrato.

As well as presenting a wealth of original material, *Basics* also features ideas and principles traditionally associated with the great violinists, many of which have never before been written down. By focusing on a single element at a time, each exercise is designed to achieve an immediately tangible and sustainable result in the shortest possible time.

Basics is intended to be the violinist's companion for life: from the early stages right up to professional concert standard. As Simon Fischer himself says: "The same basic technical exercises can be used by players at all levels because most of the technical issues remain the same."

Based on the author's celebrated series in *The Strad* magazine, *Basics* is the most comprehensive training compendium available to today's violinist.

"Original, detailed . . . useful to anyone sincerely concerned with violin technique."
Dorothy DeLay

Practice

by Simon Fischer

250 step-by-step practice methods for the violin

This essential follow-up guide extends the principles presented in *Basics* and applies them more fully to the violin repertoire. For the first time, violinists are offered an integrated resource which provides problem-solving guidance for the most awkward passages the player is likely to encounter:

- double-stopping in Wieniawski
- chromatic glissandi in Saint-Saëns
- left-hand pizzicato in Sarasate
- harmonics in Bartók
- technical control in Mozart
- chords in Bach sonatas
- improved intonation in Bruch's violin concerto
- string-crossing in Ysaÿe
- ricochet bowing in Paganini

"Fischer has provided us with a remarkable and inspirational tome"
European String Teachers' Association

LONDON · FRANKFURT/M · LEIPZIG · NEW YORK
www.editionpeters.com